LEGACY OF THE SOMME 1916

THE BATTLE IN FACT, FILM AND FICTION

GERALD GLIDDON

with a foreword by John Terraine

SUTTON PUBLISHING LIMITED

First published in 1996 by
Sutton Publishing Limited · Phoenix Mill
Thrupp · Stroud · Gloucestershire · GL5 2BU

British Library Cataloguing in Publication Data

A catalogue record for this book is available from the British Library.

ISBN 0 7509 1160 3

This bibliography is dedicated to the publisher Leo Cooper, whose books feature throughout its pages

™
ALAN SUTTON™ and SUTTON™ are
the trade marks of Sutton Publishing Limited
Typeset in 10/13 Bembo.
Typesetting and origination by
Sutton Publishing Limited.
Printed in Great Britain by
Butler & Tanner, Frome, Somerset.

CONTENTS

Author's note
Unless specified otherwise, entries are in author alphabetical order. Where an author has several titles, these appear in chronological order, unless they appeared in the same year, in which case they are in alphabetical order by title.

LIST OF ILLUSTRATIONS

FOREWORD

Gerald Gliddon has named this book *Legacy of the Somme*. That is a very large title, covering large matters; it is thought-provoking, disturbing, vibrant with unresolved disputes and passionate feelings.

To me, the most important 'legacy' of the immense battle that was fought across the smooth slopes of Picardy for four and a half bloody months in 1916 is a veritable mountain of mythology which continues to grow. For eight decades the myths of the Somme have worked their mischief, nourished and multiplied by the media in all their manifestations and by politicians of all parties. The very word 'Somme' became a synonym for the supposedly mindless repetition of totally unimaginative and hideously costly attacks which were widely believed to have been the sole significant characteristic of the conduct of the British Somme offensive.

The poison began to work quickly: Somme mythology played a big part in the 'Disenchantment' of the 1920s and 1930s. General Sir Edmund Ironside, who became Chief of the Imperial General Staff on the outbreak of the Second World War, remarked in his Diary as the birds came home to roost in the disasters of June 1940, 'The saying that we were never again to have "the bloody massacres of the Somme" has deluded the people. Nobody has been educated to the horrors of modern war.' The result of the national recoil from all forms of military preparation between the wars is all too familiar: a succession of humiliating and frightening defeats continuing until 1943. By then Churchill, a redoubtable war leader, was firmly in control, but he, too, was subject to the dangerous infection of the myths. He makes no attempt to disguise the fact. In volume V of his *History of the Second World War* (published in 1952) he admits without equivocation his reluctance to undertake the massive Allied cross-Channel assault in 1944 known as Operation Overlord:

> The fearful price we had to pay in human life and blood for the great offensives of the First World War was graven in my mind. Memories of the Somme and Passchendaele . . . were not to be blotted out by time and reflection.

The memories of the Somme were by no means blotted out; on the contrary, they flourished, not least in the 1960s, when much slanderous malice marched behind the banners of, first, the stage version, and later the film, *Oh! What a Lovely War!* My book, *Douglas Haig: The Educated Soldier*, daring to defend Field-Marshal Sir Douglas Haig in 1963, was launched in rough water. 'Somme experts' sprang up on all sides to add copiously to the already abundant mythology. The *Edinburgh Evening News* carried a review of the book which inspired a correspondent signing himself 'Footslogger 1914' to write, amid other curiosities,

After the war I was in Germany and saw a German film, *The Somme – Grave of a Million*. The battle was depicted and the respective numbers of killed given as follows: British 500,000, French 250,000, German 250,000. These round figures have never been disputed to my knowledge.

Unshakeable belief in astronomical casualty figures is part of the hard core of Somme mythology – in March 1988 a *Daily Telegraph* correspondent called it 'the battle which cost the lives of 420,000 British troops'. A difficulty in distinguishing between the living and the dead also forms part of the Somme mythology, usually extended to the entire First World War experience. The final official figure of British casualties in the 1916 Battle of the Somme (1 July–mid-November) was 419,654 of all ranks, which I would have thought was bad enough for anyone. It is quite bad enough for me, and so is the figure of approximately 131,000 dead and missing comprehended in it.

There was more to come. In the 1980s the baleful historical harmony of the politicians and the Press reached its apogee, against the troubled contemporary background of serious industrial unrest. On 2 May the *Daily Telegraph* political correspondent told readers:

'The recent steel strike was a war that everybody lost,' said Sir Geoffrey Howe, the Chancellor, last night. 'The living standards of British steelworkers were sacrificed as fruitlessly – and as surely – as the lives of soldiers on the Somme,' he added.

And to lend more emphasis to this strange analogy, Sir Geoffrey referred to the steelworkers as 'the PBI of British industry'.

It would seem that the House of Commons was taking a crash course in 'Instant History' that May, for just over a fortnight later the same newspaper reported, over the signature of Godfrey Barker, that

Mr Roy Jenkins[1] scornfully dismissed the Conservative Manifesto last night as a progress report after the Battle of the Somme. 'Casualties intolerable. Ground gained negligible. Press on and with resolution we shall secure more of the same results,' was his contemptuous version of the Prime Minister's record to an SDP meeting in Leicester.

This so delighted the *Daily Telegraph* editors that they congratulated Mr Jenkins on 'witty and apposite aphorisms', contrasting them favourably with the 'contrived and brutal vulgarities' of Mr Healey, Labour's spokesman. The curtain thus falls on a moving scene of mutual satisfaction. However, those who still care deeply about the

---

[1] Later Lord.

brave and dutiful officers and soldiers who fought the battle, and have been so glibly robbed of their due honours by sour mythology, will always be sickened by these ignorant, casual cruelties.

Perhaps a few words of fairly frigid fact are appropriate here, to end this admittedly angry indictment. First it should never be forgotten that 1 July 1916, with all its undoubted tragedy, was *not* the Battle of the Somme. It was the *first day of the Allied infantry* offensive[2]. For the British, who suffered over 57,000 casualties (21,392 killed and missing), the day was a freak: nothing like it ever happened to the British Expeditionary Force again. The 'first day' of the Somme was also the 132nd day of the Battle of Verdun, which by now had cost the French Army some 250,000 casualties.

The real Battle of the Somme, pointing with steady accuracy towards its ultimate result, began on 2 July and lasted for 140 days, during which the bulk of the losses occurred, and the result slowly came into view. An 18-year-old subaltern in the Royal Warwickshire Regiment, who lived to fight on many other days (and even in another war), Charles Carrington[3], told me twenty years ago that it was

> in the weeks of continuous close fighting along the Pozières–High Wood Ridge, throughout the whole of July and August . . . that the heart was torn out of the German Army so that they never fought so well again . . .

The most important agreement with Charles Carrington's interpretation of the Battle of the Somme is to be found in the German sources: Field-Marshal Prince Rupprecht of Bavaria tells us, 'what still remained of the old first-class peace-trained German infantry had been expended on the battlefield'. Charles himself, in *Soldier from the Wars Returning* (1965) remarks that, 'German historians admit that in the Somme fighting their great regular army bled itself to death'. A German staff officer tersely corroborates, 'The Somme was the muddy grave of the German field army.'

So we come in sight of the result; in Carrington's words, 'Enthusiastic amateurs when the fighting began, the British were soldiers at the end, with the cynical notions and the prudent habits that professionals exhibit.' But General Ludendorff's description of the Germans strikes a very different note: 'The Army had been fought to a standstill and was utterly worn out.' And looking to the future and the 1917 campaign, he flatly asserted, 'We must spare the troops a second Somme battle.'

So much for mythology. Charles Carrington hated it bitterly, and so did many of his contemporaries. One of them, Sidney Rogerson (2/West Yorkshire Regiment), in a minor classic called *Twelve Days* which Gerald Gliddon bravely reprinted in 1988, pronounced this verdict,

---

[2] The artillery bombardment opened on 24 June.
[3] C. E. Carrington was also Charles Edmonds (*A Subaltern's War*, 1929).

this post-war propaganda, piling corpse on corpse, heaping horror on futility, seems bound to fail from every point of view. *In its distortion, the soldier looks in vain for the scenes he knew.*[4]

Now Gerald has turned his hand to different work. In this book he has set out to catalogue the entire output of communication in English concerning the 1916 Battle of the Somme — a tremendous task. Here are listed the myths, the anti-myths, the distortions, the truths, the pity and the glory. Books take up a great deal of his space: books of prose and poetry, novels and history and memoirs, with plays and films, television and radio. Gerald does not, I think, indulge himself with words like 'ultimate' or 'definitive', but by whatever adjectives it may attract, this is a massive endeavour, which must be contemplated as a labour of love. We can only thank him for it.

John Terraine
1996

---

[4] My italics.

ACKNOWLEDGEMENTS

The main bibliographical references from published bibliographies that have been consulted during the research for this book include:

British Books in Print (J. Whitaker & Son)
British Library general catalogues of printed books to 1975
British Library on-line catalogue on CD-ROM up to 1995
British National Bibliography

During the preparation of this book I have received many kindnesses from both librarians and their staff and also from individuals who have been very patient with my continuous barrage of questions.

Those that I would particularly like to thank include:

Cambridge University Library, Imperial War Museum (Department of Printed Books), Ministry of Defence (Whitehall Library), The Mitchell Library (Glasgow), National Army Museum, The Prince Consort's Library (Aldershot), The Royal Artillery Institution (Woolwich), The Royal Military Academy, Sandhurst (Central Library), University of East Anglia Library (Norwich)

As for individuals, I would like to acknowledge the assistance of Maurice Johnson who helped me 'beyond the call of duty' and shared the considerable task of searching through several hundred unit histories including those which had to be rejected. Without his kindness and patience this project would have fallen behind its time schedule. Other individuals who were always keen to help were Peter Turner of the Norfolk County Library, who provided endless lists of books published on the First World War for me to search through, and the following friends: Peter Batchelor, John Bolton, Peter Harris and Bob Wyatt. My daughter Eleanor Fisher helped a great deal with keying some of the subjects into the word processor, and my wife Wynne was a great support over the five years that I spent on this book's preparation.

I would also like to thank the trustees of the John Jarrold Trust for a grant towards the cost of travel to some of the various libraries I have mentioned.

Finally I have dedicated this book to Leo Cooper, the publishing doyen of books on military history and biography in the last thirty years, and certainly on his own with the demise of William Kimber Ltd. Publishing in this specialist field is notoriously hazardous and Leo has stuck at it through thick and thin. He was also the first 'outsider' to see my manuscript of *When the Barrage Lifts* and through his enthusiasm gave me the courage to proceed with its publication.

With only a few exceptions I have not included books which are either Rolls of Honour only or books of solely educational interest. I have included a very few articles from regimental journals and have almost entirely excluded private publications.

In the cases where I was unable to complete an entry yet decided to include it anyway I have put ?. Where this information does not exist on the original material I have used square brackets.

I have 'borrowed' Cyril Falls's star rating from his bibliography *War Books* and where I have listed a book which he rated with a star rating of one to four then I have included this information at the end of the entry.

INTRODUCTION

Between 1981 and 1986 I researched in libraries and archives for material on the topography and history of the Battle of the Somme. All told I looked through well over a thousand books and documents. I used a combination of secondary as well as primary sources. This material was turned into a book called *When the Barrage Lifts* which was self-published in 1987.

I then conceived the idea of producing a bibliography of the 1916 Battle of the Somme and duly worked on it for a couple of years. This research was put to one side as I wished to work on two books about the men who won the Victoria Cross during the Great War. After the 1914 VC volume was published I took up research for the bibliography again and spent a further two years on this project.

Although the task was a daunting one, I felt that with my research for *Barrage* it would be a shame if this bibliographical material was wasted; in other words I believed that I had a head start. The only published bibliography on a Great War battle that I could trace was a book on the Battle of Jutland, and I have yet to set eyes on this. Both battles were controversial, but then there was hardly a Great War battle that was not controversial. However, it is very important that I set out the parameters that I worked to, which are as follows:

The works consulted deal with the land war only, and are all in the English language; there are a few French and German items, but only when an English translation was published. An example is Ernst Junger's *The Storm of Steel*, which is listed under biographies.

The great majority of English publications were published in London, thus the place of publication is only listed for books published outside London. For books published in the dominions, the town of publication, e.g. Sydney or Auckland, has taken precedence over any subsequent London publication.

While tracking down books that include Somme material I have looked at hundreds more that in the end have not been listed here. The reason for this is simply that there have been so many books written about the Great War which give nothing away in their titles. Take, for example, *Uncle Fred's War*; the questions asked after finding this book in a library are: just who was Uncle Fred? Did he serve on the Somme in 1916 and if so which unit did he serve with? Has the book any pictures, and what are the maps like if any are included?

It was the worth of the book to a researcher that concerned me, and not what sort of production it was. Therefore, I hope that researchers into the Battle of the Somme will be able to rely on this bibliography for the answer to most queries about whether a book on the Great War contains Somme material.

Of course, this bibliography does not include everything published on the Somme. I have yet to find a perfect bibliography, just as I have yet to find a perfect library index system. However, I can assure readers that I have spent a great many hours in trying to achieve a reasonable level of usefulness for researchers. By listing films and oral interviews as well as listing books, I have attempted to give the most comprehensive account of sources yet published. Having all this material 'under one roof' will I hope be a bonus.

Of the two thousand items listed in the following pages the first were published in 1916, including John Buchan's *The Battle of the Somme*, A.J. Dawson's *Somme Battle Stories*, M. MacDonagh's *The Irish at the Front*, *The Great Advance: Tales from the Somme Battlefield* . . . and *Sir Douglas Haig's Great Push*.

There is nothing very significant to say about these titles: what they have in common is that they were all used for propaganda purposes. As the war was barely halfway through its course, this is hardly surprising.

In 1917 there were at least six more books on the Somme published and most of these were written by official war correspondents or journalists, writers such as Philip Gibbs or H. Perry Robinson. John Masefield, who knew the old front line as well as anybody, published the first of his two Somme books with *The Old Front Line* as its title. The first of the really useful memoirs, as far as researchers are concerned, was also published and this was Bernard Adams's *Nothing of Importance*. Admittedly this book is more useful for the first months of 1916 rather than the last six months, but it is very detailed and includes maps which one would have thought would have been censored, such was the detail that they gave of the British positions.

In 1918 Edward Liveing's *Battle*, a study of a subaltern's impressions of 1 July 1916, was published having previously appeared in *Blackwood's Magazine*. Conan Doyle reached 1916 in his series *The British Campaign in France and Flanders*.

After the Armistice, in the early 1920s books on the Somme continued to be published at the rate of around six titles a year and these were now made up of memoirs, poems, novels and unofficial history volumes. For the period 1925–8 the graph of publications dipped, however, only to be followed by an explosion of publishing activity between 1928 and 1930. Publication of books about the war peaked at this time and the reading public could seemingly not get enough of them. In this short period of three years such classics as Edmund Blunden's *Undertones of War*, Siegfried Sassoon's *Memoirs of a Fox Hunting Man*, followed by his *Memoirs of an Infantry Officer*, Ernst Junger's *The Storm of Steel* and Robert Graves's *Goodbye to All That* all saw the light of day.

All of these books were in part concerned with the Somme battle and all became classics. Over the years their authors have become 'cultural heroes' and have produced a veritable industry of studies, articles and biographies. A key question about these memoirs is whether they represent the truth about the war, an issue that I have no wish to enter into here. It should be stressed that Messrs Blunden, Graves and Sassoon were all educated men who wrote their memoirs from the position of an officer; in this way they were far from typical of the 'rank and file' of the ordinary British soldier. The ranker as a writer was yet to make an appearance on the library shelves.

In 1933 this gap was rectified with the appearance of Frank Richards's *Old Soldiers Never Die*. Richards had read Graves's autobiography and other memoirs and considered that he too could turn his hand to such a book about his experiences as a regular in the

Great War. Once he had saved up enough money to cover the cost of sending his manuscript through the post, he addressed it to Robert Graves who was a former member of the same regiment, namely the 2nd Royal Welch Fusiliers. Richards asked Graves whether the book was worth publishing and Graves considered that it was and virtually took over the process of dealing with the publisher as well as 'licking it into shape'.

However, after the early 1930s a significant change occurred, for there now began a rejection of books about the war at the very time that the real possibility of a further European conflict loomed. People had read enough and wanted to forget the whole ghastly business.

It is hardly surprising that for the next twenty-odd years interest in the Great War, which had by then become the First World War, virtually disappeared altogether. A slight revival occurred with the publication of Leon Wolf's *In Flanders Fields* in 1958. In 1963 John Terraine published his life of Haig and A.J.P. Taylor published his book on the First World War.

It was to be television that created a massive increase in demand for literature about the war, combined with the fiftieth anniversary of the beginnings of the war in 1914. BBC 2 began a run of its famous Great War series in August 1964 and it was quickly repeated on BBC 1. A partwork published by Purnells ran for many weeks and provided readers of magazines with a pictorial account of the war, with a text often written by a new generation of military historians. The new men were people like Correlli Barnett, Victor Bonham Carter, Brian Gardner, Alistair Horne, Robert Kee, Barrie Pitt, John Terraine and John Williams. The historian who has stayed the course for the longest period is John Terraine, a lifelong supporter of Haig's military reputation and of the very real success of the British Army in 1918.

Captain B.H. Liddell Hart was ever present and had a team of young historians under his wing, including Brian Bond. After Hart's death his archive was transferred to King's College in London and has provided a rich mine for scholars during the last twenty years. Hart and Terraine fell out over the Somme programme in the BBC's Great War series and Terraine won that round. Not surprisingly the argument was about Hart wanting to put his own ideas across, which were very much of an anti-Haig stamp, while ignoring the views of the producer and the other scriptwriters.

In 1963 the play *Oh! What a Lovely War* opened in London in March, directed by Joan Littlewood. Although it was a very entertaining piece of theatre it was a gross caricature of the First World War and of British generals in particular. One of the reasons for the play's success was its timing, as peace was very much in vogue with the younger generation, with its love of flower power, hippies and the songs of the Beatles.

The subsequent film, directed by Richard Attenborough, was of course seen by many more thousands of people than the play, and was not only very popular but also very influential on how the First World War was perceived. As a result of this *tour de force* it was several years before the war was restored to some form of respectability as a subject for study: the debate had simply become over-simplified.

In my humble opinion it is not for one generation to pass judgement on another without being fully aware of the facts. In the question of First World War British generals, it is well known that they were relatively inexperienced as well as being untrained in scientific matters. This was not the case with their French and German counterparts.

In the late 1960s a Lincolnshire farmer visited the Somme battlefields for the first time. He was struck by the large number of cemeteries and in particular with the number of young men who had all died on one day, namely 1 July 1916. In 1971 he published a book about these men called *The First Day on the Somme*, which not only spawned a whole host of imitators but also distorted study of the battle and indeed of the Western Front. There are people who seem almost to wallow in this single-day disaster. During a lecture Charles Carrington, who served on the Somme as an officer, publicly rebuked Middlebrook for his book which over-emphasized this one day in a battle that lasted more than four and a half months, and for suggesting that as a result the heart went out of the British Army, including its New Army Battalions.

In 1976 John Keegan of the Royal Military Academy at Sandhurst published his *The Face of Battle*, a study of Waterloo and Agincourt as well as the Somme. Like Middlebrook's book it was very influential. Sandhurst also spawned Ian Beckett, Richard Holmes and Keith Simpson who have all produced excellent books concerned with the war. In 1983 Lyn Macdonald, a former BBC journalist, reached 1916 in her vernacular history of the war. With the aid of a tape recorder and concentrating on the lower ranks of the British Army, she has now covered four years of the war and is working on 1918. Again, her books are hugely popular, but do not always make for an easy read.

In the past few years a lot of very good work has been achieved by amateur historians who have attempted to fill in gaps in the records and also by academic historians such as Trevor Wilson, Robin Prior and Tim Travers. It seemed to me that as the last surviving veterans 'fade away', the First World War has become a suitable subject for academic study and many historians are digging deep into the archives and providing fresh and thought-provoking works.

Finally, I would like to end on a personal note: if I had the misfortune to have a fire in my library, which books to do with the Battle of the Somme would I rescue? The answer is that I would attempt to grab as many of the following volumes as I could:

Edmund Blunden's *Undertones of War*
J.C. Dunn's *The War the Infantry Knew 1914–1918*
Robert Graves' *Goodbye to All That*
Ernst Junger's *The Storm of Steel*
Frederic Manning's *The Middle Parts of Fortune*
Frank Richards's *Old Soldiers Never Die*
Siegfried Sassoon's *Memoirs of George Sherston*
An Anthology of Great War Poetry

As on the proverbial desert island, if I were only able to take one of these books with me, then it would be Frederic Manning's *The Middle Parts of Fortune*.

Gerald Gliddon
Brooke, Norfolk
December 1995

A Note on the Battle of the Somme

The Battle of the Somme was initially planned at an Allied conference at Chantilly on 6 December 1915. The French and the British agreed that the British would take over most of the Somme front line from the French, who in turn would be released for fighting the Germans in the Verdun region. The French contribution was 40 divisions and 1,200 heavy guns.

At the end of June 1916, after a very considerable preparation, the British began a seven-day artillery bombardment on the German lines, which because of bad weather was extended by two more days. Finally at 7.30 a.m. on 1 July 1916 the British went over the top on a front of eighteen miles with their French Allies on their right flank. As is by now very well known the expected success of a walk-over did not materialize. The Germans, who were meant to have been destroyed by the heaviness of the bombardment, were quickly at their machine-gun positions and with a slow-moving and heavily laden foe had a sitting target of a considerable magnitude. Clearly the British artillery did not have anything like the number of guns which would have silenced the German front lines.

At the end of this first day the British Army had suffered its worst day ever and there were 57,470 casualties, of whom around 19,249 were killed. The casualties included 993 officers. This tragedy has over the years distorted the writings about the battle and the true miracle is that the spirit of the British Army, including divisions of the New Army, was not broken and the battle continued for a further four and a half months before officially closing on 18 November.

On 15 September tanks were used in battle for the very first time, but their novelty was rather lost on the day. It would appear with hindsight that it would have been better to have waited until the British had a considerable number of tanks with which to surprise the enemy.

The number of casualties in the Battle of the Somme has always been an area of controversy, not least because the Germans had different counting methods from the Allies. The Germans and the British each lost around 419,000 casualties and the French around 204,000. So if it is just a question of numbers then the Germans won; however, it was not as simple as this. Both sides were equally exhausted, but more long-term damage had been done to the German Army than to the British; in particular the Germans lost many of their NCOs, who were the backbone of their army. It was the British who, despite two further dark years of trench fighting, finally succeeded in breaking the German Army during August to November 1918.

PUBLISHED WRITTEN SOURCES: BOOKS

British Official Histories

Anon
Naval and Military Despatches Relating to Operations in the War
Part VI
HMSO, 1917
Originally published in the *London Gazette*, May to December 1916.

Becke, Maj. A.F. (comp.)
The History of the Great War, Based on Official Documents: Order of battle of divisions
HMSO
Pt. 1: The regular British divisions. (1935)
Pt. 2A: The Territorial Force Mounted divisions, and the 1st Line Territorial Force divisions (42nd–56th). (1936)
Pt. 2B: The 2nd Line Territorial Force divisions (57th–69th) with the Home Service divisions (71st–73rd) and the 74th and 75th divisions. (1937)
Pt. 3A: New Army divisions (9th–26th). (1938)
Pt. 3B: New Army divisions (30th–41st) and 63rd (RN) division. (1945)
Pt. 4: The Army Council, GHQs, Armies and Corps 1914–1918. (1945)

Boraston, J.H. (ed.)
Sir Douglas Haig – Despatches (December 1915–April 1919)
Dent, 1920
Despatch titled 'The Opening of the wearing-out battle' (originally published as a supplement to the *London Gazette*, 29

December 1916) covers the period from 19 May 1916 to 23 December 1916, pp. 19–59. (Falls★)

Edmonds, Brig.-Gen. Sir James E. (comp.)
The History of the Great War, Based on Official Documents: Military operations, France and Belgium 1916, Sir Douglas Haig's command to the 1st July: Battle of the Somme
Macmillan, 1932
The purpose of the Official History series was 'to provide within reasonable compass an authoritative account, suitable for general readers and for students at military schools, of the operations of the British Army in the Western theatre of war in 1914–1918'.

Edmonds, Brig.-Gen. Sir James E. (comp.)
The History of the Great War, Based on Official Documents: Military operations, France and Belgium 1916, Sir Douglas Haig's command to the 1st July: Battle of the Somme
Macmillan, 1932
Maps and appendices to the above.

Macpherson, Maj.-Gen. Sir W.G., KCMG, CB, LLD
The History of the Great War, Based on Official Documents: Medical services general history
Vol. III
HMSO, 1924
The Somme, pp. 11–53

This is a very detailed volume and includes many photographs and diagrams. It also has a list of medical units of the BEF that served on the Western Front, ambulance trains and field ambulances.

Miles, Capt. Wilfrid (comp.)
The History of the Great War, Based on Official Documents: Miliatry operations, France and Belgium 1916, 2nd July 1916 to the end of the Battles of the Somme
Macmillan, 1938

Miles, Capt. Wilfrid (comp.)
The History of the Great War, Based on Official Documents: Military operations, France and Belgium 1916, 2nd July 1916 to the end of the Battles of the Somme
Macmillan, 1938
Maps and appendices to the above.

Ministry of Information
Chronology of the war
Vol. 2: 1916, 1917
Constable, 1919
Includes tables giving a chronology of the Battle of the Somme from 1 July to 18 November 1916, pp. 46–73. The complete work, which ran to three volumes, was reissued in a single volume by Greenhill in 1988.

British Unofficial Histories

Adams, R.J.Q.
The Great War 1914–18: Essays on the military, political and social history of the First World War
Macmillan, 1990
The Somme, pp. 16, 43 & 82

Allinson, Sidney
The Bantams: The untold story of World War I
Howard Baker, 1981
References to the Somme are scattered throughout, but are mainly on pp. 204–25
This illustrated book is rather scrappy and consists mainly of extracts from memoirs and personal interviews.

Anon
The Great Advance: Tales from the Somme battlefield told by wounded officers and men on their arrival at Southampton from the Front
Cassell, 1916
References to the Somme occur throughout.

Anon
The Illustrated War News – Being a Pictorial Record of the Great War
Vol. 1 (New Series), Pts 1 to 12
Illustrated London News & Sketch, [n.d.]
References to the Somme are scattered throughout the text; first published in magazine form.

Anon
Officers Died in the Great War, 1914–1919
HMSO, 1919
This volume was incomplete when first published. A new edition was published in 1988 by J.B. Hayward which contains twelve pages of names previously omitted and a listing of deceased European officers in the Indian Army.

Anon
Sir Douglas Haig's Great Push: The Battle of the Somme
Hutchinson, [1917] (originally issued as a part-work from late 1916)

A popular pictorial and authoritative work on one of the great battles in history, illustrated with around 700 wonderful official photographs, cinematograph films and other authentic pictures by arrangement with the War Office.

Anon
Soldiers Died in the Great War 1914–1918
HMSO, 1921
This mammoth work in 80 parts includes a listing of some 667,000 names. Each entry includes the soldier's name, number, decorations, place of enlistment and, if different, residence. The list also shows where death occurred.

Anon
The Times History of the War
Vol. IX, The Somme, pp. 477–512
Vol. X, The Somme, pp. 81–120 & 405–44
The Times, 1916 & 1917
These books are profusely illustrated and each has a Somme map.

Anon
The Western Front Then and Now
C. Arthur Pearson, 1938
The book includes many 'then and now' comparative photographs taken twenty years after the end of the war, including several of Somme villages.

Ashworth, Tony
Trench Warfare 1914–1918: The live and the let live system
Macmillan, 1980
The Somme, p. 185
When first published this book was greeted as a new interpretation of trench warfare and contains excellent references to secondary sources.

Asprey, Robert B.
German High Command at War: Hindenburg and Ludendorff and the First World War
Little Brown, 1994
The Somme, pp. 225, 243–6, 248, 255, 258, 268, 269, 273, 280, 308, 350 & 389
This book tells the story of the most famous of Commander-in-Chief and Chief of Staff relationships. In August 1916 they came to pre-eminence when Hindenburg replaced Falkenhayn as Chief of the General Staff and Ludendorff became First Quartermaster General.

Babington, A.
For the Sake of Example: Capital courts martial 1914–18, the truth
Leo Cooper, 1983
The Somme, pp. 75–84
Between the outbreak of the First World War and the end of March 1920 a total of 343 men and officers of the British Army were convicted by military courts martial and executed by being shot at dawn. The author of this book, a former judge, revealed details of these trials and executions for the first time. In 1994 he published a fully revised edition which included new information from relatives of the executed men in a new preface.

Baldwin, Hanson
World War I: An outline history
Hutchinson, 1963
The Somme, pp. 78–81
This book includes maps.

Banks, A.
A Military Atlas of the First World War
Heinemann Education, 1975
The Somme, pp. 17, 147 & 152–8

Banting, D. & Emblinton, G.A.
The Western Front, 1914–1918
Almark, 1974
The Somme, pp. 46 & 48–9

Barnett, Correlli
World War One: The story of the Great War 1914–1918
Park Lane Press, 1979
The Somme, pp. 74–8, 81, 83–4, 100–1, 103, 105, 134 & 151

Barrie, Alexander
War Underground: The tunnellers of the Great War
Muller, 1962; reprinted 1990
References to the Somme are scattered throughout the text
This book is the definitive account of tunnelling and mining operations on the Western Front. By 1916 20,000 men were involved in this underground war, including the British, Australians, Canadians and New Zealanders, as well as the Germans. The book contains maps, diagrams and other illustrations including Hawthorn Redoubt and the crater at La Boisselle.

Beckett, I.F.W. & Simpson, K.
A Nation In Arms: A social study of the British Army in the First World War
Manchester University Press, 1985
The Somme, pp. 113, 121, 137, 147, 150, 182 & 207
This excellent book is written by several contributors on various aspects of the British Army in the war years and has a particularly useful annotated bibliography compiled by Keith Simpson. It also has maps and is illustrated.

Bell, E.W.
Soldiers Killed on the First Day of The Somme
Bolton: Ernest W. Bell, 1977

This booklet is a listing of the casualties of 1 July 1916 by unit.

Bell, E.W.
Soldiers Died in the Great War
Bolton: Ernest W. Bell, 1979
This booklet is a listing of the casualties of the 1st Lancashire Fusiliers and includes those killed on the Somme.

Bidwell, Shelford & Graham, Dominick
Fire-Power: British Army weapons and theories of war 1904–1945
Allen & Unwin, 1982
The Somme, pp. 82–7

Bond, Brian (ed.)
The First World War and British Military History
Oxford: Clarendon Press, 1991
The Somme is mentioned many times, including pp. 24, 31, 32, 33, 34, 35, 45, 47, 54, 58, 78, 81, 84, 148, 155, 275, 280, 300 & 311
This is a collection of brilliant essays by different historians on the various literary aspects of the war.

Bourne, J.M.
Britain and the Great War 1914–1918
Edward Arnold/Hodder & Stoughton, 1989
The Somme, pp. 39, 51–2 & 59–67, including a map

Bredin, A.E.C.
A History of the Irish Soldier
Belfast: Century Books, 1987
The Somme, pp. 441 & 450

Brown, Malcolm
Imperial War Museum Book of the First World War
Sidgwick & Jackson, 1991

The Somme, pp. 11, 47–89, 215 & 236–9
This illustrated book tells the story of the famous film of the Battle of the Somme.

Brown, Malcolm
The Imperial War Museum of the Western Front
Sidgwick & Jackson, 1993
The Somme, pp. 111–15
This book is highly illustrated.

Browne, Lt.-Col. Archie, MM, TD
Lest We Forget: A study of human conflict on the Western Front in the First World War
Bournemouth: Self Publishing, 1985
The Somme, pp. 33–43
This is made up of material from well-known writers.

Bruce, A.
Illustrated Companion to the First World War
Michael Joseph, 1989
The Somme, pp. 352–4
This book briefly tells the story of the battle and includes a map.

Buchan, John
The Battle of the Somme: First phase
Nelson, 1916
The Battle of the Somme: Second phase
Nelson, 1917
Buchan (1875–1940) was on the intelligence staff at GHQ in June 1916, but in October was forced to return home owing to trouble with an ulcer. Very early in the war he decided to write what was to become a multi-volume work on the war, which appeared in twenty-four separate volumes and commanded high sales. Each volume was 50,000 words in length, and Buchan did all the writing himself with the assistance of one researcher. One of Buchan's reasons for writing this multi-volume work was to keep the staff of the publisher Nelson's in employment: he was a director of the firm. Buchan also wrote novels, biographies and a considerable number of articles for journals and newspapers.

Buchan, John
A History of the Great War
Vol. III
Nelson, 1922
The Somme, pp. 152–218
After Buchan had written a history of the conflict while it was in progress, he completely revised the 24-volume work (1921–2) and reproduced it in four volumes. The above is the third volume of the series and covers the period from the Battle of Verdun to the Third Battle of Ypres. Maps are included. (Falls★)

Buchan, John
Episodes of the Great War
Nelson, 1936
The Somme, pp. 207–51
This book is illustrated.

Buchan, John
A History of the First World War
Moffat: Lochnar Publishing, 1991
The Somme, pp. 113–17
This is a single-volume abridgement of Buchan's multi-volume history of the First World War and is introduced by Victor Neuburg. It is illustrated with contemporary paintings.

Burns, R.
The World War I Album
Bison, 1991
This is a picture book, including around forty of the Somme.

Cameron, James
1916: Year of decision
Oldbourne, 1962
The Somme, pp. 115–23
Cameron became a doyen of Fleet Street reporters.

Carey, G.V. & Scott, H.S.
An Outline History of the Great War
Cambridge University Press, 2nd edn, 1929
The Somme, pp. 104–18
This book is illustrated and has maps.

Carmichael, Jane
For King and Country: Battle of the Somme 1916
Imperial War Museum, 1986
This fully illustrated booklet was issued to accompany an Impressions touring exhibition which was first shown at the Impressions Gallery in York. It has 28 pages and a map.

Carmichael, Jane
First World War Photographers
Routledge, 1989
The Somme, pp. 49–53
The book examines the work of photographers both official and amateur and reproduces 100 photographs from the archive of the Imperial War Museum, where the author works.

Catto, Alexander
With the Scottish Troops in France
Aberdeen Daily Journal (printer), 1918
The Somme, pp. 27–33
This book is made up of stories from the Gordons, Seaforths, Guards, Royal Field Artillery, Royal Engineers, etc.

Cave, Nigel
Beaumont-Hamel
Leo Cooper, 1994

This illustrated paperback, the second in a series called Battleground Europe, is a guide to Beaumont-Hamel, Beaucourt and the Ancre battlefields. It is thus concerned mainly with the experiences of the 29th Div., the Newfoundland Regt., the 51st Highland Div. and the 63rd RN Div. It therefore covers Freyberg's VC and the execution of Sub-Lt. E. Dyett, one of only three officers shot by firing squad in the First World War. It includes maps.

Chappell, Michael
Scottish Units in the World Wars
Osprey, 1994
The Somme, pp. 9, 10, 20–2 & 28
This is a fully illustrated paperback.

Chappell, Michael
The Somme 1916: Crucible of a British Army
Windrow & Greene, 1995
This is a large format book which is fully illustrated and includes colour pictures and maps.

Chasseaud, Peter
Topography of Armageddon: A British trench map atlas of the Western Front 1914–1918
Lewes: Mapbooks, 1991
This A3 paperback book consists of a selection of trench map reproductions from the author's collection. Somme maps are scattered throughout the text.

Cheyne, G.Y.
The Last Great Battle of the Somme: Beaumont-Hamel 1916
Edinburgh: John Donald, 1988
The Somme, pp. 111–18
Only around a fifth of this paperback book is actually about the fighting for Beaumont-Hamel in July and November 1916.

Churchill, Winston Spencer
The World Crisis, 1916–1918
Part 1
Thornton Butterworth, 1927
The Somme, pp. 171–96

Churchill, Winston Spencer
The World Crisis, 1911–1918
Thornton Butterworth, 1931
The Somme, pp. 639–55
An abridged and revised edition, with an additional chapter on the Battle of the Marne. (Falls★★★)

Clemenceau, Georges
Grandeur and Misery of Victory
Harrap, 1930
The French leader's views on the Somme offensive, pp. 20–1.

Coombs, Rose E.B.
Before Endeavours Fade: A guide to the battlefields of the First World War
After the Battle, 1976
The Somme, pp. 73–87
After this book was first published it became *the* guide to the Western Front battlefields. However, despite being in its seventh edition (1994), it is not without inaccuracies. The layout of the guide uses maps, contempory pictures and recently taken photographs.

Crutchley, C.E. (comp.)
Machine-Gunner 1914–1918: Personal experiences of the Machine Gun Corps
Folkestone: Bailey Brothers & Swinfen, 1975
The Somme, pp. 40–74, 75–7 & 90
The book is a series of personal accounts by officers and other ranks who were members of the MGC.

Cruttwell, C.R.M.F.
A History of the Great War 1914–1918
Oxford University Press, 2nd edn, 1936
The Somme, pp. 255–79
The author served in the 1/4th Royal Berkshire Regt., a battalion which was destroyed on the Somme, and also wrote its history.

Cruttwell, C.R.M.F.
The Role of British Strategy in the Great War
Cambridge University Press, 1936
The Somme, pp. 43–71

Dewar, George A.B. & Boraston, J.H.
Sir Douglas Haig's Command, December 19th 1915 to November 11th 1918
Vol. 1
Constable, 1922
The Somme, pp. 60–83, 84–125, 126–57, 158–71 & 184–208 (Falls★)

Doherty, Richard
The Sons of Ulster: Ulstermen at war from the Somme to Korea
Belfast: Appletree Press, 1992
The Somme, pp. 17–23
This is an illustrated paperback.

Doyle, Sir Arthur Conan
The British Campaign in France and Flanders, 1916
Hodder & Stoughton, 1918
The Somme, pp. 33–309 & 310–32
At the beginning of the war Conan Doyle was a private with the Crowborough Coy., 6th Royal Sussex Volunteer Regt.

Dugmore, Capt. A. Radclyffe
When the Somme Ran Red
New York: George H. Doran, 1918
The book concentrates on the preparation

of the battle of the Somme and includes 18 photographs as well as two panoramic sketches drawn by the author.

Dungan, Myles
Irish Voices from the Great War
Dublin: Irish Academic Press, 1995
The Somme, pp. 13 & 103–50
This book attempts to fill in a gap in the history of men from an Irish nationalist tradition. It has a chapter on the 16th (Irish) Div. on the Somme.

Edmonds, Brig.-Gen. Sir James E.
A Short History of World War I
Oxford University Press, 1951
The Somme, pp. 178–96
This single-volume history of the war was compiled by the official historian of the conflict. It includes two Somme maps. In 1914 Edmonds was GSO 1 of the 4th Div.

Ellis, John
Eye-Deep in Hell: Life in the trenches 1914–1918
Croom Helm, 1976
The Somme, pp. 19, 42, 63, 94–5, 101, 113, 119, 163, 166, 168, 171, 178 & 191
This book concentrates on trench warfare and what went on behind the front line.

Ellis, John
The Social History of the Machine Gun
Pimlico, 1993
The Somme, pp. 132–9
This paperback book is illustrated.

Esposito, Vincent H. (ed.)
A Concise History of World War I
Pall Mall Press, 1964
The Somme, pp. 88–90
This book is the work of seven historians and contains 52 maps and plans.

Everett, S.
World War One
Bison, 1980
The Somme, pp. 71, 88–92 & 94–5
This is a picture book.

Falls, Cyril
The First World War
Longmans, 1960
The Somme, pp. 165–78
The author joined the Royal Inniskilling Fusiliers and later became a staff officer GSO 3 with the 36th (Ulster) Div. in 1916. This is an excellent single-volume history of the war.

Farrar-Hockley, A.H.
The Somme
Batsford, 1964
This book is illustrated and has maps.

Ferro, M.
The Great War 1914–1918
Routledge & Kegan Paul, 1973
The Somme, pp. 76–7, 80–1 & 93
The author was a foremost French historian.

Flower, Newman
The History of the Great War
Vol. IX
The Waverley Book Company, n.d.
The Somme, pp. 1579–672
This is a part of a profusely illustrated multi-volume work, with occasional maps.

French, D.
British Strategy and War Aims 1914–1916
Allen & Unwin, 1986
The Somme, pp. XI, XII, XVI, 112, 181–2, 200–5, 210, 220–2, 230–1, 234 & 246

Gardner, B.
The Big Push: A portrait of the Battle of the Somme
Cassell, 1961
This book is illustrated and has a Somme map.

Garfield, J.
The Fallen: The design and spirit of the Great War cemeteries and memorials
Leo Cooper, 1990
The Somme, pp. 106–24
This fully illustrated book has 19 Somme pictures.

Germains, Victor Wallace
The Kitchener Armies: The story of a national achievement
Peter Davies, 1930
The Somme, pp. 195–293

Gibbs, Philip
The Battles of the Somme
Heinemann, 1917

Gibbs, Philip
Now It Can Be Told
New York: Harper & Brothers, 1920
The Somme, pp. 345–446
In a chapter called 'Psychology of the Somme' Gibbs attempts to get deeper into the truth of the war, as opposed to chronicling events as he did in other books on the subject.

Gibbs, Philip
Realities of War
Heinemann, 1920
The Somme, pp. 285–366
This book could be considered to be one of the anti-Haig books, and Gibbs claimed that he had never been allowed to tell the truth about the war as an accredited war correspondent. (Falls★)

Gibbs, Sir Philip
The War Despatches
Antony Gibbs & Phillips and Times Press, 1964
The Somme, pp. 91–191

Gibson, T.A. Edwin & Ward, G. Kingsley
Courage Remembered: The story behind the construction and maintenance of the Commonwealth's Military Cemeteries and memorials of the wars of 1914–1918 and 1939–1945
HMSO, 1989
Entries on Somme cemeteries or memorials appear on pp. 114, 115, 123, 124, 127, 129, 130, 159–61, 168, 189, 192, 199, 200, 203 & 204

Gilbert, A.
Illustrated History of World War One
Brompton Books, 1988
The Somme, pp. 15, 76, 78, 82, 84 & 85–91
This is a picture book.

Gilbert, Martin
First World War Atlas
Weidenfeld & Nicolson, 1970
The Somme, p.56
This book consists of maps drawn by Arthur Banks; several are useful for study of the Somme battle. The book has an introduction by FM Montgomery.

Gilbert, Martin
First World War
Weidenfeld & Nicolson, 1994
The Somme, pp. 239, 248, 256–7, 258–72, 275–6, 280–1, 283, 285–6, 292–4 & 297–9
This illustrated book is a single-volume history by an author best known for his multi-volume work on the life and career of Winston Churchill.

Giles, John
The Somme Then and Now
Folkestone: Bailey Brothers & Swinfen, 1977
This fully illustrated book contains many of the author's photographs using the 'then and now' technique. The linking narrative is based on extracts from memoirs, diaries and contempory sources. There are 18 maps. The book was revised in 1986 and republished by After the Battle.

Gliddon, Gerald
When the Barrage Lifts: A topographical history and commentary on the Battle of the Somme 1916
Norwich: Gliddon Books, 1987
This book sets out to tell the story of the battle by indicating what happened in each village or wood etc. associated with the battle. It also has short histories of the RFC squadrons that served on the Somme and an Order of Battle. It is illustrated and uses maps from the Official History. It was reissued in its third edition in 1994 by Alan Sutton Publishing.

Glover, M.
Battlefields of Northern France and the Low Countries
Michael Joseph, 1987
The Somme, pp. 147–65

Gray, D.
No More Strangers: A record of Peterborough men killed during World War One
Peterborough: D. Gray, 1992
The Somme, pp. 41–58
This paperback includes short biographies.

Gray, R. with Argyle, C.
Chronicle of the First World War
Vol. 1: 1914–16

New York & Oxford: Facts on File, 1990
The Somme, pp. 220–74
A map is included.

Green, Lt.-Col. Howard, MC
The British Army in the First World War: the Regulars, the Territorials and Kitchener's army, with some of the campaigns into which they fitted
Clowes, 1968
The Somme, pp. 72–9

Griffith, P.
Battle Tactics of the Western Front
Yale University Press, 1994
The Somme, pp. 4–5, 8, 10, 12, 15, 17–18, 31–3, 35, 40, 44, 54, 56, 58–9, 62–78, 82–5, 87, 89–90, 100, 114, 118–119, 123–4, 130, 133, 140–5, 148–52, 154–7, 168, 171–4, 182–5, 187, 193–5, 199, 206, 208–12, 259

Guinn, Paul
British Strategy and Politics 1914 to 1918
Oxford University Press, 1965
The Somme, pp. 121–64

Haig, Sir Douglas
'The Battle of the Somme'
in *Reynold's World's War Events*, Vol. 2, 1919

Haigh, R.H. & Turner, P.W.
Training the 'New Armies' 1914–1916
Sheffield City Polytechnic, [n.d.]
This A4 booklet describes the training and build-up to the beginning of the Battle of the Somme.

Hammerton, Sir J.A.
A Popular History of the Great War
Vol. III: *The Allies at Bay 1916*

The Fleetway House, [n.d.]
The Somme, pp. 195–259
This well-illustrated book includes a diary of events of 1916.

Hammerton, Sir J.A.
The War Illustrated: A pictorial record of the conflict of nations
Vols 4 & 5
Amalgamated Press, n.d.
References to the Somme are scattered throughout the text along with photographs.

Hammerton, Sir John (ed.)
The Great War: I was there
Vol. 2: *The Somme*
Amalgamated Press, [n.d.]

Hammerton, Sir John (ed.)
World War 1914–18: a picture history
Amalgamated Press, [n.d.]
Slaughter on the Somme: pp. 630–85
More Somme fighting: pp. 855–67
Battle of the Ancre: pp. 943–54

Hankey, Lord Maurice
The Supreme Command 1914–1918
Vol. 2
Allen & Unwin, 1961
The Summer Offensive, 1916, pp. 510–16

Hardach, G.
The First World War, 1914–1918
Allen Lane, 1977
The Somme, pp. 63 & 84
This book provides a survey of the economic effects of the war.

Harris, Henry
The Irish Regiments in the First World War
Cork: Mercier Press, 1968
The Somme, pp. 69–101

Harris, John
The Somme: Death of a Generation
Hodder & Stoughton, 1966
This slim illustrated paperback is by the author of the novel *Covenant With Death*.

Haythornthwaite, P.J.
World War One 1916
Arms & Armour, 1990
This is a slim and profusely illustrated book in the Fotofax series.

Hibberd, Dominic
The First World War
Macmillan, 1990
The Somme, pp. 89–122
This book is illustrated.

Hodgson, Godfrey
People's Century
From the dawn of the century to the start of the Cold War
BBC, 1995
This book was published in conjunction with a television series, and the chapter called 'The Killing Fields' contains footage and interviews about the Somme.

Holmes, Richard
Fatal Avenue: A traveller's history of the battlefields of Northern France and Flanders, 1346–1945.
Jonathan Cape, 1992
The Somme pp. 2–3, 56–7, and 118–31. The book is illustrated and includes a Somme map.

Holt, Tonie & Valmai
The Somme
T & V. Holt Associates, 1986
This small booklet is in the Battlefield Guide series and is ideal for the pocket. It is illustrated and has maps.

Holt, Tonie & Valmai
Battlefields of the First World War: A traveller's guide
Pavilion, 1993
The Somme, pp. 65–81
The book includes a Somme map.

Horne, Alistair
Death of a Generation: From Neuve Chapelle to Verdun and the Somme
Macdonald Library of the 20th Century, 1970
The Somme, pp. 81–93
The paperback book includes photographs and drawings.

Hutchison, Graham Seton
Pilgrimage
Rich & Cowan, 1935
The Somme, a first survey, pp. 39–52; High Wood, pp. 52–78; The Somme, battle-line, 1916, pp. 79–101; A honeycomb of history: the Somme refought, 1916–1918, pp. 102–23
The author was a senior officer in the attack on High Wood in July 1916.

Johnson, Douglas Wilson
Battlefields of the World War: Western and Southern Fronts
New York: Oxford University Press, 1921
The Somme, pp. 84–133 & 134–58.
This book describes the battlefield terrain, water-table and structure of the Somme area with some illustrations. It is very detailed and there is a Somme map in the map case, No. 9. (Falls★)

Johnson, Herbert C.
Breakthrough!: Tactics, technology, and the search for victory on the Western Front in World War I
Novato, California: Presidio Press US, 1994

The Somme, pp. 87, 101, 103–4 & 106–8
The book is illustrated and also has diagrams, but not one of the Somme.

Johnson, J.H.
Stalemate!: The great trench warfare battles of 1915–1917
Arms & Armour, 1995
The Somme, pp. 53–90
This book is a fresh assessment of the thinking behind trench warfare. It is illustrated and has maps, including the Somme area.

Johnstone, Tom
Orange, Green and Khaki: The story of the Irish regiments in the Great War
Dublin: Gill & Macmillan, 1992
The Somme, pp. 224–56
This book tells the story of the 36th (Ulster) Div., 10th and 16th Divs. It is illustrated and has two Somme maps.

Jones, Sydney R. & Vince, C.
England in France
Constable and Co., 1919
Sketches mainly with the 59th Division
Drawn by Sydney R. Jones, Royal Engineers
The Somme, pp. 120–37
The drawings are superb and there is a text by Charles Vince.

Keegan, John
The Face of Battle
Cape, 1976
The Somme, pp. 207–89
This book was a very influential study of three campaigns by a former lecturer at Sandhurst. Keegan writes about Agincourt, Waterloo and the Somme, and studies the men who took part, their weapons and the type of warfare they were involved in.

Keegan, John
Soldiers: A history of men in battle
Hamish Hamilton, 1985
The Somme, pp. 32–4, 72, 104, 122 & 178
The book accompanied a television series
and is well illustrated.

Kirchberger, Joe H.
The First World War: An eyewitness history
New York: Facts on File, 1992
The Somme, pp. 191–205
The Somme material is contained in the
chapter 'Eyewitness Testimony'. The
information is taken from soldiers'
letters.

Knight, W. Stanley Macbean
*The History of the Great European War – its
Causes and Effects*
Vol. VI
Caxton, n.d.
There is Somme material in Book 111, pp.
1–13, 14–29 & 30–43
The book includes some large photographs
and maps.

Laffin, John
British Butchers and Bunglers of World War I
Gloucester: Alan Sutton Publishing, 1988
The Somme, pp. 4, 13–14, 21, 51, 62–9,
70–1, 73, 75, 77, 98–9, 149, 154, 156,
163, 166 & 192–3
The book is a pretty one-sided study of
British Army generalship, and the title of
the book gives the game away.

Laffin, John
The Western Front Illustrated 1914–1918
Stroud: Alan Sutton Publishing, 1991
This fully illustrated work contains brief
references to the Somme on pp. 10, 40,
119–20, 136 & 160.

Laffin, John
Panorama of the Western Front
Stroud: Alan Sutton Publishing, 1993
The Somme, pp. 32–41
This is a collection of Western Front
panoramas, which first appeared in a
French 1916 publication and were drawn
by the illustrator Georges Malfroy. Many of
them are double page spreads.

Liddell Hart, Capt. B.H.
*'Impressions of the Great British Offensive on
the Somme by a company commander who saw
3½ weeks of it'*
This unpublished manuscript is available in
British libraries and in it Hart is fulsome in
his praise for the organization of the
Somme battle, the use of artillery and for
the Allied mastery of the air. This entry is
included as it represents the original
thinking of a military historian who later
completely changed his views on the battle
and its leadership.

Liddell Hart, B.H.
History of the First World War
Cassell, 1934
The Somme, pp. 231–53
This book was first published as *The Real
War*. The author served as an officer with
the King's Own Yorkshire Light Infantry
at the beginning of the Battle of the
Somme. For a long time this book was
considered to be the best one-volume
history of the First World War and has
rarely been out of print. It is illustrated
and has maps.

Liddell Hart, B.H.
Through the Fog of War
Faber & Faber, 1935
The Somme, pp. 251–8

Liddle, Peter H.
Testimony of War 1914–1918
Michael Russell, 1979
The Somme, pp. 48–54
An earlier book compiled by the author from his famous archive.

Liddle, Peter H.
Home Fires & Foreign Fields: British social and military experience in the First World War
Brasseys Defence Publishers, 1985
This book was based on a collection of conference papers given at a conference in Sunderland in 1984. The Somme is mentioned in Chapters 3, 4, 10 & 14.

Liddle, Peter H.
The Soldier's War 1914–1918
Blandford, 1988
The Somme, pp. 94–110
This book is one of a trilogy written up from a comprehensive archive on the First World War formed by the author and now housed at Leeds University.

Liddle, Peter H.
1916 – Battle of the Somme: A reappraisal
Leo Cooper, 1992
This book draws heavily on the Liddle archive based at Leeds University, and compares what actually happened with what was recorded at the time. It is illustrated and has maps.

Livesey, Anthony
Viking Atlas of World War I
Penguin, 1994
The Somme, pp. 100–1 & 106–7
This is a well-produced atlas of the war, but a reviewer in *The Times Literary Supplement* (18 November 1994) described the text as being 'the usual mixture of half-truth and generalization, based on a relatively out-of-date bibliography'.

Lloyd, Alan
The War in the Trenches
Granada, 1976
The Somme, pp. 7, 79, 83, 84, 85–9, 89–95, 95–6, 99, 101, 103, 108–110, 113–19, 121, 124–5 & 141
The book is illustrated and has maps. It is a volume in The British at War series (general editor Ludovic Kennedy).

London County Council
Record of Service in the Great War 1914–18 by Members of the Council's Staff
London County Council, 1922
The Somme, pp. 35–52
This book is an extremely comprehensive work and contains a full record of what happened to members of the LCC who served in the war. The book reveals that 168 men from the council were killed in the period from 1 July to 16 November 1916.

Longworth, Philip
The Unending Vigil: A history of the Commonwealth War Graves Commission 1917–1967
Constable, 1967
The Somme, pp. 17, 18, 66, 74, 82, 86, 101, 102, 103, 126, 127, 130, 137, 165 & 168
The book has an introduction by Edmund Blunden.

McCarthy, C.
The Somme: The day-by-day account
Arms & Armour, 1993
This book is a chronology of the battle and is fully illustrated with maps used from the

Official History. It has an introduction by Peter Simkins; he and the author are both on the staff of the Imperial War Museum.

MacDonagh, Michael
The Irish on the Somme
Hodder & Stoughton, 1917
The Somme, pp. 24–46, 67–83 & 138–51
This book has an introduction by John Redmond, MP, who died of wounds received on 7 June 1917 when leading his men in an attack on Wytschaete Wood. The book mentions the Somme elsewhere than on the above pages and describes VC actions.

Macdonald, Lyn
Somme
Michael Joseph, 1983
This book is one of Lyn Macdonald's vernacular histories of the First World War. It makes extensive use of the recollections, diaries and letters of men who served in the campaign, and the text is often vivid and harrowing but occasionally touched by humour. The book is illustrated and has maps.

Macdonald, Lyn
1914–1918 Voices and Images of the Great War
Michael Joseph, 1988
The Somme, pp. 143, 152–89, 190, 196, 210 & 215
This book is fully illustrated.

McEntee, Girard Lindsley
Military History of the World War: A complete account of the campaigns on all fronts accompanied by 456 maps and diagrams
New York: Scribners, 1937
The Somme, pp. 285–94

Martin, Christopher
Battle of the Somme
Wayland, 1973
This is an educational book for schools. It is illustrated and has maps.

Masefield, John
The Old Front Line: Or the Beginning of the Battle of the Somme
Heinemann, 1917
This illustrated book covers the British positions as at the beginning of the battle, and is dedicated to Neville Lytton. It was reissued by Spurbooks in 1972, when the subtitle was dropped and the pictures altered. This new edition also has a 63-page introduction by Col. Howard Green, MC and a bibliography. (Falls★)

Masefield, John
The Battle of the Somme
Heinemann, 1919
This short book only covers the July 1916 fighting. It was initially published as a limited edition of 250 copies.

Masters, John
Fourteen Eighteen
Michael Joseph, 1965
The Somme, p. 73
This book is a picture history by the famous novelist.

Maurice, Sir Frederick, KCMG, CB
Lessons of Allied Co-operation: Naval, Military and Air 1914–1918
Royal Institute of International Affairs/Oxford University Press, 1942
The Somme, pp. 16, 25, 27, 28, 29, 30, 33, 34, 72, 73, 76, 77, 84, 89, 124, 130, 133, 137, 139, 143, 149, 152, 160 & 161

Messenger, C.
Trench Fighting 1914–1918
Pan paperback, 1973
The Somme, pp. 66 & 80–7

Michelin Guides
The Somme
Vol. 1: *The First Battle of the Somme 1916–1917*
Clermont-Ferrand: Michelin, 1919

Middlebrook, Martin
The First Day on the Somme 1 July 1916
Allen Lane, 1971
This book was based on interviews with several hundred survivors of the Somme battle together with unit war diaries. It was acclaimed as a masterly account of the opening hours of the Battle of the Somme, but has often been criticized for concentrating on one day of a battle which lasted until mid-November 1916. It is illustrated and has 11 maps, together with some useful appendices.

Middlebrook, Martin & Mary
The Somme Battlefields: A comprehensive guide from Crecy to the two world wars
Viking, 1991
Martin Middlebrook was joined by his wife to produce a guidebook which was partly based on experiences of tours run to the Western Front. It covers the two Somme battles of the First World War as well as earlier and later periods. It has maps and illustrations.

Millett, Allan, R. & Murray, Williamson
Military Effectiveness
Vol. 1: *The First World War*
Boston, USA: Allen & Unwin, 1988
The Somme, pp. 18, 37, 42, 50–1, 55, 59, 64–7, 69–70, 95, 213, 333, 337–9 & 343–7

Moore, W.
The Thin Yellow Line
Leo Cooper, 1974
The Somme, pp. 83–5
The book covers the cause and effect of war on men of the British Army who were executed for misdemeanours.

Moore, W.
Gas Attack: Chemical warfare 1914–1918 and afterwards
Leo Cooper, 1987
The Somme, pp. 106, 107 & 111

Mumby, Frank A. (ed.)
The Great War: a history
Vol. 6
Gresham, [n.d.]
The Somme, pp. 113–206

Neame, Philip
German Strategy in the Great War
Edward Arnold, 1923
The Somme, pp. 87–9; Falkenhayn, pp. 89–90; Ludendorff and the Somme, pp. 90–1; Observations, p. 91

Neuberg, Victor
A Guide to the Western Front
Penguin, 1988
The Somme, pp. 147–65
This paperback was withdrawn from sale because of plagiarism.

Norman, T.
The Hell they Called High Wood: The Somme 1916
Kimber, 1984
This book is a complete account of the history of the attempts to capture High Wood in July 1916, and of its eventual fall in September of that year. It is profusely illustrated and also has maps.

Occleshaw, M.
Armour Against Fate: British Military Intelligence in the First World War
Columbus, 1989
The Somme, pp. 5, 58, 120, 127–8, 140, 164, 168–9, 355 & 358

Oldham, Peter
Pill Boxes on the Western Front: A guide to the design, construction and use of concrete pill boxes, 1914–1918
Leo Cooper, 1995
The book has Somme references scattered throughout the text and is fully illustrated with pictures and diagrams. There is also a gazetteer of pill boxes which still exist on the Western Front.

Oman, Sir Charles
'The German Losses on the Somme, July–December 1916'
in *Lord Sydenham of Combe and others, a criticism of 'The World Crisis' by Winston Churchill*
Hutchinson, n.d.
The Somme, pp. 40–65

Palmer, Frederick
With the New Army on the Somme: My second year of the war
Murray, 1917
Palmer was an accredited American war correspondent at the British Front, attached to the BEF. He was later on Gen. Pershing's staff.

Parks, Maj. Edwin (late Royal Horse Artillery)
Diex Aïx! God Help Us: The Guernseymen who marched away, 1914–1918
Guernsey Museums & Galleries, 1992
The Somme, pp. 7, 8 & 10

This illustrated paperback with maps traces the history of some 3,000 Guernseymen who served abroad during the war, and lists the units from Guernsey.

Pétain, Henri Philippe
Verdun: Authorized translation by Margaret MacVeagh
Elkin Mathews & Marrot, 1930
Opening of the Battle of the Somme: pp. 197–205

Plumbridge, J.
Hospital Ships and Ambulance Trains
Seeley, Service, & Co., 1975
The Somme, pp. 40, 118, 132 & 178–80

Pollard, A.F.
A Short History of the Great War
Methuen, 1920
The Somme, pp. 211–21 & 284

Pound, Reginald
The Lost Generation
Constable, 1964
The Somme, pp. 251–61
The book is illustrated.

Prior, Robin
Churchill's 'World Crisis' as History
Croom Helm, 1983
The Somme, pp. 210–30
The above chapter deals with casualty figures on the Western Front and especially those for the Somme.

Prior, Robin & Wilson, Trevor
Command on the Western Front: The military career of Sir Henry Rawlinson, 1914–18
Blackwell, 1992
The Somme, pp. 135–260
This is a study of tactics and command

seen through the eyes of Rawlinson, Commander of the Allied Fourth Army in 1916. It is not a biography.

Puleston, William Dilworth
High Command in the World War
New York: Scribners, 1934
Verdun and the Somme, pp. 193–201 & 237–47

Punch
Published at the *Punch* Office, 1916.
This is a bound work of half a year's issues of the famous humorous magazine. References to the Somme occur throughout the text.

Putkowski, Julian & Sykes, Julian
Shot at Dawn: Executions in World War One by authority of the British Army Act
Barnsley: Wharncliffe, 1989
The Somme, pp. 99–166
The first book published that actually 'names names' of the 343 officers and men of the British and Empire forces who were executed by firing squad.

Redmond, Maj. William, MP
Trench Pictures from France
A. Melrose, 1917
The Somme, pp. 73–101
This book was based on articles mostly contributed to the *Daily Chronicle* before the author's death in 1917.

Reeves, Nicholas
Official British Film Propaganda During the First World War
Croom Helm, 1986, in association with the Imperial War Museum
The Somme entries are mostly on the Battle of the Somme official film, which

was first shown in August 1916: pp. 59, 61, 70, 96, 101–3, 104, 141, 148, 157–64, 166, 169, 183, 217, 223–4, 225, 227, 231, 232, 234, 235, 236, 238, 239, 240, 243–7 & 260

Regan, Geoffrey
The Guinness Book of Military Blunders
Guinness Publishing (paperback), 1991
The Somme, pp. 113 & 114–15
The Somme section is called 'The Butchers'.

Regan, Geoffrey
The Guinness Book of More Military Blunders
Guinness Publishing (paperback), 1993
The Somme, pp. 153–9

Richter, Donald
Chemical Soldiers: British gas warfare in World War I
Cooper, 1994
The Somme, pp. 127–8, 130–2 & 137
This book was first published in the USA in 1992. It is illustrated and has maps.

Robbins, Keith
The First World War
Oxford University Press, 1984
The Somme, pp. 53, 55–7, 68, 73 & 86
This short paperback deals with the main military operations of the war.

Robinson, H. Perry
The Turning Point: The Battle of the Somme
Heinemann, 1917
The author was war correspondent of *The Times* and this book consists of dispatches to that newspaper. The Battle of the Somme might have been conceived as a one-day battle but it turned out to be no 'turning point' at all except that it banished forever the expectation of one.

Rowe, R.P.P.
A Concise Chronicle of Events of the Great War
Philip Allan, 1920
The Somme, pp. 91–108 & 110–12

Scott-Daniel, David
World War I: An illustrated history
Benn, 1965
The Somme, pp. 64–72

Sellers, Revd William E.
With our Heroes in Khaki: The story of Christian work with our soldiers and sailors — and some of its results
R.T.S., [n.d. or details]
The Somme, pp. 139–56

Sellman, R.R.
The First World War
Methuen, 1961
The Somme, pp. 37–9

Seton, Brev. Col. Sir Bruce, Bt & Pipe, Maj. John Grant
The Pipes of War: A record of the achievements of pipers of Scottish and overseas regiments during the war 1914–18
Glasgow: Maclehose Jackson, 1920
The Somme, pp. 24–8
This book includes some superb paintings, including one of Piper James Richardson, VC at Regina Trench in 1916. There are also rolls of honour of pipers from the regiments.

Sheffield, G.D.
The Pictorial History of World War I
Bison, 1987
The Somme, pp. 116–25

Shermer, D.
World War I
Octopus, 1973

The Somme, pp. 114–33
This is a picture book.

Sillars, S.
Art and Survival in First World War Britain
Macmillan, 1987
The Somme, pp. 1–2 & 48–89
Reproductions of paintings and posters of the period provide the illustrations for this book.

Simkins, P.
World War I 1914–1918: The Western Front
Colour Library Books, 1992
The Somme, pp. 108–23
This large format book is one of the very best of the illustrated books published, if only simply because the photographs have been reproduced so well.

Simpson, Andy
Hot Blood and Cold Steel
Tom Donovan Publishing, 1993
The Somme, pp. 172–98
The book includes maps and illustrations.

Simpson, Andy
The Evolution of Victory: British battles on the Western Front 1914–1918
Tom Donovan Publishing, 1995
The Somme, pp. 50–74
This book contains two chapters on the Somme campaign and has some maps, including one of the Somme battlefield and some illustrations that do not relate to the Somme.

Slowe, Peter & Woods, Richard
Fields of Death: Battle scenes of the First World War
Robert Hale, 1986
The Somme, pp. 139–76
A book using contemporary accounts with newly drawn maps.

Smith, Percy John Delf
Sixteen Drypoints and Etchings: A record of the Great War
Soncino Press, 1930
Smith was a gunner and most of the drawings are of the old front line. The book was printed on handmade paper in an edition of 22 copies, with a foreword by William Rothenstein and an introduction by H.M. Tomlinson.

Smyth, J.
In This Sign Conquer: The story of the army chaplains
Mowbray, 1968
The Somme, p. 190

Smyth, Sir J.
Leadership in Battle, 1914–1918: Commanders in action
Newton Abbot: David & Charles, 1975
The Somme, pp. 109–32

Spiers, E.
Chemical Weapons: A Continuing Challenge
Macmillan, 1989
The Somme, pp. 72 & 74

Stallings, Laurence (ed.)
The First World War: A photographic history
Heinemann, 1934
The book contains several Somme photographs with captions.

Stedman, Michael
Thiepval: Somme
Leo Cooper, 1995
This small paperback is a volume in the Battleground Europe series. It is illustrated and has maps.

Stokesbury, James L.
A Short History of World War I

Robert Hale, 1982
The Somme, pp. 261–7

Swinton, Maj.-Gen. Sir Ernest
Twenty Years After: The battlefields of 1914–18 then and now
Newnes, 1936–8
This three-volume work has Somme information and illustrations throughout the text.

Tames, R.
The Somme
Jackdaw/Jonathan Cape, 1972
This is a collection of copies of original documents gathered together in a folder for educational use.

Taylor, A.J.P.
The First World War: An illustrated history
Hamish Hamilton, 1963
The Somme, pp. 90, 91, 96, 98, 99–105 & 214
This book was published in time for the 50th anniversary of the beginning of the First World War, and has proved to be enormously popular, especially in paperback.

Taylor, A.J.P.
English History
Oxford University Press, 1965
The Somme, pp. 59–61
This book is part of the Oxford History of England series.

Taylor, H.A.
Goodbye to the Battlefields: To-day and yesterday on the Western Front
Stanley Paul, 1928
The Somme, pp. 19–73

Written by a former captain in the Royal Fusiliers and General Staff, this book is particularly useful for a description of the battlefields just a few years after the war ended. It is illustrated with many postwar photographs.

Taylorson, Keith
Narrow Gauge at War
Croydon: Plateway Press, 1987
The Somme, p. 28
This paperback covers the use of light railways in the First World War and has many superb photographs.

Terraine, John
The First World War
Macmillan/Hutchinson, 1965
The Somme, pp. 114–23
This book was reissued in 1983 by Leo Cooper with new maps and a fresh introduction.

Terraine, John
The Great War 1914–1918: A pictorial history
Hutchinson, 1965
The Somme, pp. 214, 244, 246, 251, 258–9, 261, 269 & 273
Terraine was already at work on this illustrated book, commissioned by Macmillan, New York, when he was invited to join the BBC TV Great War team as scriptwriter and associate producer. The book was reprinting before it was even published and became a 'tie-in' with the successful BBC series.

Terraine, John
Impacts of War 1914 and 1918
Hutchinson, 1970
The Somme, pp. 107, 114, 120, 198 & 210
This book is illustrated.

Terraine, John
The Smoke and the Fire: Myths and anti-myths of war 1861–1945
Sidgwick & Jackson, 1980
The Somme, pp. 41, 46, 89, 90, 91, 92, 100, 102–9, 111–25, 128, 130–65 & 195
In this illustrated book Terraine looks back to earlier wars to find clues to the British success on the Western Front in 1918.

Terraine, John
White Heat: The new warfare 1914–18
Sidgwick & Jackson, 1982
The Somme, pp. 190, 204, 209–11, 214, 215, 228, 231, 240, 255, 264, 279, 280 & 322
The book has many illustrations.

Thierry, Jean-Pierre
The Somme: paths of memory
Amiens: Comité Départemental du Tourisme de la Somme, 1991
This is a small 32-page illustrated guidebook.

Thomas, W. Beach
With the British on the Somme
Methuen, 1917
The Somme, pp. 14–285
The author was a correspondent with the *Daily Mail*.

Thompson, P.A.
Lions Led by Donkeys: Showing how victory in the Great War was achieved by those who made the fewest mistakes
Werner Laurie, 1927
The Somme, pp. 225–35

Thoumin, Richard
The First World War
Secker & Warburg, 1963
The Somme, p 219–49
This translation from French is a volume in

the History in the Making series. It is based on accounts of 'those who were there'.

Travers, Tim
The Killing Ground: The British Army, the Western Front and the emergence of modern warfare, 1900–1918
Unwin Hyman, 1987
The Somme, pp. 127–99 & 203–5
This book by a Canadian professor is a fresh approach, as the author has gone back to the original source material. It attempts to cast new light on the command structure of the British Army. The book makes solid but worthwhile reading, providing a case study of the Somme battle and describing how it was written up by the official historian after the war.

Wade, Aubrey
The War of the Guns: Western Front 1917 and 1918
Batsford, 1936
This book, which contains an introduction by Edmund Blunden, does not cover the 1916 battles. Nevertheless, it does have some excellent photographs, some of which date from the 1916 Somme fighting.

Walsh, Colin
Mud Songs and Blighty: A scrapbook of the First World War
Hutchinson, 1975
This illustrated A4 paperback is a miscellany of songs, poems, pictures, articles, advertisements, drawings, etc. The Somme is interspersed throughout the text.

Ward, Cyril & Finch, Evelyn
Leigh and the Somme
Leigh Local History Society, 1986
(Publication No. 14)

This small booklet attempts to trace the Somme casualties as listed on the Leigh War Memorial. It includes a Somme map.

Warner, Philip
World War I: A chronological narrative
Arms & Armour, 1995
The Somme, pp. 45, 94, 95–100, 102–6, 135, 155 & 165
The book contains maps and illustrations, and attempts an 'overview of the motives and reactions of those involved, so enabling the reader to follow strategies and tactics'.

Westlake, Ray
Kitchener's Army, 1914–18
Tunbridge Wells: Nutshell Publishing, 1989
This fully illustrated book deals with Kitchener's 'New Army' divisions and is laid out in numerical order. The references to the Somme battle therefore occur within these brief divisional histories.

Westlake, Ray
British Battalions on the Somme
Leo Cooper, 1994
The illustrated book covers the engagements and movements within the Somme area of the 616 British battalions involved in the battle.

Williams, I.
Newspapers of the First World War
Newton Abbot: David & Charles, [n.d.]
The book includes reproductions of parts of the *Daily Telegraph* of 4 September 1916 and of the *Daily Mirror* of 22 November 1916.

Wilson, H.W. & Hammerton, J.A. (eds)
The Great War: A standard history of the All Europe Conflict
Vol. 8

Amalgamated Press, 1917
The Somme, pp. 1–185 & 233–46
This volume is one of a profusely illustrated series with photographs and maps.

Wilson, Trevor
The Myriad Faces of War
Blackwell/Polity, 1985
The Somme, pp. 2, 309, 312–22, 323–31, 331–7, 338–45, 346–8, 349–52, 354–61, 368–9, 371, 395–6, 459 & 533
The author, a professor at the University of Adelaide, has attempted to write a complete history of the war from the Allied point of view, and says that 'he is addressing readers who are not trained historians'. He has not only used documentary evidence, but has also used diaries and memoirs to reconstruct images of how the war was experienced, producing a very compassionate study of the conflict.

Winter, Denis
Death's Men: Soldiers of the Great War
Allen Lane, 1978
The Somme, pp. 40, 56, 82, 96, 103, 184, 187, 203, 212 & 218
This illustrated book provides a fresh approach to a study of the ordinary British soldier.

Winter, J.M.
The Great War and the British People
Basingstoke: Macmillan, 1986
The Somme, pp. 32, 52, 164, 166, 254, 288 & 291
This book attempts show the real effect of the war on the British people. It has many statistical tables and figures.

Winter, J.M.
The Experience of World War I
Macmillan, 1988
The Somme, pp. 17–18, 49–50, 84, 88, 92–4, 100, 107, 122, 131, 138, 140, 148–9 & 153
This book is fully illustrated.

Winter, Jay
Sites of Memory. Sites of Mourning: The Great War in European cultural history
Cambridge University Press, 1995
The Somme, pp. 1, 52, 133, 146, 161, 192, 193, 201 & 228
This illustrated book is made up of a series of cultural essays. It has an excellent 22-page bibliography.

Woodward, David
Lloyd George and the Generals
USA: University of Delaware Press, 1983
The Somme, pp. 74–97

Young, Peter (ed.)
History of the First World War
Vol. 4
Purnell for BPC Publishing
This is a book made up from a part-work of magazines and the Somme is mentioned. The books are fully illustrated and include maps with some pictures of equipment reproduced in colour. The part-work began in October 1969 and ran for 128 weekly parts, finishing in April 1971. It was published by Purnell in association with the Imperial War Museum.

British Unit Histories

ARMIES

Gough, Sir Hubert
The Fifth Army
Hodder & Stoughton, 1931
The Somme, pp. 136–62

DIVISIONS
Guards Division

Headlam, Lt.-Col. Cuthbert, BEF
History of the Guards Division in the Great War, 1915–1918
Vol. 1
John Murray, 1924
The Somme, pp. 135–86
The book includes a Somme map. (Falls★)

2nd Division

Wyrall, Everard
The History of the Second Division, 1914–18
Vol. 1
Thomas Nelson, 1921
The Somme, pp. 265–305
The book has some good maps and a list of officers killed in the Somme battle. The foreword is by FM Earl Haig.

5th Division

Hussey, Brig.-Gen. A.H., CB, CMG & Inman, Maj. D.S.
The Fifth Division in the Great War
Nisbet, 1921
The Somme, pp. 107–34
The book is illustrated with pictures and maps. It also has the Order of Battle for the 5th Division and the composition of divisional staff. The foreword is by FM Earl Haig.

6th Division

Marden, Maj.-Gen. T.O. (ed.)
A Short History of the 6th Division, August 1914 – March 1919
Hugh Rees, 1920
The Somme, pp. 20–7
The book includes a list of battle casualties and diary movements and actions, as well as giving a list of battalion commanders. It also has maps.

7th Division

Atkinson, C.T.
The Seventh Division 1914–1918
John Murray, 1927
The Somme, pp. 243–338
The appendices include a list of changes in the composition of the division and in command staff. The book is illustrated and has maps. (Falls★)

8th Division

Boraston, Lt.-Col. J.H. & Bax, Capt. C.E.O.
The Eighth Division in the War, 1914–1918
Medici Society, 1926
The Somme, pp. 65–95
The book includes some good maps and illustrations as well as the composition of the HQ in the appendix. (Falls★)

9th (Scottish) Division

Croft, Lt.-Col. W.D., CMG, DSO (late Commander 27th (Lowland Brigade))
Three Years with the Ninth (Scottish) Division
John Murray, 1919
The Somme, pp. 48–67 & 79–80
Maps and illustrations are included.

Ewing, Brev. Maj. John (late 6th KOSB)
The History of the Ninth (Scottish) Division 1914–1919
John Murray, 1921
The Somme, pp. 84–168
The book includes a list of VC winners, some good maps and some excellent water-colours of the battlefield.

12th (Eastern) Division

Scott, Maj.-Gen. Sir Arthur, BEd
History of the 12th (Eastern) Division in the Great War, 1914–1918
Nisbet, 1923
The Somme, pp. 47–85
This illustrated book, with maps, includes a list of staff and a list of VC winners and their actions.

15th (Scottish) Division

Stewart, Lt.-Col. J. & Buchan, John
The Fifteenth (Scottish) Division 1914–1919
Edinburgh: Blackwood, 1926
The Somme, pp. 77–112
This illustrated book includes lists of casualties by battalion. It has some maps in a pocket at the end. (Falls★)

16th (Irish) Division

Denman, T.
Ireland's Unknown Soldiers: The 16th (Irish) Division in the Great War

Dublin: Irish Academic Press, 1992
The Somme, pp. 78–103
This illustrated book has a Somme map. The division served on the Western Front from early 1916.

17th (Northern) Division

Atteridge, A. Hilliard
History of the 17th (Northern) Division
Glasgow: Robert Maclehose, 1929
The Somme, pp. 98–175
The book includes maps and casualty numbers.

18th Division

Maxse, Lt.-Gen. Iver
18th Division in the Battle of Ancre, 1916
n.p., 1917
This book has some excellent fold-out maps.

Nichols, Capt. G.H.F.
The 18th Division in the Great War
Blackwood, 1922
The Somme, pp. 35–153
This illustrated book includes a list of VC winners and two excellent maps. It also contains a good chapter on the Battle of Boom Ravine (pp. 139–53), which was just outside the time of the first Somme battle. Capt. Nichols was also known as 'Quex' who wrote *Pushed and The Return Push*. (Falls★★)

19th (Western) Division

Jeffreys, Maj.-Gen. G.D.
A Short History of the 19th (Western) Division, 1914–1918
John Murray, 1919
The Somme, p. 9

Wyrall, Everard
The History of the 19th Division 1914–1918
Bradford: Edward Arnold & Humphries,
1932
The Somme, pp. 30–68
This illustrated book, with maps, includes a
list of awards of VC winners and their
actions.

20th (Light) Division

Inglefield, Capt. V.E.
The History of the Twentieth (Light) Division
Nisbet, 1921
The Somme, pp. 61–113
This illustrated book includes some good
maps.

23rd Division

Sandiland, Lt.-Col. H.R. (Northum-
berland Fusiliers)
The Twenty-third Division 1914–19
Blackwood, 1925
The Somme, pp. 62–120
The book includes some rare battlefield
photographs and a list of divisional staff as
well as some maps.

25th Division

Kincaid-Smith, Lt.-Col. M.
*The Twenty-fifth Division in France and
Flanders*
Harrison, 1919
The Somme, pp. 9–36

29th Division

Gillon, Capt. Stair
The Story of the 29th Division
Thomas Nelson, 1925
The Somme, pp. 75–96
This illustrated book has maps, and

includes a list of VC winners and of reliefs
when the division took over a new sector.
It also lists red-letter days and the words of
a divisional song.

33rd Division

Hutchison, Lt.-Col. Graham Seton, DSO,
MC, FRGS
*The Thirty-third Division in France and
Flanders 1915–1919*
Waterlow, 1921
The Somme, pp. 12–32
The book includes a photograph of a
group of officers in Mametz Wood, a
hand-drawn map and many paintings by
the author, including the Somme.

34th Division

Shakespear, Lt.-Col. J.
*The Thirty-fourth Division 1915–1919: The
story of its career from Ripon to the Rhine*
Witherby, 1921
The Somme, pp. 33–73
This illustrated book includes some good
maps. (Falls★)

35th Division

Davson, H.M.
*The History of the 35th Division in the Great
War*
Sifton Praed, 1926
The Somme, pp. 27–54
The book includes maps, plans and lists of
casualties by battalions and RFA.

36th (Ulster) Division

Falls, Cyril
The History of the 36th (Ulster) Division
Belfast: McCaw, Stevenson & Orr, 1922
The Somme, pp. 41–62

The book includes a list of VC winners and citations, as well as a photograph of them and some other illustrations. The author was formerly a lieutenant in the Royal Inniskilling Fusiliers and later Captain General Staff 36th Div. A new edition of this excellent history was issued in 1991, which includes an eight-page colour photo section depicting battlefield scenes today.

Orr, Philip
The Road to the Somme
Men of the Ulster Division tell their story
Belfast: Blackstaff Press, 1987
The author, an Ulster schoolteacher, set out to interview as many survivors as possible and wove their experiences into a very moving text. The division, which had its origins as the Ulster Volunteers, suffered grievous casualties on 1 July 1916 in the attempt to capture the fortress village of Thiepval. The book contains many illustrations and some maps.

Shooter, W.A.
50th Anniversary of the Battle of the Somme
Ulster's part in the Battle of the Somme 1st July to 15th November 1916
Belfast: Northern Whig Press, 1966
This is a small booklet.

38th (Welsh) Division

Hughes, C.
Mametz: Lloyd George's 'Welsh Army' at the Battle of the Somme
Gerrards Cross: Orion Press, 1982
The majority of the book tells of the forming of the 38th Welsh Division and its role in the Battle of the Somme. This illustrated book has 14 maps, and was reissued by Gliddon Books of Norwich in 1990.

Munby, Lt.-Col. J.E., CMG, DSO (ed.)
A History of the 38th (Welsh) Division
Hugh Rees, 1920
The Somme, pp. 17–20

39th Division

Jobson, Allan (72109)
Via Ypres: The story of the 39th Divisional Field Ambulances
London: Westminster City Publishing, 1934
The Somme, pp. 52–78
The book includes many illustrations of battle areas not usually seen.

42nd (East Lancashire) Division

Fox, J.
Two Forgotten Divisions: The First World War from both sides of No Man's Land
Wilmslow, Cheshire: Sigma Leisure, 1993
The Somme, pp. 46–8 & 52–3
The 'forgotten divisions' are the 42nd (East Lancashire) Division and the German 121 (Independent) Division. The paperback is illustrated.

Gibbon, Frederick P.
The 42nd (East Lancashire) Division 1914–1918
Country Life, 1920
The Somme, p. 96
The book includes rolls of honour by battalion.

46th (North Midland) Division

Priestley, Maj. R.E.
Breaking the Hindenburg Line: The story of the 46th (North Midland) Division
Fisher Unwin, 1919
The Somme, p. 19

47th (London) Division

Maude, Alan H. (ed.)
The 47th (London) Division, 1914–1919
Stapleton, 1922
The Somme, pp. 61–78
The book includes some good photographs. In the 1920s a slim souvenir book was issued by this division to commemorate the unveiling of memorials at High Wood and in the village of Martinpuich; it is illustrated but undated.

48th Division (Territorial Army)

Anon
A Short History of the 48th Division (Territorial Army) 1914–1918, 1939–1945
Private publication, n.d.
The Somme, p. 9
This small, illustrated book, with maps, gives brief histories of units and a list of commanding officers.

Dopson, F.W.
The 48th Divisional Signal Company in the Great War
Bristol: Arrowsmith, 1938
The Somme, pp. 49–73
The book includes some good drawings by the author, some of which are of the Somme.

49th West Riding & Midland Infantry Division (Territorial Army)

Hughes, Lt.-Col. F.K.
A Short History of the 49th West Riding and Midland Infantry Division (Territorial Army)
Barnet: Stellar Press, 1957
The Somme, p. 7
This small book includes a list of divisional commanders and their dates, as well as illustrations and maps.

50th (Northumbrian) Division

Baker, Maj. A.H.R. & Rust, Maj. B.
A Short History of the 50th Northumbrian Division
Berwick-upon-Tweed: Tweedale Press, 1966
The Somme, pp. 18 & 21
This small, illustrated book, with maps, lists commanders and includes the order of battle.

Wyrall, Everard
The History of the Fiftieth Division, 1914–1919
Lund Humphries, 1939
The Somme, pp. 135–91
This illustrated book, with maps, includes mention of the reorganization of the artillery in 1916.

51st (Highland) Division

Anon
The 51st (Highland) Division War Memorial Beaumont Hamel (Somme)
Glasgow: Aird & Coghill (printer), n.d.
A superb book of photographs commemorating the 51st (Highland) Division memorial at what is known as Newfoundland Park. The book also contains some poetry.

Bewsher, Maj. F.W. (Brigade Maj. 152nd Infantry Brigade, GSO 2nd Grade 51st (Highland) Division)
The History of the 51st Highland Division, 1914–1918
Blackwood, 1921
The Somme, pp. 73–86 & 100–37
This author certainly pulled no punches in his writing, and of the Western Front at the end of 1917 he wrote for the benefit of a real understanding of conditions: 'Visualize two teams dressed in battle order playing football in the dark on a ploughed field in a clay soil after three weeks' steady rain'.

Farrell, Fred A.
The 51st Division War sketches
Edinburgh: T.C. & E.C. Jack, 1920
The Somme, pp. 21 & 22
The book contains a number of superb sketches of places and men associated with the role of the division on the Somme, including Plate 35 of Beaumont-Hamel, dated 13 November 1916. It has an introduction by Neil Munro.

Ross, Capt. Robert B. (Gordon Highlanders)
The Fifty-first in France
Hodder & Stoughton, 1918
The Somme, pp. 106–238 & 283–313
The book includes some very good drawings.

55th (West Lancashire) Division

Coop, Revd J.O., DSO, TD, MA (Chaplain to the Forces First Class (T.F.), Senior Chaplain of the Division)
The Story of the 55th (West Lancashire) Division
Liverpool: Daily Post, 1919
The Somme, pp. 30–45
The book includes maps, an order of battle and pictures of divisional staff.

56th (1st London Territorial Division)

Ward, Maj. C.H. Dudley
The 56th Division (1st London Territorial Division)
John Murray, 1921
The Somme, pp. 1–100
This illustrated book has maps. (Falls★)

Royal Naval Division

Jerrold, Douglas
The Royal Naval Division
Hutchinson, 1923; reissued Imperial War Museum, 1995

The Somme, pp. 183–207 & 208–22
The Ancre, pp. 171–91
This illustrated book has some maps. It also lists the names of officers killed in the Battle of the Ancre on 13 & 14 November 1916. The Royal Naval Division became the 63rd (Royal Naval) Division in July 1916 when it was transferred from Admiralty control to the responsibility of the War Office. As a consequence, casualties were not listed in 'Officers Died' or 'Soldiers Died'. This deficiency is in the process of being rectified by the Imperial War Museum who, working from returns to the Divisional Record Office, have so far issued lists for the following: Drake, Hawke, Hood, Howe and Nelson. The author was adjutant with the Hawke Bn. (Falls★)

Sparrow, Geoffrey & Macbean-Ross, J.N.
On Four Fronts with the Royal Naval Division
Hodder & Stoughton, 1918
The Ancre, pp. 171–91
The two authors were surgeons who served with the division.

Territorial Divisions

Magnus, L.
The West Riding Territorials in the Great War
Kegan Paul, Trench & Trubner, 1920
The Somme, pp. 83–110
This illustrated book has maps and a foreword by FM Earl Haig, and deals with the history of the 49th Div. who were on the Somme, and the 62nd Div. who weren't.

Stirling, J. (late Maj. 8th Bn. Royal Scots)
The Territorial Divisions 1914–1918
Dent, 1922
The appendix shows the battles in which these divisions took part.

BRIGADES

50th Infantry Brigade

Anon
History of the 50th Infantry Brigade 1914–1919
Oxford University Press, 1919 (private printing)
The Somme, pp. 23–36
The book includes maps and a list of casualties in a statistical breakdown. It also has a list of serving officers.

54th Infantry Brigade

E.R. (pseud.)
The 54th Infantry Brigade 1914–1918
Some records of battle and laughter in France
Aldershot: Gale & Polden, 1919 (private printing)
The Somme, pp. 31–74
This book is illustrated and includes a list of senior officers as well as a list of VC winners.

55th Infantry Brigade

Anon
A Short History of the 55th Infantry Brigade in the War of 1914–1918
Burt & Sons, [n.d.] (private printing)
The Somme, pp. 10–13

89th Brigade

Stanley, Brig.-Gen. F.C.
The History of the 89th Brigade, 1914–1918
Liverpool: Daily Post, 1919
The Somme, pp. 116–74
The book has portrait illustrations and a foreword by Lord Derby.

104th Infantry Brigade

Sandilands, J.W.
A Lancashire Brigade (104th Infantry Brigade) in France

Business Newspapers, [n.d.]
The Somme, pp. 12–16

ARTILLERY

Bidwell, Shelford
Gunners At War: A tactical study of the Royal Artillery in the twentieth century
Arms & Armour, 1970
The Somme, pp. 35, 39, 65 & 201

Farndale, Gen. Sir Martin, KCB
History of the Royal Regiment of Artillery: Western Front 1914–18
The Royal Artillery Institution, 1986
The Somme, pp. 141–57
Amazingly, considering the publication date, this was the first published history of the role of the artillery on the Western Front, and was the first of a series.

The following artillery units are listed by their number or letter rather than by the size of their guns and by unit (i.e. Divisional before Brigade).

Divisional Artillery

Hussey, Brig.-Gen. A.H., CB, CMG
Narrative of the Fifth Divisional Artillery 1914–1918
Woolwich: Royal Artillery Institution, 1919
The Somme, pp. 22–4
This book includes a list of casualties.

Johnson, Lt.-Col. R.M., CMG, DSO
29th Divisional Artillery, War Record and Honours Book 1915–1918
Woolwich: Royal Artillery Institution, 1921
The Somme, pp. 184–7
The book includes a roll of honour of all those who were killed, wounded or missing when serving with the 29th Divisional Artillery.

Scott, A.B., RE, Grice Hutchinson, L. Heathcote Amory, *et al.*
Artillery and Trench Mortar Memories – 32nd Division
Unwin, 1932
This large book is made up of accounts by men of the Division, and the Somme is mentioned throughout the text.

Macartney-Filgate, J.
The History of the 33rd Divisional Artillery in the War 1914–1918
Vacher, 1921
The Somme, pp. 24–51, 52–60, & 62–77
The book contains maps and a list of casualties of officers and men.

Wiebkin, Lt.-Col. H.W.
A Short History of the 39th Deptford Divisional Artillery 1915–1918
Berryman, 1923
The Somme, pp. 14–18
This small book covers the history of 186 (Deptford) Bde, RFA, and includes a roll of honour.

Artillery Brigade

Wadsworth, Capt. W.W., MC
War Diary of the 1st West Lancashire Brigade RFA
Liverpool: Daily Post, 1923
The Somme, pp. 28–37 & 38–47
The book is well illustrated.

Ommanney, C.M. (author/ed.)
The War History of the 1st Northumbrian Brigade RFA (TF) August 1914 – July 1919
Newcastle-upon-Tyne: J.W. Hindson (brigade printer), 1927
The Somme, pp. 93–134

Stirling, Brig.-Gen. J.W. & Richey, Lt.-Col. F.W.
A Short History of the 72nd Brigade R.F.A. 1914–1919
Woolwich: Royal Artillery Institution, 1920
The Somme, pp. 2 & 15–19

James, N.D.G.
Before the Echoes Die Away: The story of a Warwickshire Territorial Gunner Regiment 1892–1969
Torquay: Devonshire Press, 1980
The Somme, pp. 57–60
The book includes a roll of honour of officers and other ranks and a list of guns used by the regiment.

Battery

Grant, D.F., MC (late Maj. RFA)
History of 'A' Battery 84th Brigade RFA 1914–1919
Marshall Brothers, 1922?
The Somme, pp. 33–43
The short book has a foreword by Lt.-Gen. Sir Ivor Maxse and describes the events of 1 July 1916. It also has a fold-out list of the names of officers who served with the battery.

Gedye, F.S.
An Outline of the War History of the 240th (1st South Midland: Gloucestershire) Brigade R.F.A.
[n.p., n.d.]
The Somme, pp. 16–21
This slim pamphlet was reprinted from articles which first appeared in the *Bristol Evening World* in 1933.

Royal Horse Artillery

Burne, A.H.
Some Pages from the History of 'Q' Battery R.H.A. in the Great War
Woolwich: Royal Artillery Institution, 1922

The Somme, pp. 5–8

This short book has two illustrations and some fold-out maps which are not Somme.

Royal Field Artillery

Horsfall, Jack

The Long March: The story of the 'Devil's Own' B/210 Burnley Battery Royal Field Artillery 1914–1919

Lancashire: Lancashire Library, 1986

The Somme, pp. 150–66

This A4 paperback is a work of great enthusiasm and dedication, compiled by the son of one of the members of the battery.

Blore, J.E. & Sherratt, J.R.

Over There: C Battery 231st Brigade RFA TF 46th North Midland Division TF. A commemorative history 1908–1919

Fairway Press (printer), 1991

The Somme, pp. 92–6

The book covers the history of the 3rd (Leek) Bty. T.F. from its beginning in 1908. It was part of 46th (N. Mid.) Div. the first T.F. Division to land in France in early 1915. The history deals with the Gommecourt area and the northern end of the British front line. It has many illustrations and a Somme map.

Gee, Sgt. A.E., MM & Shaw, Cpl. A.E.

A Record of D245 Battery 1914–1919

London: Renwick of Otley, 1931

The Somme, pp. 69–90

At 184 pages, this excellent history is much longer than average and has a foreword by Maj. Petrie, DSO, MC. The illustrations are by Bdr. Norman Tennant, DCM. It has three maps plus a fold-out colour map of the route taken by the battery year by year, and a comprehensive roll of honour.

Royal Garrison Artillery

Berdinner, H.F.

With the Heavies in Flanders 1914 – '15', '16', '17', '18', '19': A record of active service of the 24th Heavy Battery RGA

Botolph Printing Works, 1922

The Somme, pp. 91–102

The author was wireless officer to the battery 1916–1919. The book is illustrated.

Penstone, L.F.

The History of 76 Siege Battery RGA

[n.p., n.d.]

The Somme, pp. 15–43

The book includes a roll of honour.

Hinderlich, A.

History of 88 Siege Battery RGA: 1 December 1915 – 5 July 1919

Hinderlich, 1920 (private printing)

The Somme, pp. 8–11

The author was the printer. The booklet includes a roll of honour.

Christian, Maj. W.F.A., DSO, RGA

History of the 91st (Siege) Battery RGA: December 1915 – 11 November 1918

Woolwich: Royal Artillery Institution, 1920

The Somme, pp. 3–11

This small book has a foreword by the battery CO and information on battery personnel and casualties.

Berkeley Lowe, Maj. Charles E., DSO, MC

Siege Battery 94: Diary of the World War 1914–1918

Werner Laurie, 1919

The Somme, pp. 17–32

The book includes a roll of honour, a picture of battery personnel and other excellent photographs.

Walters, Lt. D.J., MC, RGA & Hobbs, C.R. Hurle, RGA
History of the 135th Siege Battery
Hartley Robinson, 1921
The Somme, pp. 24–8
This book is well illustrated with a small map and also has a roll of honour.

Walker, Capt. Maurice C., MC, RGA
A History of 154 Siege Battery RGA France 1916–1919
Dublin: John T. Drought (printer), 1919?
The Somme, pp. 3–7
The author wrote this short, illustrated account from battery records and a personal diary.

Anon
The Royal Artillery War Commemoration Book: Written and illustrated for the most part by artillerymen serving in line during the Great War
G. Bell, 1920
The Somme, Pt. 5, pp. 115–54 (January to September 1916); Pt. 6, pp. 155–76 (November to December 1916)
On p. 135 there is a poem by Maj. C.L. Penrose, and there is an extract from the diary of the Master of Belhaven on pp. 139–51. The book includes a roll of honour and some excellent drawings and paintings.

CAVALRY

Bickersteth, Lt. J.B., MC
History of the 6th Cavalry Brigade 1914–1918
The Baynard Press (Sanders Phillips), 1920
The Somme, pp. 48–54
The foreword is by FM Sir Douglas Haig.

Mann, M.
The Regimental History of 1st the Queen's Dragoon Guards
Norwich: Michael Russell, 1993
The Somme, p. 358

Oatts, Lt.-Col. L.B., DSO
I Serve: Regimental history of 3rd Carabiniers (Prince of Wales's Dragoon Guards)
Norwich: Jarrold & Sons, 1966
The Somme, pp. 220–32

d'Avigdor-Goldsmid, Maj. J.A.
Short History of the 4th Royal Irish Dragoon Guards 1685–1922: 7th (Princess Royal's) Dragoon Guards 1688–1922. 4th/7th Royal Dragoon Guards 1922–1939
Aldershot: Gale & Polden, 1949
The Somme, pp. 23 & 48–9

Brereton, J.M.
History of the 4th/7th Royal Dragoon Guards
Banbury: Cheney (printer), [n.d.]
The Somme, pp. 326–7
This was published by the regiment.

Scott, Capt. F.J., MC
Records of the Seventh Dragoon Guards (Princess Royal's) during the Great War
Sherborne: F. Bennett, 1923
The Somme, pp. 69–75 & 80–3
The book includes a roll of honour of officers and men.

Hardy, S.J.
The History of the Royal Scots Greys (The Second Dragoons) August 1914 – March 1919
[n.p.], 1928
The Somme, pp. 99–101
This book was compiled by officers of the regiment and lists casualties by number as well as giving a list of officers who served from 1914 to 1931.

Willcox, Lt.-Col. Walter Temple, CMG
(commanded the regiment 1915–21)
*The 3rd (Kings Own) Hussars in the Great
War (1914–1919)*
John Murray, 1925
The Somme, pp. 156–63
This book includes a detailed roll of
honour for officers and men and has details
of officers who were wounded. It also lists
prisoners of war.

Evans, Capt. H.K.D., MC & Laing, Maj.
N.O., DSO
The 4th (Queen's Own) Hussars in the Great War
Aldershot: Gale & Polden, 1920
The Somme, pp. 77–8
This book includes a roll of honour.

Harvey, Col. J.R., DSO & Cape, Lt.-Col.
H.A., DSO
*The History of the 5th (Royal Irish) Regiment
of Dragoons 1698–1798: Afterwards the 5th
Royal Irish Lancers 1858–1921*
Aldershot: Gale & Polden, 1923
The Somme, pp. 325–37

Murray, Revd R.H., LittD
*The History of VIII King's Royal Irish Hussars
1693–1927*
Vol. II
Cambridge: W. Heffer, 1928
The Somme, pp. 585–90

Whitmore, F.H.D.C.
*The 10th (P.W.O.) Royal Hussars and Essex
Yeomanry During the European War 1914–1918*
Colchester: Benham, [n.d.]
The Somme, pp. 73–5
This book is illustrated.

Anon
*Regimental History of the 11th Hussars (Prince
Albert's Own)*

Aldershot: Gale & Polden, 1925
The Somme, pp. 36–7

Lumley, Capt. L.R., JP
*History of the Eleventh Hussars (Prince Albert's
Own) 1908–1934*
Royal United Service Institution, 1936
The Somme, pp. 248–56
This book includes a roll of honour.

Mallinson, A.
The Light Dragoons: The origins of a new regiment
Leo Cooper, 1993
The Somme, pp. 188-9

Lunt, J.
*The Scarlet Lancers: The story of the 16th/5th
the Queen's Royal Lancers 1689–1992*
Leo Cooper, 1993
The Somme, p. 115

Micholls, Maj. Gilbert
*A History of the 17th Lancers (Duke of
Cambridge's Own)*
Vol. II: *1895–1924*
Macmillan, 1931
The Somme, p. 107
The book includes illustrations, maps, and pen
pictures of the officers who died in the war.

Burnett, Brig.-Gen. C., CB, CMG
*The Memoirs of the 18th (Queen Mary's Own)
Royal Hussars 1906–1922*
Winchester: Warren, n.d.
The Somme, p. 120
The book includes a list of officers and
NCOs who became casualties in the war.

Darling, Maj. J.C., DSO
20th Hussars in the Great War
Lyndhurst: Darling, 1923 (private printing)
The Somme, pp. 70–1

Aquila [pseud.]
With The Cavalry in the West
John Lane, Bodley Head, 1922
The Somme, pp. 71–80
The book includes eight illustrations and two maps.

Yeomanry

Southern, L.J.C. *et al.*
The Bedfordshire Yeomanry in the Great War
Bedford: Rush & Warwick, 1935
The Somme, pp. 39, 43 & 45
This book includes rolls of honour of officers and men as well as a list of those men who were wounded. It also has a map.

Burrows, John W.M.
The Essex Yeomanry: Essex Units in the War 1914–1919
Vol. 3
Southend-on-Sea: Burrows (by arrangement with the Essex Territorial Association), 1929?
The Somme, p. 112
The book includes a roll of honour of officers and men killed or wounded.

Pease, Howard, MA, FSA
History of the Northumberland Hussars Yeomanry 1819–1919
Constable, 1924
The Somme, pp. 141–4
This book was issued with a supplement for 1923. The foreword is by FM the Earl of Ypres.

Keith-Falconer, Adrian
The Oxfordshire Hussars in the Great War (1914–1918)
John Murray, 1927
The Somme, pp. 164–73 & 182

This book includes a list of officers who served with the regiment during the war and a roll of honour of officers and men killed and wounded which gives the place of death or wounding. It is illustrated and has maps. (Falls★)

Platt, Brig. J.R., DSO, OBE
The Royal Wiltshire Yeomanry Prince of Wales's Own 1907–1967
Garnstone Press, 1972
The Somme, pp. 36–7
The book includes a list of officers commissioned in the Yeomanry.

INFANTRY AND OTHER UNITS

For five years after the end of the war a considerable number of unit histories were published; the urgency was a result of authors not wanting to lose contact with former comrades before it was too late. These histories were of variable quality but they did serve as mementos for the men who had served and also as souvenirs or 'comforting texts' for those who had been bereaved. Their publication was also an attempt to come to terms with the long casualty lists published during the war. They also served very often as part of the memorial to those men who were never to return to their families.

Many of these histories were, not surprisingly, very biased and this should be noted by readers and researchers. Nevertheless they are still an excellent source and many of them have become highly collectible. Some too have been reissued in recent years.

Everard Wyrall wrote seven regimental histories as well as three divisional ones, and also contributed an article to the *Army*

Quarterly magazine (Vol. 6/2) in July 1923, called 'On the Writing of "Unit" War Histories'. The guidelines in this article suggested that the first draft should be based on the General Staff Diary and that certain types of material, such as lists of casualties, should not 'lumber the text'. Personal material on how a VC was won should also not appear in the main body of the text but rather at the foot of the appropriate page.

Argyll & Sutherland Highlanders

Mileham, P.J.R.
Fighting Highlanders!: The history of the Argyll & Sutherland Highlanders
Arms & Armour, 1993
The Somme, pp. 96–9
This illustrated book includes a map.

Sutherland, D.
The Argyll & Sutherland Highlanders (The 91st and 93rd Highlanders)
Leo Cooper, 1969 (Famous Regiments series)
The Somme, pp. 72–4
Anderson, Brig. R.C.B., DSO, MC
History of the Argyll and Sutherland Highlanders 1st Battalion 1909–1939
Edinburgh: Constable, 1954
The Somme, pp. 44–5

Cavendish, Brig.-Gen. A.E.J., CMG
An Reisimeid Chataich: The 93rd Sutherland Highlanders now 2nd Bn. the Argyll and Sutherland Highlanders (Princess Louise's), 1799–1927
Butler & Tanner, 1928 (private printing)
The Somme, pp. 253–5

Sotheby, Lt.-Col. H.G., DSO, MVO
The 10th Battalion Argyll and Sutherland Highlanders 1914–1919

John Murray, 1931
The Somme, pp. 18–28 & 32–5
The book includes lists of officer casualties and very good group photographs of officers.

Artists' Rifles

Anon
The Regimental Roll of Honour and War Record of the Artists' Rifles
Howlett, 1922
As indicated from the title the book is mainly a roll of honour.

May, Col. H.A.R., CB, VD
Memories of the Artists' Rifles
Howlett, 1929
The book contains very little information on the Somme.

Bedfordshire & Hertfordshire Regiment

Maurice, Maj.-Gen. Sir F.K., CMG, DLit
The 16th Foot: A history of the Bedfordshire and Hertfordshire Regiment
Constable, 1931
The Somme, pp. 151–72
The book includes a list of colonels of the regiment and an appendix with a list of battalions in the regiment together with a brief history of each one.

Peters, G.W.H.
The Bedfordshire & Hertfordshire Regiment
Leo Cooper, 1970 (Famous Regiments series)
The Somme, pp. 69–71

Black Watch

Ferguson, B.
The Black Watch: A short history
Perth: printed for the regiment, [n.d.]
The Somme, pp. 88–9

Howard, P.
The Black Watch (Royal Highland Regiment) (The 42nd Regiment)
Hamish Hamilton, 1968 (Famous Regiments series)
The Somme, pp. 96–7

Linklater, E. & A.
The Black Watch: The history of the Royal Highland Regiment
Barrie & Jenkins, 1977
The Somme, pp. 148–55

Wauchope, Maj.-Gen. A.C., CB (ed.)
A History of the Black Watch (Royal Highlanders) in the Great War 1914–1918
Medici Society, 1925–6, 3 vols
Vol. I: The Somme, pp. 56–64
The book includes a superb map of the actions of the 1st Battalion, a roll of honour and some drawings.
Vol. II: 4/5th Bn., pp. 69–77; 6th Bn., pp. 135–56; 7th Bn., pp. 255–77
The book tells the history of the Territorial Force in the First World War. It includes numerous records and summaries.
Vol. III: The Somme: 8th Bn., pp. 22–5; 9th Bn., pp. 138–44 & 12th Bn., pp. 286 & 287
The book deals with the history of the New Army battalions. It includes maps and illustrations.
All three volumes include records of service, casualties and lists of operations, etc. (Falls★)

Border Regiment

Anon
A Short History of the Border Regiment
Aldershot: [n.p.], 1944, 6th edn
The Somme, pp. 20–1
This is a small booklet.

Sutherland, D.
Tried and Valiant: History of the Border Regiment (The 34th and 55th Regiments of Foot) 1702–1959
Leo Cooper, 1972 (Famous Regiments series)
The Somme, pp. 141–4

Wylly, Col. H.C.
The Border Regiment in the Great War
Aldershot: Gale & Polden, 1924
The Somme, pp. 73–104 & 112–15

Bardgett, Colin
The Lonsdale or XI (Service) Battalion Border Regiment (Lonsdale)
Wigtown: G.C. Book Publishers, 1993
The Somme, pp. 16–29
The book has rolls of honour of officers and men and casualty lists from 1 July 1916, along with some photographs of members of the battalion with pen portraits.

V.M. (comp.)
Records of the XIth (Service) Battalion Border Regiment (Lonsdale), from September, 1914 to July 1st 1916
Appleby: J. Whitehead & Son (printer) [1916]
This small book was compiled from notes by the C.O., Lt.-Col. P.W. Machell, and officers of the battalion. It has a map and some portrait illustrations.

Buckinghamshire

Swann, Maj.-Gen. J.C., CB, DL
Citizen Soldiers of Buckinghamshire 1795–1926
London & Aylesbury: Hazel, Watson & Viney, 1930
The Somme, pp. 95–104
Casualties are mentioned in each chapter.

Wright, Capt. P.L., DSO, MC
The First Buckinghamshire Battalion 1914–1919
London & Aylesbury: Hazell, Watson & Viney, 1920
The Somme, pp. 13–53
This book is illustrated with maps and photographs and has a very detailed roll of officers.

Buffs (Royal East Kent Regiment)

Blaxland, G.
The Buffs
Cooper, 1972 (Famous Regiments series)
The Somme, pp. 82–3

Blaxland, G.
The Buffs (Royal East Kent Regiment) (The 3rd Regiment of Foot)
Osprey, 1972 (Men at Arms series)
The Somme, pp. 26–7
This is a short paperback which is highly illustrated.

Moody, R.S.H.
Historical Records of the Buffs Royal East Kent Regiment 3rd Foot 1914–1919
Medici Society, 1922
The Somme, pp. 134–73
The book includes a roll of honour of officers and men, and also some good pictures and maps.

Cambridgeshire Regiment

Riddell, Brig.-Gen. E., CMG, DSO & Clayton, Col. M.C., DSO, DL
The Cambridgeshires 1914–1919
Cambridge: Bowes & Bowes, 1934
The Somme, pp. 41–89
The book is illustrated.

The Cameronians (Scottish Rifles)

Story, H.H.
History of The Cameronians (Scottish Rifles) 1910–1933
Aylesbury: Hazell, Watson & Viney, 1961
The Somme, pp. 109–26 & 132–44
This book includes extracts from the army lists of 1914 and 1919 and a useful map.

Whyte, Wolmer (ed.)
The Roll of the Drum: The Cameronians – The story of the Scottish Rifles
Hutchinson, [n.d.]
The Somme, pp. 64–9

Wylly, Col. H.C., CB
A Short History of The Cameronians (Scottish Rifles)
Aldershot: Gale & Polden, 1924
The Somme, pp. 30 & 36

Wylly, Col. H.C., CB
A Short History of The Cameronians (Scottish Rifles)
Aldershot: Gale & Polden, 1939
The Somme, 1st Bn., p. 16; 2nd Bn., p. 32

Anon
The Cameronians Fifth Battalion, The Cameronians (Scottish Rifles), 1914–1919
Glasgow: Jackson, 1936
The Somme, pp. 70–97
The book includes a roll of honour and excellent maps.

Anon
The Tenth Battalion Cameronians (Scottish Rifles)
A record and a memorial, 1914–1918
Edinburgh: Edinburgh Press, [n.d.]
The Somme, pp. 50–70
This book contains excellent portraits of individual officers who served with the battalion in France 1915–1918.

Cheshire Regiment

Crookenden, Arthur
The History of the Cheshire Regiment in the Great War
Chester: W.H. Evans, 1939, 2nd edn
The Somme, pp. 64–98
This book includes a roll of honour of officers and other ranks. The author was the colonel of the regiment.

Kelsall, D.
Stockport Lads Together. The 6th Cheshire Territorials 1908–1919
Stockport: Leisure Services Division, 1989
The Somme, pp. 30–6
This illustrated A4 booklet was one of many produced in the United Kingdom in the 1980s and reflects the renewed interest in local history and wider events. The 1/6th Bn. Cheshire served on the Western Front from November 1914.

Churton, Lt.-Col. W.A.V., DSO, TD
The War Record of the 1/5th (Earl of Chester's Battalion): The Cheshire Regiment August 1914 – June 1919
Chester: Phillipson & Golder, 1920
The Somme, pp. 44–58
This book includes a roll of honour of officers and men, along with a location table of battalion HQs during the war. It also has some superb maps.

Johnston, Lt.-Col. Harrison
Extracts from an Officer's Diary, 1914–1918: Being the story of the 15th and 16th Service Battalions the Cheshire Regiment (originally Bantams)
Manchester: Geo Falkner & Sons, 1919
The Somme, pp. 84–124

Coldstream Guards

Anon
The Record of the Coldstream Guards 1650–1918
Vacher, 1923
The Somme, pp. 67–9
This small book includes a list of commanding officers and accounts of VC actions.

Hill, E.R.
The Record of the Coldstream Guards 1650–1950
William Clowes, 1950
The Somme, pp. 40, 41 & 42

Ross-of-Bladensburg, Sir John
The Coldstream Guards, 1914–1918
Oxford University Press, 1928, 2 vols
The Somme, Vol. 1, Ch. 14–15, pp. 450–519
Casualties are included in the text. An accompanying map volume includes three maps on the Somme. (Falls★)

Connaught Rangers

Jourdain, Lt.-Col. H.F.N., CMG & Fraser, Edward
The Connaught Rangers
Vol. III
Royal United Services Institution, 1928
The Somme, 6th Bn., pp. 221–40
The book also includes a list of officers belonging to the 1st, 2nd, 3rd, 4th, 5th and 6th Bns. between 1914 and 1918. (Falls★)

Pollock, S.
Mutiny for the Cause: (Connaught Rangers)
Leo Cooper, 1969

Devonshire Regiment

Aggett, W.J.P.
The Bloody Eleventh
Vol. III 1915–1969

Exeter: The Devonshire and Dorset Regiment, 1995
The Somme, pp. 49–67
This book complements the Atkinson entry, and is a large book which includes maps and illustrations.

Anon
A Short History of the Devonshire Regiment
Aldershot: Gale & Polden, 1940
The Somme, pp. 27–9
This is a small book.

Atkinson, C.T.
The Devonshire Regiment, 1914–1918
Exeter: Eland Brothers, 1926
The Somme, pp. 143–95
The book includes lists of casualties of officers and men.

Dorset Regiment

Anon
History of the Dorsetshire Regiment, 1914–1919
Dorchester: Henry Ling; London: Simpkin Marshall, 1937, compiled for the Regimental History Committee
The Somme, 1st Bn., pp. 78–99; 5th Bn., pp. 48–57; 6th (Service) Bn., pp. 116–26
This excellent unit history includes rolls of honour.

Atkinson, C.T.
The Dorsetshire Regiment
Oxford University Press, 1947 (private printing), 2 vols
The Somme, Vol. 2, Pt. III, pp. 126–7

Popham, H.
The Dorset Regiment (The 39th/54th Regiment of Foot)
Leo Cooper, 1970 (Famous Regiments series)
The Somme, pp. 96–7

Duke of Cornwall's Light Infantry

Goldsmith, R.F.K.
Duke of Cornwall's Light Infantry (The 32nd and 46th Regiments of Foot)
Leo Cooper, 1970 (Famous Regiments series)
The Somme, pp. 94–5

Snell, L.S. (comp.)
A Short History of the Duke of Cornwall's Light Infantry 1702–1945
Aldershot: Gale & Polden, 1945
The Somme, p. 36

Wyrall, Everard
The History of the Duke of Cornwall's Light Infantry 1914–1919
Methuen, 1932
The Somme, pp. 158–95
This book includes a superb Somme map, a roll of honour and a good photograph of Delville Wood.

Newey, H.N.
The Story of the 1st Battalion the Duke of Cornwall's Light Infantry (32nd Foot)
Aldershot: Gale & Polden, 1924
The Somme, p. 42

Matthews, E.C. (comp.)
With the Cornwall Territorials on the Western Front: Being the history of the Fifth Battalion Duke of Cornwall's Light Infantry in the Great War
Cambridge: W.P. Spalding, 1921
The Somme, pp. 13–18
This book includes a roll of honour.

Duke Of Wellington's (West Riding) Regiment

Anon
The Duke of Wellington's Regiment (West Riding)
London: M. Page, *c.* 1958
The Somme, pp. 33 & 43

Brereton, J.M. & Savory, A.C.S.
History of the Duke of Wellington's Regiment (West Riding) 1702–1992
Halifax: The Duke of Wellington's Regiment (West Riding), 1993
The Somme, pp. 242–4
The foreword is by Brig. His Grace The Duke of Wellington.

Bales, Capt. P.G., MC
The History of the 1/4th Duke of Wellington's (West Riding) Regiment 1914–1919
Halifax & London: Mortimer, 1920
The Somme, pp. 69–99 & 103–7
This book includes maps and summaries of casualties and photographs of officers.

Fisher, J.J. (Military Correspondent)
History of the Duke of Wellington's West Riding Regiment (The Iron Duke's Own) during the First Three Years of the Great War from August 1914 to December 1917
Halifax: Fisher, 1918
The Somme, pp. 44–51
The book has a roll of honour, and includes some photographic portraits of officers, a list of POWs and where they were imprisoned, and a note on casualties.

Bruce, C.D.
History of the Duke of Wellington's Regiment (1st and 2nd Battalions) 1881–1923
Medici Society, 1927
The Somme, pp. 147–56
This book includes a roll of honour of officers and men.

Durham Light Infantry

Moore, W.
The Durham Light Infantry
Leo Cooper, 1975 (Famous Regiments series)
The Somme, pp. 27–30

Ward, S.G.P.
Faithful: The story of the Durham Light Infantry
Nelson, 1962
The Somme, pp. 363–75

Miles, Capt. Wilfrid (late 13th Durham Light Infantry)
The Durham Forces in the Field, 1914–1918
Vol. 2: *The Service Battalions of the Durham Light Infantry*
Cassell, 1920
The Somme, pp. 45–104
The book includes a map case in the back, portraits and illustrations.

Raimes, Maj. A.L., DSO, TD
The Fifth Battalion the Durham Light Infantry 1914–1918
Published by a committee of past and present officers of the battalion, 1931
The Somme, pp. 53–76
This illustrated book includes a map and rolls of honour of officers and men.

Ainsworth, Capt. R.B., MC
The Story of the 6th Battalion the Durham Light Infantry France April 1915 – November 1918
St Catherine's Press, 1919
The Somme, pp. 25–34
This book includes a roll of honour of officers and a list of commanding officers.

Veitch, Maj. E. Hardinge
8th Battalion Durham Light Infantry
Veitch, 1926
The Somme, pp. 88–111
This book contains portraits, plates and maps.

Lowe, Lt.-Col. W.D., DSO, MC
War History of the 18th (Service) Battalion Durham Light Infantry
Oxford University Press, 1920
The Somme, pp. 28–47 & 56–66
This book includes a roll of honour of officers and warrant officers, and a casualty list. Profits from the sale of this book went towards the Battalion relief fund.

East Lancashire Regiment

Nicholson, C. Lothian & Macmullen, H.T.
History of the East Lancashire Regiment in the Great War, 1914–1918
Liverpool: Littlebury, 1936
The Somme, 1st Bn., Pt. I, pp. 71–5; 2nd Bn., Pt. II, pp. 142–9; 7th Bn., Pt. VIII, pp. 419–29
The book includes some photographs of officers in the battalion and some good maps.

Lewis, A.S.
The Lilywhite 59th: The 2nd Nottinghamshire and 2nd Battalion East Lancashire Regiment
Blackburn Borough Council, 1986
The Somme, pp. 69–70

Garwood, John M.
Chorley Pals: 'Y' Company, 11th (Service) Battalion, East Lancashire Regiment. A short history of the company in the Great War, 1914–1919
Manchester: Neil Richardson, 1989
The Somme, pp. 13–19 including Serre, & p. 21
This is one of three books published in the 1980s about units of the 11th East Lancashires. The illustrated A4 booklet has a list of the Chorley Pals that formed 'Y' Coy. of the 11th (Accrington Pals) Bn. East Lancs. Regt. The book includes information on graves and memorials.

Turner, William
The 'Accrington Pals': A tribute to the men of Accrington and District, Blackburn, Burnley, Chorley and the neighbouring villages, who volunteered, fought and died in 'The Great War' 1914–1918
Lancashire Library, 1986
The Somme, pp. 27–31
This is a pictorial history of one of the Pals battalions. They suffered 585 casualties at Serre on 1 July 1916.

Turner, William
Accrington Pals: The 11th (Service) Battalion (Accrington) East Lancashire Regiment. A history of the battalion raised from Accrington, Blackburn, Burnley & Chorley in World War One
Barnsley: Wharncliffe, 1987
The Somme, pp. 137–78
This is one of a series of books compiled since the 1980s about certain Pals units. It is very well illustrated and includes maps, and a nominal roll of those who died between 1 and 5 July 1916 with their place of burial or memorial.

East Surrey Regiment

Anon
A Short History of the East Surrey Regiment
Aldershot: Gale & Polden, n.d.
The Somme, pp. 11 & 13

Langley, M.
The East Surrey Regiment (The 31st and 70th Regiments of Foot)
Leo Cooper, 1972 (Famous Regiments series)
The Somme, pp. 72–3

Pearse, H.W. & Sloman, H.S.
History of the East Surrey Regiment
Medici Society, 1933, 3 vols

The Somme, Vol. 2: 1st Bn., pp. 187–202; 7th Bn., pp. 209–21; 8th Bn., pp. 222–40; 9th Bn., pp. 241–51; 12th Bn., pp. 254–7; 13th Bn., p. 260
The book includes maps.

Aston, J. & Duggan, L.M. (comps)
The History of the 12th (Bermondsey) Battalion East Surrey Regiment
Finsbury: Union Press, 1936
The Somme, pp. 33–63
This book includes a roll of honour and has maps and illustrations. Letters from Sir Sydney T.B. Lawford and Brig.-Gen. F.W. Towsey are also included.

East Yorkshire Regiment

Wyrall, Everard
The East Yorkshire Regiment in the Great War, 1914–1918
Harrison, 1928
The Somme, pp. 135–85
The book includes a good map and rolls of honour by battalions and a VC listing.

Hadrill, C.I. (ed.)
A History of the 10th (Service) Battalion The East Yorkshire Regiment (Hull Commercials), 1914–1919
Hull: Brown, 1937
The Somme, pp. 68–107
The book includes a roll of honour and some illustrations and maps.

Barnes, B.S.
This Righteous War
Huddersfield: Richard Netherwood, 1990
The Somme, pp. 69–84
This book tells the story of the Hull Pals, the 10th, 11th, 12th and 13th Bns. of the East Yorkshire Regt. who were part of

92nd Bde. 31st Div. The book is illustrated and has a Somme map.

'Some of Them' (comp.)
A Short Diary of the 11th (Service) Battalion the East Yorkshire Regiment, 1914–1919
Hull: Goddard, Walker & Brown, 1921
The Somme, pp. 13–24
The book is illustrated.

Essex Regiment

Burrows, J.W.
The Essex Regiment 1st Battalion
Southend, John H. Burrows, 1923
The Somme, pp. 204–14
The book includes pictures of officers.

Burrows, J.W.
Essex Units in the War 1914–1919: 2nd Battalion the Essex Regiment
Vol. 2
Southend: John H. Burrows, 1927
The Somme, pp. 139–48
The book includes pictures of officers.

Burrows, J.W.
The Essex Regiment: 9th, 10th, 11th, 13th and 15th Battalions
Southend: John H. Burrows, 1935
(Essex Units in the War, 1914–1919, Vol 6)
The Somme, 9th Bn., pp. 36–51; 10th Bn., pp. 158–89; 11th Bn., pp. 292–308; 13th & 15th Bns., pp. 393–8
This is an excellent historical source, in three books that are fully illustrated and have maps.

Banks, Lt.-Col. T.M., DSO, MC & Chell, Capt. R.A., DSO, MC
With the 10th Essex in France
London: 10th Essex Old Comrades Association, 1921

The Somme, pp. 116–85
This book, which also includes some drawings, sold out very quickly on publication and was reprinted in 1924.

Gloucestershire Regiment

Newbould, Christopher & Beresford, Christine
The Glosters: An illustrated history of a county regiment
Stroud: Alan Sutton Publishing
The book includes a few pictures of the Somme.

Daniel, David Scott
Cap of Honour: The story of the Gloucestershire Regiment (The 28th/61st Foot), 1694–1950
Harrap, 1951
The Somme, pp. 220–33
The book includes a list of battalions and where they served.

Anon
A Short History of the Gloucester Regiment (28th/61st Foot)
[n.p., n.d.]
The Somme, pp. 20–1
This is a small book.

Pagan, Brig.-Gen. A.W., DSO, DL
Infantry: An account of the 1st Bn Gloucestershire Regiment during the war 1914–1918
Aldershot: Gale & Polden, 1951
The Somme, pp. 93–119 & 120–32
This book is a superb account of the battalion. It was issued with a separate case of 15 maps, two of which are for the Somme battle. The text includes locations and moves of the battalion.

Wyrall, Everard
The Gloucestershire Regiment in the War, 1914–1918: The records of the 1st (28th),

2nd (61st), 3rd (Special Reserve) and 4th, 5th and 6th Battalions (First Line T.A.)
Methuen, 1931
The Somme, pp. 147–78

Barnes, A.F., MC
The Story of the 2/5th Battalion Gloucester Regiment 1914–1918
Gloucester: Crypt House, 1930
The Somme, pp. 53–7
This book has illustrations and includes a list of unit casualties.

Beresford, Christine & Newbould, Christopher
The Fifth Gloster Gazette: A trench magazine of the First World War
Stroud: Alan Sutton Publishing, 1993
The articles and illustrations include references to the Somme throughout the text. The 1/5th Gloucesters was a Territorial battalion that went to France as part of the 48th (South Midland) Division in May 1915. It later became part of 25th Div. The last issue of the gazette was published in January 1919.

Gordon Highlanders

Falls, C.
The Gordon Highlanders in the First World War 1914–1919: The life of a regiment
Vol. 4
Aberdeen University Press, 1958
The Somme, pp. 80–113
This book has four Somme maps and includes a summary of casualties and details of VC actions.

Pratt, Paul W.
Glory of the Gordons
Inverness: Highland Printers (for the author), 1966
The Somme, p. 61

Stevenson, C. Sinclair
The Gordon Highlanders
Hamish Hamilton, 1968 (Famous Regiments series)
The Somme, pp. 97–101

Thomson, Revd P.D., MA, Hon. CF (sometime chaplain with the 1st & 4th Bns. in the field)
The Gordon Highlanders: Being a short record of the services of the regiment
Devonport: Swiss, 1921
The Somme, pp. 77–91
This book includes a list of casualties of the Gordon Highlanders in major battles, a list of VC winners to the end of the war and a list of commanding officer casualties.

Mackenzie, Capt. D., MA, MC
The Sixth Gordons in France and Flanders (with the 7th and 51st Divisions)
Aberdeen: Rosemount Press, 1921, printed for the War Memorial Committee
The Somme, pp. 88–106
The book includes a roll of honour.

Green Howards

Anon
The Green Howards (Alexandra, Princess of Wales's Own Yorkshire Regiment) For Valour 1914–1918
[n.p.], 1964
This booklet concerns the men who won the VC with the regiment and includes their photographs.

Powell, G.
The Green Howards
Hamish Hamilton, 1968 (Famous Regiments series)
The Somme, pp. 90–2

Powell, G.
The History of the Green Howards
Arms & Armour, 1992
The Somme, pp. 148–52 & 159
This book includes a list of regimental colonels and VC pen pictures.

Wylly, Col. H.C., CB
The Green Howards in the Great War 1914–1919
Richmond, Yorks: n.p., 1926
The Somme, 2nd Bn., pp. 73–82; 1/4th (T) Bn., pp. 132–3; 1/5th (T) Bn., pp. 156–7; 6th (Service) Bn., pp. 192–5; 7th (Service) Bn., pp. 212–29; 8th (Service) Bn., pp. 251–61; 9th (Service) Bn., pp. 293–302; 10th (Service) Bn., pp. 334–42; 12th (Service) Bn., pp. 349–51; 13th (Service) Bn., pp. 361–5
The book includes pen pictures of VC award winners and, in an appendix, a reference to the regimental war memorial at Richmond.

Fife, Lt.-Col. R.
History of the 7th Battalion Green Howards
York & London: Herald Printing Works, n.d.
The Somme, pp. 14–35
The narrative is taken from the *The Green Howards Gazette*.

Grenadier Guards

Ponsonby, Sir Frederick
The Grenadier Guards in the Great War of 1914–1918
Macmillan, 1920, 3 vols
The Somme, Vol. 2: 1st, 2nd, 3rd & 4th Bns., pp. 27–159

Whitworth, R.H.
The Grenadier Guards (The First or Grenadier Regiment of Foot Guards)
Leo Cooper, 1974 (Famous Regiments series)
The Somme, pp. 87–90

Guards

Paget, J.
The Story of the Guards
Osprey, 1976
The Somme, pp. 164–5

Hertfordshire Regiment

Sainsbury, Lt.-Col. J.D., TD
The Hertfordshire Regiment: An illustrated history
Ware: Castlemead, 1988
The Somme, pp. 57–8

Highland Light Infantry

Oatts, L.B.
Proud Heritage: The story of the Highland Light Infantry
Vol. 3: *The Regular, Militia, Volunteer, T.A. and Service Battalions 1882–1918*
Glasgow: House of Grant, 1961
The Somme, pp. 259–86

Oatts, L.B.
The Highland Light Infantry (The 71st Highland Light Infantry and 74th Highlanders)
Leo Cooper, 1969 (Famous Regiments series)
The Somme, pp. 75–7

Aiken, Alex
Courage Past: A duty done
Glasgow: Aiken & Alex, 1971
This is the story of the Glasgow Highlanders (1/9 Highland Light Infantry) and in particular of their experiences at High Wood on 15 July 1916. The book includes a roll of honour for officers and NCOs.

Telfer-Smollett, Maj. A.D., Wallace, Maj. C.J. & Skinner, Capt. H. Ross (comps.)
The 2nd Battalion Highland Light Infantry in the Great War

Glasgow: John Horn, 1929
The Somme, pp. 59–79
This illustrated book also has plans and maps.

Chalmers, Thomas (ed.)
An Epic of Glasgow: History of the 15th Battalion the Highland Light Infantry (City of Glasgow Regiment)
Glasgow: John McCallum, 1934
The Somme, pp. 63–115
This book has maps and illustrations including pictures by A.M. Burnie.

Chalmers, Thomas (ed.)
A Saga of Scotland: History of the 16th Battalion the Highland Light Infantry (City of Glasgow Regiment)
Glasgow: John McCallum, 1930
The Somme, pp. 31–55
The book has an excellent account of day-by-day movements and also drawings, maps and a roll of honour. The foreword is by Principal R.S. Rait of the University of Glasgow.

Arthur, John W. & Munro, Ian S. (eds.)
The Seventeenth Highland Light Infantry (Glasgow Chamber of Commerce Battalion): Record of War Service 1914–1918
Glasgow: David J. Clark, 1920
The Somme, pp. 39–52
This book is illustrated and includes a map.

Munro, Ian S.
Youth of Yesteryear: Campaigns, battles, service and exploits of the Glasgow Territorials in the last Great War
Edinburgh: William Hodge, 1939
The Somme, pp. 79–80
The foreword is by Ian Hay.

Honourable Artillery Company

Goold Walker, G., DSO, MC (Maj. Reserve of Officers)
The Honourable Artillery Company 1537–1926
John Lane, Bodley Head, 1926
The Somme, pp. 268, 269 & 271
The book includes a roll of honour, a roll of the VCs and a description of how the medals were gained.

Goold Walker, G., DSO, MC
The Honourable Artillery Company in the Great War 1914–1919
Seeley, Service & Co., 1930
The Somme, 1st Bn., pp. 61–77
This book is the war history of the oldest of the territorial regiments and includes a roll of honour.

Irish Guards

Verney, P.
The Micks: The story of the Irish Guards
Peter Davies, 1970
The Somme, pp. 46–53

Kipling, Rudyard
The Irish Guards in the Great War: Edited and compiled from their diaries and papers
Vol. 1: *The 1st Battalion*
Macmillan, 1923, 2 vols
The Somme, pp. 134–95
This book includes a list of 1st Battalion commanding officers. (Falls★★)

King's Liverpool Regiment

Burke-Gaffney, Lt.-Col. J.J., MC
The Story of the King's Regiment 1914–1948
Liverpool: King's Regiment (printed by Sharpe & Kellet), 1954
The Somme, pp. 34–46

Macdonald, R.P.
A Short History of the King's Regiment (Manchester & Liverpool)
Aldershot: Gale & Polden, 1962
The Somme, p. 14 (Regular Battalions series)
This is a small booklet.

Wyrall, Everard
The History of the King's Regiment (Liverpool) 1914–1919
Vol. 2
Arnold, 1928
The Somme, pp. 258–354
The book contains good maps and photographs and a roll of honour by battalion as well as VC citations. (Falls★)

MacGilchrist, A.M.
The Liverpool Scottish 1900–1919
Liverpool: Henry Young, 1930
The Somme, pp. 74–88
This is a history of the 1/10th (Scottish) Bn. T.F. with some superb maps and a roll of honour.

Wurtzburg, Capt. C.E., MC
The History of the 2/6th (Rifle) Battalion: 'The King's' (Liverpool Regiment) 1914–1919
Aldershot: Gale & Polden, 1920
The Somme, pp. 180–98
This book includes illustrations and maps, a list of senior officers and a nominal roll of officers and men giving dates of death or of being wounded.

Roberts, E.H.G.
The Story of the 9th King's in France
Liverpool: Northern Publishing, 1922
The Somme, pp. 47–58

Anon
The Record of the 11th Battalion of the King's (Liverpool) Regiment, subsequently the 15th Battalion of the Loyal North Lancs. Regiment Pioneers 14th Light Division August 1914–March 1919
R.E. Thomas, 1920
The Somme, pp. 20–2
This small book includes a map.

Maddocks, Graham
Liverpool Pals: A History of the 17th, 18th, 19th and 20th (Service) Battalions the King's (Liverpool Regiment) 1914–1919
Barnsley: Wharncliffe, 1991
The Somme, pp. 77–138
This book is fully illustrated in the same style as others in the Pals series and includes a full listing of those Liverpool Pals who died during the First World War and where they are commemorated. There are four Somme maps.

King's Own Royal Border Regiment

Anon
The King's Own Royal Border Regiment
Morecambe: Morecambe Bay Printers, 1963
The Somme, p. 21

King's Own Royal Regiment (Lancaster)

Cowper, J.M. (comp.)
The King's Own: The story of a royal regiment
Aldershot: Gale & Polden, 1957, 3 vols
Vol. 3, 1914–50
The Somme, pp. 111–27 & 134–42
The book includes maps and a list of commanding officers.

Eastwood, Stuart
Lions of England: A pictorial history of the King's Own Royal Regiment (Lancaster) 1680–1980

Kettering: Silver Link, 1991
There is a brief mention of the Somme on p. 72 and a picture of men at Hawthorn Ridge on p. 88, as well as pictures of 1/4th Bn. on the Somme on p. 91.

Green, H.
The King's Own Royal Regiment (Lancaster) (The 4th Regiment of Foot)
Leo Cooper, 1972 (Famous Regiments series)
The Somme, pp. 114–16 and 119–20

Wadham, Lt.-Col. W.F.A. & Crossley, Capt. J.
The Fourth Battalion the King's Own Royal Lancaster Regiment and the Great War
Crowther Goodman (printer), 1920
The Somme, pp. 58–72

Hodgkinson, Albert
The King's Own 1/5 Battalion T.F.: Being a record of the 1/5th Battalion King's Own Royal Lancaster Regiment in the European War 1914–18
Lewes: Lewes Press, 1921
The Somme, pp. 58–71
This book includes a list of officers commanding, and a list of officers and other ranks who were killed or died of wounds.

King's Own Scottish Borderers

Gillon, Capt. S.
The K.O.S.B. in the Great War
Nelson, 1930
The Somme, 1st Bn., Book 2, Pt. 2, pp. 176–88; 2nd Bn., Book 1, pp. 76–85; 6th Bn., Book 4, pp. 331–42; 7th & 8th Bns., Book 5, pp. 400–8
This book has good maps.

Woollcombe, R.
All the Blue Bonnets: The history of the King's Own Scottish Borderers

Arms & Armour, 1980
The Somme, pp. 98 & 186

Goss, J. (comp.)
A Border Battalion: The history of the 7th/8th (Service) Battalion, King's Own Scottish Borderers
Edinburgh: T.N. Foulis, 1920
The Somme, pp. 83–117
This book includes pictures of groups of officers, a list of commanding officers and information on casualties.

King's Own Yorkshire Light Infantry

Bond, Lt.-Col. Reginald C., DSO
History of the King's Own Yorkshire Light Infantry in the Great War, 1914–1918
Lund Humphries, 1929, 3 vols
The Somme, Vol. 3, pp. 802–40
The book includes mentions of casualties.

King's Royal Rifle Corps

Compiled by committee of officers of corps
King's Royal Rifle Corps Chronicle 1916
Winchester: Warren, 1919
The Somme, 1st Bn., pp. 50–7; 2nd Bn., pp. 76–84; 7th Bn., pp. 122–6; 8th Bn., pp. 143–50; 9th Bn., pp. 170–7; 10th Bn., pp. 200–9; 11th Bn., p. 217; 12th Bn., pp. 224–5; 13th Bn., pp. 230–5; 16th Bn., pp. 247–54; 17th Bn., pp. 267–9; 18th Bn., pp. 276–7; 20th Bn., p. 291
The book gives the war records of the 21 battalions during 1916 and includes rolls of honour.

Hare, Maj.-Gen. Sir Steuart S.
The Annals of the King's Royal Rifle Corps
Vol. 5: *The Great War*
Murray, 1932
The Somme, pp. 118–80
This book includes a list of VC winners with their citations and a list of officer casualties listed by name and date.

Wood, H.F.
The King's Royal Rifle Corps (The 60th Regiment of Foot)
Hamish Hamilton, 1967 (Famous Regiments series)
The Somme, pp. 87–8

Turberville, Capt. A.S., MC
A Short History of the 20th Battalion the King's Royal Rifle Corps. (B.E.L. Pioneers)
Hull: Goddard, Walker & Brown, 1923
The Somme, pp. 16–44

King's Shropshire Light Infantry

Anon
The History of the Corps of the King's Shropshire Light Infantry
Vol. 3
Shrewsbury Regimental Secretary, [n.d.]
The Somme, 1st Bn., pp. 91–2; 2nd Bn., p. 103; 5th Bn., pp. 120–1; 6th Bn., p. 130; 7th Bn., pp. 139–40
This is a typescript covering the period 1881–1968.

Anon
A Short History of the King's Shropshire Light Infantry (53rd and 85th Foot)
Aldershot: Gale & Polden, n.d.
The Somme, pp. 23 & 26

Moulsdale, J.R.B.
The King's Shropshire Light Infantry
Leo Cooper, 1972 (Famous Regiments series)
The Somme, p. 45

Wood, Maj. W. de B.
The History of the King's Shropshire Light Infantry in the Great War 1914–1918
Medici Society, 1925

The Somme, 1st Bn., pp. 30–5; 5th Bn., pp. 141–5; 6th Bn., pp. 178–80; 7th Bn., pp. 226–34
This book includes a nominal roll of officers killed or wounded.

Lancashire Fusiliers

Latter, Maj.-Gen. J.C., CBE, MC
The History of the Lancashire Fusiliers
Aldershot: Gale & Polden, 1949, 2 vols
The Somme, Vol. 1, pp. 129–74
This book gives the history of nine battalions.

Barlow, Sir C.A. Montague
The Lancashire Fusiliers: The roll of honour of the Salford Brigade (15th, 16th, 19th, 20th and 21st Lancashire Fusiliers)
Manchester: Sherratt & Hughes, 1919
The Somme, pp. 57–85
This illustrated book includes portraits.

Leicestershire Regiment

Kelly, D.V.
39 Months with the 'Tigers', 1915–1918
Benn, 1930
The Somme, pp. 25–35 & 43–9
This book has two Somme maps.

Wylly, Col. H.C.
History of the 1st and 2nd Battalions the Leicestershire Regiment in the Great War
Aldershot: Gale & Polden, [n.d.]
The Somme, pp. 27–42
This book contains maps.

Milne, Capt. J. (formerly a captain with the 4th Bn. Leicester Regt.)
Footprints of the 1/4th Leicestershire Regiment, August 1914 to November 1918
Leicester: Edgar Backus, 1935
The Somme, pp. 82–5 & 92–7

Hills, Capt. J.D., MC, Croix de Guerre
The Fifth Leicestershire: A record of the 1/5th Battalion the Leicestershire Regiment T.F. during the War 1914–1919
Loughborough: Echo Press, 1919
The Somme, pp. 127–78
This book includes a list of officers who went to France in 1915.

Leinster Regiment

Whitton, Lt.-Col. F.E., CMG
The History of the Prince of Wales's Leinster Regiment (Royal Canadians)
Aldershot: Gale & Polden, 1924, 2 vols
The Somme, pp. 217–60
The book describes the history of the 2nd Bn. on the Somme at Guillemont and Delville Wood and includes a sketch of the sunken road at Guillemont by Capt. Frank Hitchcock.

Lincolnshire Regiment

Anon
A Short History of the Lincolnshire Regiment
Aldershot: Gale & Polden, 1926
The Somme, pp. 53–4 & 60–1
This book includes an order of battle for the Lincolnshire Regiment.

Simpson, Maj.-Gen. C.R., CB (ed.)
The History of the Lincolnshire Regiment, 1914–1918: Compiled from war diaries, despatches, officers' notes and other sources
Medici Society, 1931
The Somme, pp. 159–99
This book contains histories of the 1st, 6th, 7th, 8th and 10th Bns. and also has maps, drawings, and rolls of honour by battalion.

Sandall, Col. T.E. (late commanding the Battalion)
A History of the 5th Battalion The Lincolnshire

Regiment: With a chapter on its reconstruction by Maj. G.H. Teall (Adjutant)
Oxford: Blackwell, 1922
The Somme, pp. 66–82
This book is illustrated.

Anon
8th (S.) Battalion, Lincolnshire Regiment, 1914–1919
Aldershot: Gale & Polden, 1919
The Somme, pp. 4–5
An abridged form of war diary, this is a small booklet with portrait illustrations.

Bryant, Peter
Grimsby Chums: The story of the 10th Lincolnshires in the Great War
Hull: Humberside Leisure Services, 1991
The Somme, pp. 49–74
This book is a history of a Pals unit formed in September 1914, which became part of 34th Div. It is well produced with illustrations and some excellent maps. For readers interested in the Somme battle it provides an excellent account of the fight to capture the Lochnagar Crater at La Boisselle. It also has a roll of honour.

London Regiment

Martin, Col. A.R., OBE, TD
Historical Records of the London Regiment
[n.p., n.d.]
The Somme, p. 12
After p. 34 the pages are unnumbered and the text gives brief histories of each battalion in the London Regiment.

1st Londons

Handley, R.E., FRICS
The First Londons
Dover: Littledown Publishing, 1986
The Somme, pp. 170–3
The book is illustrated.

2nd Londons

Grey, Maj. W.E.
The 2nd City of London Regiment (Royal Fusiliers) in the Great War (1914–1919)
London Regiment, 1929
The Somme, pp. 110–43
The book has rolls of honour and good maps. (Falls★)

3rd Londons

Kelleher, J.P.
The 3rd London Regiment
Private publication, 1984
This A4 typed history gives a brief account of the 1/3rd Bn. action on 1 July 1916 and on the Transloy Ridges during 6–10 October (p. 5).

4th Londons

Grimwade, Capt. F.C.
The War History of the 4th Battalion the London Regiment (Royal Fusiliers) 1914–1919
Headquarters of the 4th London Regiment, 1922
The Somme, pp. 139–216
This illustrated book has 21 maps including four of the Somme.

5th Londons

Anon
The History of the London Rifle Brigade 1859–1919
Constable, 1921
The Somme, 1st Bn., pp. 130–74
This is a very detailed book with the regiment's history shown by battalions. A roll of honour of officers lists when they were wounded or killed. The introduction is by Maj.-Gen. Sir Frederick Maurice, KC, MG, CB.

Mitchinson, K.W.
Gentlemen and Officers: The impact and experience of war on a Territorial Regiment 1914–1918
Imperial War Museum, 1995
The Somme, pp. 112–50
This book was based on the archives of the London Rifle Brigade (5th London Regiment) deposited at the Imperial War Museum. The foreword is by Peter Simkins, who describes the book 'as a most welcome addition to the new generation of scholarly unit studies'. It is illustrated and has maps, a roll of honour and other useful appendices.

6th Londons

Godfrey, Capt. E.G., MC
The 'Cast Iron' Sixth: A history of the 6th Battalion London Regiment (The City of London Rifles)
F.S. Stapleton, 1938
The Somme, pp. 82–99
This book includes group pictures of officers and men.

7th Londons

Planck, C. Digby (comp.)
History of the 7th (City of London) Battalion London Regiment
The Old Comrades Association, 1946
The Somme, pp. 75–90
This book has some excellent photographs of officers belonging to the battalion and a roll of honour of officers and men.

8th Londons

Messenger, C.
Terriers in the Trenches: The Post Office Rifles at War 1914–1918
Chippenham: Picton, 1982
The Somme, pp. 52–61

The Post Office Rifles were the 8th Bn., City of London Regt. (TA). This illustrated book includes a roll of honour and a small Somme map.

9th Londons

Keeson, Maj. C.A. Cuthbert, VD
The History and Records of the Queen Victoria's Rifles 1792–1922
Constable, 1923
The Somme, pp. 146–92
The unit was part of the London Regiment. This illustrated book includes a roll of honour of officers and other ranks, and some excellent maps.

12th Londons

Wheeler-Holohan, Capt. A.V.
The Rangers' Historical Records from 1859 to Conclusion of the Great War
Harrison, 1921
The Somme, pp. 42–74
This unit is also known as the 12th London Regiment.

13th Londons

Bailey, Sgt. O.F. & Hollier, Sgt. H.M.
'The Kensingtons' 13th London Regiment
Published for the Regimental Old Comrades Association, 1936
The Somme, pp. 72–101
This book includes portraits, plates and maps.

14th Londons

Lindsay, Lt.-Col. J.H., DSO
The London Scottish in the Great War
London Scottish Regiment, 1925
The Somme, 1st Bn., pp. 103–36
This was the 14th London Regt. The book

has a foreword by FM Earl Haig and includes a map of Gommecourt and a map of later Somme operations. It also contains photographs of regimental war memorials and rolls of honour.

15th Londons

Anon
The History of the Prince of Wales's Own Civil Service Rifles
Wyman (for the regiment), 1921
The Somme, pp. 111–22
The unit was part of the London Regiment. This book describes action at High Wood, Eaucourt l'Abbé and the Butte de Warlencourt.

16th Londons

Henriques, Maj. J.Q.
The War History of the 1st Battalion Queen's Westminster Rifles, 1914–1918
Medici Society, 1923
The Somme, pp. 61–129
This book is illustrated and included a panorama dated 20 May 1916 of the Gommecourt sector, two Somme maps and a roll of honour. In the appendices is a useful itinerary of the 16th London regiment.

Loyal North Lancashire Regiment

Anon
A Short History of the Loyal Regiment (North Lancashire)
Malcolm Page, [n.d.]
The Somme, p. 32

Langley, M.
The Loyal Regiment (North Lancashire): The 47th and 81st Regiments of Foot
Leo Cooper, 1976 (Famous Regiments series)
The Somme, pp. 72–5

Wylly, Col. H.C.
The Loyal North Lancashire Regiment, 1914–1919
R.U.S.I., 1933, 2 vols
The Somme, 1st Bn., pp. 35–44; 1/4 T Bn., pp. 166–71; 1/5 T Bn., pp. 206–8; 7th (S) Bn., pp. 270–7; 8th (S) Bn., pp. 292–6; 9th (S) Bn., pp. 307–9; 10th (S) Bn., pp. 327–30; 1/12th T Bn. The Pioneers, pp. 343–4
This book also includes a list of winners of the VC.

Anon
The War History of the 1/4th Battalion the Loyal North Lancashire Regiment, now the Loyal Regiment (North Lancashire) 1914–1918
Preston: Toulmin/Battalion History Committee, [n.d.]
The Somme, pp. 31–9
This illustrated book has maps, casualty lists and an abridgement of the war diary.

Machine Gun Corps

Crutchley C.E. (ed.)
The Machine Gun Corps 1914–18
Northampton: Mercury Press, 1973
The Somme, pp. 18–51

Hutchison, Lt.-Col. G.S., DSO, MC
Machine Guns, their History and Tactical Movement (being the history of the Machine Gun Corps 1916–1922)
Macmillan, 1938
The Somme, pp. 162–8

Members of the Battalion
History and Memoir of the 33rd Battalion Machine Gun Corps and of the 19th, 98th, 100th and 248th MG Companies
Waterloo Brothers & Layton, 1919

The Somme, pp. 4–12
The book includes some excellent photographs and paintings of the Somme area. The book was fully subscribed within 24 hours of being announced; of the 1,600 copies printed, 500 were given to soldiers' next of kin.

Stevens, F.A.
The Machine Gun Corps: a short history
Tonbridge: F.A. Stevens, 1981
The Somme, p. 10

Manchester Regiment

Campbell, Capt. G.L. (RFA) (comp.)
The Manchesters: A history of the Regular, Militia, Special Reserve, Territorial and New Army Battalions since their formation; with a record of the officers now serving and the honours and casualties of the War 1914–1916
Picture Advertising, 1916
The Somme, p. 14
The book gives brief histories of each battalion and includes lists of officers and men killed.

Wylly, Col. H.C., CB (comp.)
History of the Manchester Regiment
Vol. 2: *1883–1922*
Forster & Groom, 1925, 2 vols
The Somme, pp. 133–40
This illustrated book includes lists of VC winners and senior officers.

Wylly, Col. H.C., CB
A Short History of the Manchester Regiment
Aldershot: Gale & Polden, 1950 (Regular Battalions series)
The Somme, p. 27
Contains a brief mention of the 2nd Bn.

Borland, W.J.
Memories – The Battle of the Somme 1916
Manchester: James Lord, [n.d.]
This book is a souvenir and roll of honour for the Manchester Regiment. It includes some portraits of senior officers in the regiment.

Westropp, H.C.E.
To Manchester, a Tribute to 'The Fallen' and to 'The Spirit' of her Great Regiment
Manchester: Sherratt & Hughes, 1920
The Somme, pp. 12–13

Bonner, Robert (ed.)
The 12th Battalion the Manchester Regiment 1914–1919
Knutsford: Fleur de Lys, 1994 (Manchester Regiment Collection)
The Somme, pp. 8–12
This small booklet includes a roll of honour.

Anon
Sixteenth, Seventeenth, Eighteenth, Nineteenth Battalions, The Manchester Regiment (1st City Brigade): a record, 1914–1918
Manchester: Sherratt & Hughes, 1923
The Somme, pp. 23–35

Anon
The Manchester Regiment 16th, 17th, 18th and 19th Battalions 1914–1918
Manchester, Sherratt & Hughes, 1923
The Somme, 16th Bn., pp. 13–32 & 43–53; 17th Bn., pp. 116–28; 18th Bn., pp. 191–217; 19th Bn., pp. 292–305
The book includes rolls of honour of officers and men, and excellent maps in the 16th Bn. section.

Stedman, M.
Manchester Pals: 16th, 17th, 18th, 19th, 20th, 21st, 22nd and 23rd Battalions of the

Manchester Regiment. A history of the two Manchester brigades
Leo Cooper, 1994
The Somme, pp. 97–154
This book tells the stories of eight battalions of the Manchester Regiment that served with the 7th, 30th and 35th Divs. Except for the 23rd, all were in action on 1 July 1916 on the Somme. The book is fully illustrated and has several Somme maps and a listing of unit fatalities.

Compiled by a committee of the old members of the regiment
The 21st Battalion of the Manchester Regiment
Manchester: Sherratt & Hughes, 1934
The Somme, pp. 40–60
The book includes a roll of honour of officers and men.

Anon
The 21st Battalion The Manchester Regiment: A history
Knutsford: Fleur de Lys, 1994 (Manchester Regiment Collection)
The Somme, pp. 12–18
This small booklet has a roll of honour.

Mitchinson, K.W. & McInnes, I.
Cotton Town Comrades: The story of the 24th Bn. the Manchester Regt. 'The Oldham Pals', 1914–1919
Oldham: Bayonet, 1993
The Somme, pp. 69–83
This Pals history lists the original 1,500 men of the battalion as well as casualty rolls. It is illustrated and includes maps.

Wilde, Alderman Herbert (ed.)
The Oldham Battalion of comrades (24th Battalion Manchester Regiment) Book of Honour
Manchester: Sherratt & Hughes, 1920

The Somme, pp. 20–34
This is a small book with portrait illustrations.

Kempster, Brig.-Gen. F., DSO
Manchester City Battalions of the 90th and 91st Infantry Brigades: Book of Honour
Manchester: Sherratt & Hughes, 1916
This hugely comprehensive book includes lists of men by the firms and institutions in Manchester that they worked for, along with the name of the battalion in which they later served. There are also many illustrations, but no account of actual war actions.

Middlesex Regiment

Anon
Roll of Honour of Officers, Warrant Officers, Non Commissioned Officers and Men of the Middlesex Regiment (Duke of Cambridge's Own)
Aldershot: Gale & Polden, [n.d.]
Produced in tandem with the unveiling of the War Memorial Tablets at the Church of St Paul, Mill Hill, on 5 November 1922.

Blaxland, G.
The Middlesex Regiment (Duke of Cambridge's Own)
Leo Cooper, 1977 (Famous Regiments series)
The Somme, pp. 83–6

Whyte, Wolmer
The Diehards: The story of the Middlesex Regiment
Hutchinson, [n.d.]
The Somme, pp. 63–74

Wyrall, Everard
The Die-hards in the Great War: A history of the Duke of Cambridge's Own (Middlesex Regiment) 1914–1919. Compiled from the

records of the line, special reserve, service and
Territorial Battalions
Harrison, [n.d.], 2 vols
The Somme, pp. 243–330
The book is a day-by-day account and
includes some maps. (Falls★)

King, Col. E.J., CMG, FSA
History of the 7th Middlesex
Harrison, 1927
The Somme, pp. 185–97, 198–208 & 209–17
The book includes various statistical tables
including casualties.

Grain, H.W. Wallis
The 16th (Public Schools) Service Battalion
Middlesex Regiment
F.P. Lewington (printer), [n.d.]
The Somme, pp. 38–44
The book includes a roll of honour of
officers and men.

Monmouthshire Regiment

Dixon, J. & J.
With Rifle and Pick
Cardiff: CWM Press, 1991
The Somme, pp. 105–17
The book mainly deals with the Monmouth-
shire Regt. and includes rolls of honour.

Hughes, I. and Dixon, J.
'Surrender be Damned': A history of the
Monmouthshire Regiment, 1914–1918
Caerphilly: CWM Press, 1985
The Somme, pp. 114–28
Illustrated and includes a map of the
Gommecourt sector.

Somerset, W.H.B., Tyler, H.G. and
Whitehead, L.I.
On the Western Front – 1/3rd Bn. Monmouth
Regiment

Abergavenny: Sergeant Bros. Ltd, [n.d.]
The Somme, pp. 85–93
The book includes an excellent map of the
Somme area and a detailed roll of honour
of officers and men.

Norfolk Regiment

Carew, T.
The Royal Norfolk Regiment (The 9th
Regiment of Foot)
Leo Cooper/Hamish Hamilton, 1967
(Famous Regiments series)
The Somme, pp. 93–5

Petre, F. Loraine, OBE
The History of the Norfolk Regiment,
1685–1918
Jarrold, 1924, 2 vols
The Somme, Vol. 2: 1st Bn., pp. 19–35; 7th
(Service) Bn., pp. 175–83; 8th (Service) Bn.,
pp. 214–27; 9th (Service) Bn., pp. 252–62
The book includes a roll of honour of officers.

Northamptonshire Regiment

Anon
The Northamptonshire Regiment 1914–1918
Aldershot: Gale & Polden, [n.d.], compiled
for the Regimental History Committee
The Somme, pp. 153–86

Barthorp, M.
The Northamptonshire Regiment (The
48th/58th Regiment of Foot)
Leo Cooper, 1974 (Famous Regiments series)
The Somme, pp. 62–3

Wyatt, Capt. J.D.
A Short History of the Northamptonshire
Regiment
Aldershot: Gale & Polden, 1933
The Somme, pp. 40–1

Moore, Geoffrey (late Northamptonshire Regiment)
Kitchener's Pioneers: The story of one battalion formed from Kitchener's first 100,000 – August 1914: 5th (Service) Bn. the Northamptonshire Regiment (Pioneers)
[n.p., n.d.]
The Somme, pp. 19–22
This booklet has a foreword by Brig. W.J. Jervois, MC, Colonel of the Northamptonshire Regiment 1953–6, and a list of casualties in chronological order.

King, H.B., MC (late Capt.)
7th (S) Battalion Northamptonshire Regiment, 1914–1919
Aldershot: Gale & Polden, 1919
The author was a former member of the regiment and the book has illustrations and maps. One of the men to whose memory it is jointly dedicated is Lt.-Col. E.R. Mobbs.

North Staffordshire

Cook, H.C.B.
The North Staffordshire Regiment (The Prince of Wales's)
Leo Cooper, 1970 (Famous Regiments series)
The Somme, pp. 83–7

Taylor, A.D.
A Short History of the North Staffordshire Regiment, 64th, 1756–1945
Hednesford: [n.p.], 1948
The Somme, p. 13

Anon
History of the 1st and 2nd Battalions the North Staffordshire Regiment ('The Prince of Wales's) 1914–1923
Longton: Hughes & Harber, 1932
The Somme, pp. 34–44

Meakin, Lt. Walter
The 5th North Staffords and the North Midland Territorials (The 46th and 59th Divisions), 1914–1919
Longton: Hughes & Harber (The Royal Press), 1920
The Somme, pp. 64–78
This book is illustrated and includes maps.

Anon
History of the 8th North Staffordshire Regiment
Longton: Hughes & Harber, 1921
The Somme, pp. 35–55
This illustrated book has maps.

Northumberland Fusiliers

Peacock, B.
The Royal Northumberland Fusiliers
Leo Cooper, 1970 (Famous Regiments series)
The Somme, pp. 89–90

Sandilands, Brig. H.R.
The Fifth in the Great War: A history of the 1st and 2nd Northumberland Fusiliers 1914–1918
Dover: St George's Press, 1938
The Somme, 1st Bn., pp. 146–68
The book includes a list of officers who served with these units in the First World War. An accompanying slip case contains two Somme maps.

Buckley, Capt. F. (ed.)
War History of the 7th Northumberland Fusiliers
Newcastle-upon-Tyne: T.M. Grierson (printer), 1919
The Somme, pp. 41–52

Cooke, Capt. C.H., MC
Historical records of the 9th (Service) Battalion Northumberland Fusiliers

Newcastle & Gateshead Incorporated Chamber of Commerce, 1928
The Somme, pp. 35–54
The book includes an embarkation roll for 'B' Company and photographs of officers. The Newcastle Chamber of Commerce published a history of each of the three battalions it had raised, and presented a copy to surviving serving men and the families of those who died.

Cooke, Capt. C.H., MC
Historical Records of the 16th (Service) Battalion Northumberland Fusiliers
Newcastle & Gateshead Incorporated Chamber of Commerce, 1923
The Somme, pp. 43–60 & 64–8
The book includes an embarkation roll of November 1915 by company and platoon, and a list of casualties on 1 July 1916, together with a roll of honour.

Shakespear, Lt.-Col. John, CMG, CIE, DSO
A Record of the 17th and 32nd Battalions Northumberland Fusiliers 1914–1919
Newcastle-upon-Tyne: Northumberland Press, 1926
The Somme, pp. 30–41
This is a very comprehensive work, including rarely used illustrations of the Somme area and some very good maps. It also has a list of men who served with the two battalions.

Shakespear, Lt.-Col. John, CMG, CIE, DSO
Historical Records of the 18th Battalion Northumberland Fusiliers
Plymouth: William Brendon, 1920
The Somme, pp. 33–49
The book includes an itinerary of the battalion, a roll of honour and a good photograph of La Boisselle.

Cooke, Capt. C.H., MC (Adj.)
Historical Records of the 19th Battalion Northumberland Fusiliers
Newcastle-upon-Tyne: Newcastle & Gateshead Incorporated Chamber of Commerce, 1920 (private printing)
The Somme, pp. 27–38
This illustrated book has maps, including one of the Somme.

Ternan, Brig.-Gen. Trevor
The Story of the Tyneside Scottish: 20th, 21st, 22nd and 23rd (S.) Battalions
Newcastle-upon-Tyne: Northumberland Press, 1919
The Somme, pp. 82–103
This illustrated book has a foreword by FM Douglas Haig. The Tyneside Scottish were part of the Northumberland Fusiliers.

Army Ordnance

Forbes, A.
A History of the Army Ordnance Services
Medici Society, 1929
The Somme, pp. 124–8
This section deals with ammunition supply.

Oxford and Buckinghamshire Light Infantry

Booth, P.
The Oxfordshire & Buckinghamshire Light Infantry (The 43rd/52nd Regiments of Foot)
Leo Cooper, 1971 (Famous Regiments series)
The Somme, pp. 101–2

Crosse, Lt.-Col. R.B., DSO
A Short History of the Oxfordshire and Buckinghamshire Light Infantry 1741–1922
Aldershot: Gale & Polden, [n.d.]
The Somme is mentioned briefly by battalion service on pp. 33, 35, 37, 38, 39 & 40.

Mockler-Ferryman, Lt.-Col. A.F.
Regimental War Tales 1741–1919
Oxford: Slatter & Rose, 1915 & 1942
The Somme (briefly), pp. 231, 234, 235, 237 & 238

Mockler-Ferryman, Lt.-Col. A.F. (comp.)
The Oxfordshire and Buckinghamshire Light Infantry Chronicle, 1916–1917: An annual record of the 1st and 2nd Battalions together with war records of the other battalions of the regiment
Vol. 26: *1 July 1916 – 30 June 1917*
Eyre & Spottiswoode, [n.d.]
The Somme, 2nd Bn., pp. 113–30; 1/4th Bn., pp. 210–22; 1st Bucks. Bn., pp. 247–58; 5th (Service) Bn., pp. 282–314; 6th (Service) Bn., pp. 335–49
The book includes a roll of honour for officers, and some pictures of them with places associated with the Somme battle.

Pickford, Maj. F., DSO, MC
War Record of the 1/4th Oxfordshire and Buckinghamshire Light Infantry
Banbury: Banbury Guardian, 1919
The Somme, pp. 15–25
The book includes very detailed information about men killed and their place of burial.

Swann, Maj.-Gen. J.C., CB, DL, JP
The 2nd Bucks Battalion Oxfordshire and Buckinghamshire, Light Infantry 1914–1918
[n.p.], 1929
The Somme, pp. 16–17
A small book.

Rose, Capt. G.K., MC
The Story of the 2/4th Oxford and Bucks Lt. Infantry
Oxford: Blackwell, 1920

The Somme, pp. 19–52
The book includes some small drawings, but not of the Somme area.

Queen's Own Cameron Highlanders

Anon
Historical Records of the Queen's Own Cameron Highlanders
Vol. III
Blackwood, 1931
The Somme, pp. 187–94, 197–211 & 214–27
The book includes some good maps.

Queen's Royal Regiment (West Surrey)

Anon
A Short History of the Queen's Royal Regiment
Aldershot: Gale & Polden, 1941
The Somme (briefly), pp. 47 & 48

Haswell, J.
The Queen's Royal Regiment (West Surrey)
Leo Cooper/Hamish Hamilton, 1967
(Famous Regiments series)
The Somme, pp. 125–6

Wylly, Col. H.C., CB
History of the Queen's Royal Regiment
Gale & Polden, 1924, 9 vols
The Somme, Vol. VII: 1st Bn., pp. 38–48; 2nd Bn., pp. 101–8; 6th (Service) Bn., pp. 193–7; 7th (Service) Bn., pp. 211–19; 8th (Service) Bn., pp. 241–2; 10th (Service) Bn., pp. 252–4; 11th (Service) Bn., pp. 267–9
The accompanying map volume has a map of the Somme battlefield, No. VII.

Neave, E.W.J. Capt., MC (comp.)
History of the 11th Battalion, 'The Queen's'
London: Brixton 'Free Press', 1931

The Somme, pp. 10–14
This illustrated book has maps and a foreword by Lt.-Gen. Sir Sydney Lawford.

Queen's Own Highlanders

Fairrie, Lt.-Col. Angus
'Cuidich 'N Righ': A history of the Queen's Own Highlanders. Seaforths & Camerons
Queen's Own Highlanders, 1983
The Somme, pp. 60, 62, 65, 66–8, 70, 74–8 & 80
This A4 paperback tells the story of the regiment from before 1881 to after the Second World War.

Queen's Own Royal West Kent Regiment

Anon
A Short History of the Queen's Own Royal West Kent Regiment
Maidstone: Kent Messenger, 1930
The Somme (briefly), pp. 42–3

Atkinson, C.T. (late Capt. Oxford University OTC)
The Queen's Own Royal West Kent Regiment, 1914–1919
Simpkin Marshall, 1924
The Somme, pp. 180–224 & 370–86
The illustrated book has maps. (Falls★)

Holloway, Roger
The Queen's Own Royal West Kent Regiment
Leo Cooper, 1973 (Famous Regiments series)
The Somme, pp. 62–4 & 65

Molony, Maj. C.V.
'Invicta': With the First Battalion the Queen's Own Royal West Kent Regiment in the Great War
Nisbet, 1923
The Somme, Ch. VIII, pp. 138–59 & Appendix Pt. III, pp. 248–58

This book includes maps and portraits of senior officers. It was compiled from war diaries and eyewitness accounts.

Wenyon, Lt.-Col H.J. & Brown, Maj. H.S.
The History of the Eighth Battalion The Queen's Own Royal West Kent Regiment, 1914–1919
London & Aylesbury: Hazell, Watson & Viney, 1921 (private printing)
The Somme, pp. 45–60
This illustrated book has maps.

Russell, Capt. R.O., MC
The History of the 11th (Service) Battalion, the Queen's Own Royal West Kent Regiment
Lewisham Newspaper Co., 1934
The Somme, Ch. 10–12, pp. 56–83
The book is illustrated with photographs including those of officers and men, and also has a roll of honour and some maps.

Gould, E. *et al.*
Lewisham's Own Battalion: The story of the gallant 11th (Service) Battalion, Queen's Own Royal West Kent Regiment
Kentish Mercury, 1920
Printed as 'The Somme' in the *Kentish Mercury*, 22 October 1920.

Rifle Brigade (Prince Consort's Own)

Berkeley, Capt. R., MC
The History of the Rifle Brigade in the War of 1914–1918
London: Rifle Brigade Club, 1927, 2 vols
The Somme, Vol. 1, pp. 151–239
The book includes maps.

Eastwood, Lt.-Col. T.R., DSO, MC & Parkin, Maj. H.G., OBE (comps.)
List of Officers and Other Ranks of the Rifle

Brigade Awarded Decorations or Mentioned in Despatches for Service During the Great War
London: Rifle Brigade Club, 1936
The book is a complete listing, occasionally giving the name of the place of action.

Harvey, Basil
The Rifle Brigade (Prince Consort's Own)
Leo Cooper, 1975 (Famous Regiments series)
The Somme (briefly), pp. 74–5

Verner, Col. Willoughby (comp. & ed.)
The Rifle Brigade Chronicle for 1916
John Bale & Danielsson, 1917
The Somme, pp. 173–90
The book has very detailed rolls of honour.

Rowlands, D.H.
For the Duration: The story of the Thirteenth Battalion the Rifle Brigade
Simpkin, Marshall, 1932 (for the 13th Bn. The R.B. Old Comrades Association)
The Somme, Chs. 5–6, pp. 66–89
This illustrated book has a foreword by Capt. W.B. Maxwell.

Royal Armoured Corps

Macksey, Maj. (retd) Kenneth, MC, RTR
A History of the Royal Armoured Corps 1914–1917
Beaminster: Newtown Publications, 1983
The Somme, pp. 11 & 16–18

Murland, Capt. J.R.W.
The Royal Armoured Corps
Methuen, 1943
The Somme, pp. 20–2
This illustrated book was written by a member of the 5th Royal Inniskilling Dragoon Guards.

Royal Army Medical Corps

Atkinson, A.
Unarmed Comrades: 2/3rd City of London Field Ambulance
Errington & Martin, 1969?
The Somme, pp. 22–34
This book is based on the diaries of Pte. A.L. Ellis of 'C' Section and describes the activities of one of the three field ambulances which served with 56th Division.

Brereton, F.S.
The Great War and the R.A.M.C.
Constable, 1919
The Somme, pp. 22 & 86

Chase, H.L.
The 2/1st London Field Ambulance: An outline of the 4½ years service of a unit of the 56th Division at home and abroad during the Great War, 1914–1919
Morton: Burt & Sons, 1924
The Somme, pp. 27–40
This book is illustrated and has two Somme pictures.

Foster, George W. (ed.)
The History of the First London (City of London) Sanitary Company R.A.M.C. (T), with a record of its activities in the Great War, 1914–1919
Grimsby: Burnetts, 1926?
The Somme, pp. 45–50
This illustrated book has a foreword by P.S. Lelean. There is a chapter on the 35th Sanitary Section.

Laffin, J.
Surgeons in the Field
Dent, 1970
The Somme, pp. 21–2, 211 & 273

McLaughlin, R.
The Royal Army Medical Corps
Leo Cooper, 1972 (Famous Regiments series)
The Somme, pp. 51–3

Royal Army Medical Corps
Roll of Honour 1914–1919
Chiswick Press (for the RAMC Memorial Fund), 1924
The book is a complete listing of officers and men.

Royal Army Service Corps

Crew, G.
The Royal Army Service Corps
Leo Cooper, 1970 (Famous Regiments series)
The Somme, p. 129

Royal Army Veterinary Corps

Clabby, Brig. J., OBE, MRCVS
The History of the Royal Army Veterinary Corps 1919–1961
J.A. Allen, 1963
The Somme, p. 17
This gives details of equine casualties.

Royal Berkshire Regiment

Petrie, F.L.
The Royal Berkshire Regiment
Reading: The Barracks, 1925, 2 vols
The Somme, Vol. 2: 1st Bn., Ch. 26, pp. 25–31; 2nd Bn., Ch. 27, pp. 80–2; 1st/4th (Territorial) Bn., Ch. 29, pp. 140–51; 5th (Service) Bn., Ch. 31, pp. 214–21; 6th (Service) Bn., Ch. 32, pp. 252–67; 8th (Service) Bn., Ch. 34, pp. 328–37
A list of regimental colonels is in the appendices.

Cruttwell, C.R.M.F.
The War Service of the 1/4 Royal Berkshire Regiment (T.F.)
Oxford: Blackwells, 1922
The Somme, pp. 67–99
The book includes a roll of honour of officers and men. Cruttwell went on to write a single-volume history of the war (see Unofficial History section, p. 12). The author was late Capt. 1/4 Royal Berks. Regt., Fellow of Hertford College, and formerly Fellow of All Souls College, Oxford.

Pawle, Capt. H. & Stokes, Capt. V.G.
Notes for Instructors on the History of the 49th and 66th, 1st and 2nd Battalions The Royal Berkshire Regiment (Princess Charlotte of Wales's)
Reading: Bradley (printer), 1925
The Somme, pp. 70–3
This is a small book.

Royal Dublin Fusiliers

Wylly, Col. H.C., CB
Neill's 'Blue Caps' (The Royal Dublin Fusiliers)
Aldershot: Gale & Polden, 1923, 3 vols
The Somme, Vol. 3, Ch. 4, pp. 64–76
The book includes a roll of honour of officers and other ranks by numbers. Many photographs of groups of men are included along with descriptions of memorials.

Wylly, Col. H.C., CB
Crown and Company of the 2nd Battalion Royal Dublin Fusiliers
Aldershot: Gale & Polden, [n.d.]
The Somme, pp. 64–76

Royal Engineers

Anon
The Work of the Royal Engineers in the European War, 1914–19: Military mining

Chatham: Institution of Royal Engineers, 1922
The Somme, pp. 33–6
This is a technical book with many plans of mining activity.

Grieve, Capt. W. Grant & Newman, Bernard
Tunnellers: The story of the tunnelling companies, Royal Engineers, during the World War
Herbert Jenkins, 1936
The Somme, pp. 112–38
The book has many maps of mining activity and a few illustrations.

Pritchard, H.L. (ed.)
History of the Corps of Royal Engineers
Vol. 5: *The Home Front, France, Flanders and Italy in the First World War*
Chatham: Royal Engineers, 1952
The Somme, pp. 88, 165, 245, 253–76, 435, 447, 501, 535 & 605–7
This book covers the organization of the Royal Engineers in various theatres. There is a map pocket at the back.

Fox, Maj. C.L., MC, RE
Narrative of 502 (Wessex) Field Company Royal Engineers 1915–1919
Hugh Rees, 1920
The Somme, pp. 123–7

Royal Fusiliers (City of London Regiment)

Foss, Michael
The Royal Fusiliers (The 7th Regiment of Foot)
Leo Cooper/Hamish Hamilton, 1967 (Famous Regiments series)
The Somme, pp. 89–90

O'Neill, H.C.
The Royal Fusiliers in the Great War
Heinemann, 1922
The Somme, Ch. 7, pp. 109–51

Wyrall, Everard
The 17th (Service) Battalion, the Royal Fusiliers, 1914–1919
Methuen, 1930
The Somme, pp. 32–96
The book includes a nominal roll of officers and men who went to France on 16 November 1915, and a very comprehensive roll of honour of officers.

Stone, Maj. Christopher, DSO, MC (ed.)
A History of the 22nd (Service) Battalion, the Royal Fusiliers (Kensington)
Old Comrades Association of the Battalion, 1923 (private printing)
The Somme, pp. 34–42
The book includes a roll of honour.

Ward, Capt. Fred W.
The 23rd (Service) Battalion Royal Fusiliers (First Sportsman's): A record of its services in the Great War 1914–1919
Sidgwick & Jackson, 1920
The Somme, pp. 44–5, 83–92
The book includes a roll of honour of officers and men.

Royal Hampshire Regiment

Atkinson, C.T.
Regimental History, the Royal Hampshire Regiment
Glasgow: Robert Maclehose (printer; for the regiment), 1950–2, 3 vols
The Somme, Vol. 2, pp. 169–201
The book includes a roll of officers from the Regular Battalion.

Stevens, F.E.
The Battle Story of the Hampshire Regiment, 1702–1919
Southampton: Hampshire Advertiser, 1919

The Somme, 1st Bn., pp. 20–1; 2nd & 14th Bns., pp. 22–3
This small, illustrated book has maps and a foreword by the Rt. Hon. The Earl of Selborne.

Royal Inniskilling Fusiliers

Fox, Sir Frank (late of the RFA of QMG Staff GHQ, BEF & General Staff War Office)
The Royal Inniskilling Fusiliers in the World War: A record of the war as seen by the Royal Inniskilling Regiment of Fusiliers, thirteen battalions of which served
Constable, 1928
The Somme, pp. 63–86
The book includes a roll of honour for officers and of other ranks by battalion.

Alexander, Maj. C.A.M.
With the 2nd Battalion the Royal Inniskilling Fusiliers in France, 1914–16
Omagh: Tyrone Constitution, 1916
The Somme, pp. 72–80
This small book is illustrated and was compiled from official records.

Walker, C.A. Cooper
The Book of the 7th (Service) Battalion, the Royal Inniskilling Fusiliers from Tipperary to Ypres
Dublin: Brindley, 1920
The Somme, pp. 61–73
The book includes a good picture of the destroyed village of Guillemont. It also has a roll of honour of officers and men, and a listing from the battalion cemetery with names by row, including cause of death.

Mitchell, Gardiner S.
'Three Cheers for the Derrys': A history of the 10th Royal Inniskilling Fusiliers in the 1914–18 War based on the recollections of veterans Jim Donaghy and Leslie Bell
Derry: Yes! Publications, 1991
The Somme, pp. 71–120
The battalion was part of the 36th (Ulster) Div. The book has maps, illustrations and a roll of honour.

Royal Irish Fusiliers

Anon
Outline History of the Royal Irish Fusiliers (Princess Victoria's)
Armagh: Armagh Guardian, 1944
The Somme, pp. 18 & 20
This a small book.

Anon
Outline History of the Royal Irish Fusiliers (Princess Victoria's)
Aldershot: Gale & Polden, 1948
The Somme (briefly), pp. 17, 19 & 20
This is a small book.

Cunliffe, Marcus
The Royal Irish Fusiliers, 1793–1950
Oxford University Press, 1952
The Somme, pp. 299–315
This large book has illustrations and maps.

Harris, H.
The Royal Irish Fusiliers (The 87th and 89th Regiments of Foot)
Leo Cooper, 1972 (Famous Regiments series)
The Somme, pp. 94–7

Burrows, Brig.-Gen. A.R., CMG, DSO (late of the Royal Irish Fusiliers)
The 1st Battalion the Faugh-a-Ballaghs (The Royal Irish Fusiliers in the Great War)

Aldershot: Gale & Polden, 1925
The Somme, pp. 73–83
The book includes a roll of honour of officers and men, an aerial photograph of Redan Ridge and some maps, including one of Beaumont-Hamel. (Falls★)

Royal Irish Rifles

Anon
A Short History of the Royal Irish Rifles (The 83rd & 86th Regiment of Foot)
Aldershot: Gale & Polden, 1920
The Somme (briefly), pp. 21–2
This is a small book.

Georghegan, Brig.-Gen. S., CB (late Indian Army & 1st Bn. the Royal Irish)
The Campaigns and History of the Royal Irish Regiment
Vol. II, *1900–22*
William Blackwood, 1927
The Somme, pp. 35–44
The book includes a roll of honour of officers and men.

Falls, C. (formerly Capt. General Staff 36th (Ulster Division))
The History of the first seven battalions, the Royal Irish Rifles (later the Royal Ulster Rifles) in the Great War
Aldershot: Gale & Polden, 1925
The Somme, pp. 69–79
The book includes a roll of honour for officers, and of other ranks by numbers.

A.P.I.S. & D.G.S. [Capt. Samuels, A.P.I. & D.G.S.]
With the Ulster Division in France: A story of the 11th Battalion Royal Irish Rifles (South Antrim Volunteers)

Belfast: William Mullan, 1918
The Somme, pp. 37–56
The book includes a list of casualties by company, some good photographs of officers and men and some hand-drawn maps including one of Thiepval Wood (1 July 1916).

Royal Military Police

Sheffield, G.D.
The Redcaps: A history of the Royal Military Police and its antecedents from the Middle Ages to the Gulf War
Brasseys, 1994
The Somme, pp. 63–6

Royal Munster Fusiliers

McCance Capt. S.
History of the Royal Munster Fusiliers
Aldershot: Gale & Polden, 1927, 2 vols
The Somme, Vol. 2: 1st Bn., pp. 64–6; 2nd Bn., pp. 134–41; 8th (Service) Bn., pp. 201–2
The illustrated book has maps, a list of actions and a list of officer and other rank casualties by battalion.

Jervis, Lt.-Col. H.S., MC
The 2nd Munsters in France
Aldershot: Gale & Polden, 1922
The Somme, pp. 29–36
The book includes some very good maps.

Royal Naval Division

Blumberg, Sir H.E., KCB (comp.)
Britain's Sea Soldiers: A record of the Royal Marines during the War 1914–1919
Devonport: Swiss, 1927
The Somme, pp. 283, 286–8, 316–21 & 322–5
There is also a Somme map in the accompanying map case.

Grover, Col. G.W.M., OBE
A Short History of the Royal Marines
Aldershot: Gale & Polden, 1959
The Somme, pp. 36

Moulton, J.L.
The Royal Marines
Leo Cooper, 1972 (Famous Regiments series)
The Somme, pp. 59–60

Smith, Peter C.
Per Mare Per Terram: A history of the Royal Marines
St Ives: Photo Precision, 1974
The Somme, pp. 105–6

Jerrold, Douglas
The Hawke Battalion: Some personal records of four years, 1914–1918
Ernest Benn, 1925
The Somme, pp. 126–42
This book is illustrated with maps and photographs of the Somme. (Falls★)

Sellers, Leonard
Hood Battalion: Royal Naval Division: Antwerp, Gallipoli, France 1914–1918
Leo Cooper, 1995
The Somme, pp. 163–202
This is the history of what became the 63rd (RN) Div., which was formed in 1914, served in Gallipoli, and was transferred to France in May 1916. It won five VCs including one by Lt.-Col. Freyberg, the CO of Hood Bn. The illustrated book has maps, including one of the Battle of the Ancre.

Royal Regiment Of Wales

Brereton, J.M.
A History of the Royal Regiment of Wales (24th/41st Foot) 1689–1989
Cardiff: Royal Regiment, 1989
The Somme, pp. 234–6

Royal Scots

Brander, A.M.
The Royal Scots (The Royal Regiment)
Leo Cooper, 1976 (Famous Regiments series)
The Somme, pp. 60–1

Ewing, Maj. J., MC
The Royal Scots, 1914–1919
Oliver & Boyd, 1925
The Somme, Vol. 1, pp. 265–342
The book includes a map of the Somme sector and some photographs and drawings of officers.

Royal Scots Fusiliers

Anon
A Short History of the Royal Scots Fusiliers
Aldershot: Gale & Polden, [n.d.]
The Somme, pp. 38, 39 & 40

Buchan, J.
The History of the Royal Scots Fusiliers, 1678–1918
Nelson, 1925
The Somme, pp. 348–62
The book includes lists of senior officers.

Royal Sussex Regiment

Anon
A Short History of the Royal Sussex Regiment (35th Foot – 107th Foot)
Aldershot: Gale & Polden, 1941
The Somme, pp. 36–7
This is a small book.

Martineau, G.D.
A History of the Royal Sussex Regiment
Chichester: Moore & Tillyer, 1955
The Somme, pp. 176–9

Readman, A.E., BA
The Royal Sussex Regiment: A catalogue of records
Chichester: West Sussex County Council, 1985
The Somme, pp. 35, 36, 39, 40, 81, 94,
97, 100, 112 & 129
This book lists documents and photographs.

Fazan, Col. E.A.C., MC, TD, DL
*Cinque Ports Battalion: The story of the 5th
(Cinque Ports) Battalion the Royal Sussex
Regiment (T.A.), formerly 1st Cinque Ports
Rifle Volunteer Corps*
Chichester: Royal Sussex Regimental
Association, 1971
The Somme, pp. 112–14
The book includes a list of battalion
commanding officers.

Rutter, Owen (ed.)
*The History of the 7th (Service) Battalion, the
Royal Sussex Regiment, 1914–1919*
Times, 1934
The Somme, pp. 77–108
The book provides a diary of battalion
movements in France, a summary of
casualties and a roll of honour.

Royal Tank Regiment

Liddell Hart, B.H.
*The Tanks: The history of the Royal Tank
Regiment and its predecessors; Heavy Branch
Machine Gun Corps, Tanks Corps and Royal
Tank Corps, 1914–1945*
Cassell, 1959, 2 vols
The Somme, vol. 1, pp. 71–9
The book includes several pictures of the
development of the tank.

Royal Ulster Rifles

Anon
*The Royal Ulster Rifles: A short history of the
83rd Foot and 86th Foot*

Belfast: J. Aiken, 1937
The Somme, pp. 66–7

Royal Warwickshire Regiment

Kingsford, C.L.
*The Story of the Royal Warwickshire Regiment
(formerly the Sixth Foot)*
Newnes, 1921
The Somme, pp. 148–67
The book includes a roll of honour and a
list of battalions that served in France.

Carrington, Lt. C.E., MC
*The War Record of the 1/5th Battalion the
Royal Warwickshire Regiment*
Birmingham: Cornish Brothers, 1922
The Somme, pp. 21–39
This is a small paperback.

Anon
*Forward with the Fifth: History of the 1/6th
Battalion the Royal Warwickshire Regiment*
Birmingham: Cornish Brothers, 1922
The Somme, pp. 21–32
This small booklet includes a roll of officers
and men killed.

Collison, Brev. Col. C.S.
*The 11th Royal Warwicks in France 1915–16:
From the personal diary of its commanding officer*
Birmingham: Cornish Brothers, 1928
The Somme, pp. 67–108
The foreword is by Maj.-Gen. Lord
Edward Gleichen.

Fairclough, J.E.B.
*The First Birmingham Battalion in the Great War
1914–1919: Being a history of the 14th (Service)
Battalion of the Royal Warwickshire Regiment*
Birmingham: Cornish Brothers, 1933
The Somme, pp. 31–44 & 55–76
These pages include the period before the

battle. The foreword is by Gen. Sir R.B. Stevens and Col. G. White Lewis, and the book contains a roll of honour of officers and men and their date of death. It is also illustrated with portraits, plates and maps.

Bill, Maj. C.A.
The 15th Battalion Royal Warwickshire Regiment (2nd Birmingham Battalion) in the Great War
Birmingham: Cornish Brothers, 1932
The Somme, pp. 39–59
This illustrated book has maps and a foreword by Lt.-Col. Colin Harding.

Royal Welch Fusiliers

Glover, Michael
That Astonishing Infantry: Three hundred years of the history of the Royal Welch Fusiliers (23rd Regiment of Foot) 1689–1989
Leo Cooper, 1989
The Somme, pp. 132–48
This book is illustrated.

Skaife, Col. E.O., OBE
A Short History of the Royal Welch Fusiliers
Aldershot: Gale & Polden, 1940
The Somme, p. 55

Ward, Maj. C.H. Dudley, DSO, MC (late Welsh Guards)
Regimental Records of the Royal Welch Fusiliers
Vol. 3: *1914–1918 France and Flanders*
Forster & Groom, 1928
The Somme, pp. 189–258
The book contains nine maps concerning the battle and several photographs of regimental personalities.

[Dunn, Capt. J.C. (ed.)]
The War the Infantry Knew, 1914–1919: A chronicle of service in France and Belgium with the Second Battalion His Majesty's Twenty-third Foot, the Royal Welch Fusiliers founded on personal records, recollections and reflections assembled, edited and partly written by one of their medical officers
P.S. King, 1938
The Somme, pp. 222–83
This chronicle is based on the editor's diaries and on contributions from fifty officers and men who served with the battalion as well as with other units. In later editions the editor's name was revealed as being Capt. J.C. Dunn and one of the book's special qualities, apart from its wealth of detail, are the references to well-known writers such as Robert Graves, Frank Richards and Siegfried Sassoon. Dunn rejected Graves's contributions as he did not like the 'theatrical tone' of Graves's autobiography *Goodbye to All That*. Dunn was a Scot, and won the DCM in the Boer War and a DSO, MC and Bar in the First World War.

The book is a glorious mosaic of the history of the war from the point of view of one unit. It was originally issued in an edition of 500 copies and became much sought, after it went out of print. For the 1987 edition, published by Jane's Publishing Company, Keith Simpson wrote a fine introduction. This book has maps and illustrations. The Royal Welch Fusiliers is one of the oldest regiments in the British Army and a flash of black ribbons is worn on their collars as a regimental tradition dating back to 1808.

Ellis, Capt. C.
The 4th (Denbighshire) Battalion Royal Welch Fusiliers in the Great War
Wrexham: Woodall, Minshall & Thomas, 1926
The Somme, pp. 39–48
This book is illustrated.

Burton, Lt.-Col. F.N. (ed., assisted by Lt. A.P. Comyns)
The War Diary (1914–1918) of 10th (Service) Battalion Royal Welch Fusiliers
Plymouth: William Brendon & Sons, 1926
The Somme, pp. 37–63

Scots Guards

Goodinge, A.
The Scots Guards (The 3rd Guards)
Leo Cooper, 1969 (Famous Regiments series)
The Somme, p. 90

Petre, F. Loraine, Ewart, Wilfrid & Lowther, Maj.-Gen. Sir Cecil, CB, CVO, DSO
The Scots Guards in the Great War 1914–1918
Murray, 1925
The Somme, pp. 144–68
This book includes maps.

Swinton, J.
A Short History of the Scots Guards, 1642–1962: With some notes on the colours, badges and customs of the regiment
Aldershot: Gale & Polden, 1963
The Somme, pp. 16 & 22

Seaforth Highlanders

Anon
Short History of the Seaforth Highlanders
Dingwell: Ross Shire Printing, 1928
The Somme, 2nd Bn., pp. 55–6; Territorial Bns., pp. 65–6; Service Bn., pp. 74–5; Dominion Bn., pp. 84–5
This is a small booklet.

Nairns, C.S.
The Seaforth Highlanders
[n.p.], 1928
The Somme, pp. 55, 65, 66, 74, 75, 84 & 85

Sym, John (ed.)
Seaforth Highlanders
Aldershot: Gale & Polden, 1962
The Somme, pp. 173–9
The appendices include lists of senior officers and details of VC awards.

Haldane, Lt.-Col. M.M.
A History of the Fourth Battalion Seaforth Highlanders
Witherby, 1928
The Somme, pp. 146–84
Good maps and small paintings are included. (Falls★)

Sutherland, Capt. D., MC, TD
War Diary of the Fifth Seaforth Highlanders, 51st (Highland) Division
Bodley Head, [n.d.]
The Somme, pp. 72–94

Peel, Capt. R.T., MC & Macdonald, Capt. A.H., MC
6th Seaforth Highlanders Campaign Reminiscences
Elgin: W.R. Walker, 1923
The Somme, pp. 13–17, 23–6 & 30–4
This book includes some good individual photographs of officers and men.

Sherwood Foresters

Anon
A Short History of the Sherwood Foresters (Nottinghamshire and Derbyshire Regiment)
Aldershot: Gale & Polden, 1940
The Somme, p. 18

Wylly, Col. H.C., CB (late of the Regiment) (comp.)
The 1st and 2nd Battalions the Sherwood Foresters in the Great War (Nottinghamshire and Derbyshire Regiment)

Aldershot: Gale & Polden, 1925
The Somme, 1st Bn. (with illustrations), pp. 27–40; 2nd Bn. (with a map of the Quadrilateral), pp. 122–30
The book includes information on VC winners.

Brewill, A.W. *et al.*
'The Robin Hoods': 1/7th, 2/7th, 3/7th Battalions, the Sherwood Foresters, 1914–1918
Nottingham: J.H. Bell, 1921
The Somme, Section 1, pp. 194–255
The book includes a roll of honour of officers and men by battalion.

Weetman, Capt. W.C.C., MC, Croix de Guerre
The Sherwood Foresters in the Great War, 1914–1919, 1/8th Battalion
Nottingham: T. Forman, 1920
The Somme, pp. 128–74
This illustrated book has a roll of honour of officers and men and a summary of regimental events.

De Grave, L.W.
The War History of the Fifth Battalion, the Sherwood Foresters, Notts & Derby Regiment, 1914–1918
Derby: Bernrose, 1930
The Somme, pp. 72–89
This book includes a roll of honour and has some excellent maps and illustrations.

Jamieson, Capt. W.D.
6th Battalion the Sherwood Foresters 1914–1918
Chesterfield: Jamieson, 1958 (private printing)
The Somme, pp. 37–51
This illustrated typescript has maps.

Fryer, Percy
The Men from the Greenwood: Being the war history of the 11th (Service) Battalion Sherwood Foresters
Nottingham: Cresswell & Oaksford, 1919
The Somme, pp. 42–76
This illustrated book has maps and plans.

Bacon, M. & Langley, D.
The Blast of War: A history of Nottinghamshire Bantams 15th (S) Battalion Sherwood Foresters 1915–1919
Nottingham: Sherwood Press, 1986
The Somme, pp. 25–8 & 37
This illustrated book includes a roll of honour.

Truscott, Lt.-Col. R.F.
A Short History of the 16th Battalion, the Sherwood Foresters (Chatsworth Rifles)
Truscotts, 1928
The Somme, pp. 52–83
This book is illustrated with plates, portraits and maps.

Royal Corps of Signals

Nalder, Maj.-Gen. R.F.H., CB, OBE
The Royal Corps of Signals: A history of its antecedents and development (c. 1800–1955)
Aldershot: Gale & Polden, 1958
The Somme, pp. 59, 63, 67, 114–17 & 123
This book includes biographies of senior officers and some illustrations, and covers the development of the signals section of the Royal Engineers.

Priestley, R.E., MC, BA
The Signal Service in the European War of 1914 to 1918
Chatham: Royal Engineers/Mackay, 1921

The Somme, pp. 120, 121, 123, 127, 132 & 133
This book is particularly good at explaining the communication problems that the war produced.

Somerset Light Infantry

Popham, H.
The Somerset Light Infantry
Hamish Hamilton, 1968 (Famous Regiments series)
The Somme, pp. 108–10

Wyrall, Everard
The History of the Somerset Light Infantry (Prince Albert's) 1914–1919
Methuen, 1927
The Somme, pp. 114–53
This book has very good maps and includes photographs of some commanding officers.

Majendie, Maj. V.H.B., DSO
History of the 1st Battalion Somerset Light Infantry: 1st July to the end of the war
Taunton: Phoenix Press, 1921
The Somme, pp. 1–8
This book includes a roll of honour of officers and a good map of the Somme area.

Foley, H.A. (ed.)
Scrap Book of the 7th Battalion, Somerset Light Infantry (13th Foot): Being a chronicle of their experiences in the Great War, 1914–1918, contributed by officers and other ranks of the 7th (Service) Battalion the Somerset Light Infantry (Prince Albert's), with a foreword by Col. C.J. Troyte-Bullock
n.p., 1931
The Somme, pp. 13, 23–31 & 37–64
The book has one illustration and some maps.

South Lancashire Regiment (Prince Of Wales's Volunteers)

Mullaly, Col. B.R.
The South Lancashire Regiment
Bristol: The White Swan, 1952
The Somme, pp. 199–224
The book includes a list of lieutenant-colonels.

Whalley-Kelly, Capt. H.
'Ich Dien': The Prince of Wales's Volunteers (South Lancashire), 1914–1934
Aldershot: Gale & Polden, 1935
The Somme, 2nd Bn., pp. 36–42; 4th Bn. (TA), Ch. 5, Pt. 1, pp. 82–4; 5th (Rifle) Bn. (TA), Ch. 6, Pt. 1, pp. 112–15; 8th (Service) Bn., Ch. 9, pp. 206–13; 11th (Service) Bn. (St Helens Pioneers), Ch. 10, pp. 246–8

South Staffordshire Regiment

Jones, James P.
History of the South Staffordshire Regiment
Wolverhampton: Whitehead Brothers (Wolverton), 1923
The Somme, pp. 175–92, 193–6 & 327–40
The book includes a list of commanding officers.

Page, M.
The South Staffordshire Regiment
London: [n.p.], 1953
The Somme, p. 99

Vale, Col. W.L.
History of the South Staffordshire Regiment
Aldershot: Gale & Polden, 1969
The Somme, pp. 324–6

Beauman, Lt.-Col. A.B., DSO
With the 38th in France and Italy: Being a

record of the doings of the 1st Battalion South
Staffordshire Regiment from the 26th September
1916 to 26th May 1918
Lichfield: A.C. Lomax, 1919
The Somme, pp. 7–13

A committee of officers who served with
the battalion
The War History of the Sixth Battalion, the
South Staffordshire Regiment (T.F.)
Heinemann, 1924
The Somme, pp. 129–40
This book includes very detailed rolls of
honour and many good photographs.

Ashcroft, Maj. A.H., DSO (ed.)
The History of the Seventh South Staffordshire
Regiment
Boyle, Son & Watchurst, 1919
The Somme, pp. 60–75 & 81–90
The book includes a list of officers who
served with the battalion, together with
their home address and whether they were
killed or wounded.

South Wales Borderers

Atkinson, C.T. (late Capt. Oxford
University OTC)
The History of the South Wales Borderers,
1914–1918
Medici Society, 1931
The Somme, pp. 212–69
This book includes a roll of honour of
officers and men.

Atkinson, C.T.
The South Wales Borderers, 24th Foot,
1689–1937
Cambridge University Press, 1937
The Somme, 1st Bn., p. 425; 2nd Bn., pp.
427–8; 1st & 2nd Monmouthshires, p.

434; 3rd Monmouthshires, p. 435; 5th
(Service) Bn., p. 439; 6th (Service) Bn., p.
442; 10th & 11th (Service) Bns., pp.
447–8
The book includes a roll of honour of
officers and a list of war memorials.

Special Brigade

Foulkes, Maj.-Gen. C.H., CB, CMG,
DSO (late Royal Engineers)
'Gas!': The story of the Special Brigade
William Blackwood, 1934
The Somme, pp. 120–58
This secret unit was raised in June 1915 to
carry out gas operations against the
Germans. This book includes illustrations,
graphs and folding maps, some of which
show gas preparations. The author was
Commander of the Special Brigade from
January 1916 to June 1917, and then
served at GHQ.

Suffolk Regiment

Moir, G.
The Suffolk Regiment (The 12th Regiment of
Foot)
Leo Cooper, 1969 (Famous Regiments
series)
The Somme, pp. 95–8

Murphy, Lt.-Col. C.C.R. (late of Suffolk
Regiment)
The History of the Suffolk Regiment,
1914–1927
Hutchinson, 1928
The Somme, pp. 120–54; 2nd Bn., pp.
182–7; 4th Bn., pp. 189–92; 7th Bn., pp.
177–81; 8th Bn., pp. 165–72; 9th Bn., pp.
194–9; 11th Bn., pp. 172–7
This book includes several regimental
portraits of commanding officers.

Welsh Guards

Retallack, J.
The Welsh Guards
Leo Cooper/Warne, 1981 (Famous Regiments series)
The Somme, pp. 13–19

Ward, Maj. C.H. Dudley, DSO, MC
History of the Welsh Guards
Murray, 1920
The Somme, pp. 111–41
This book is illustrated, mainly with regimental portraits, and includes the movements of the 1st Bn. It also has some good maps and records of the Welsh Guards officers. (The Welsh Guards had only been formed in 1915, and hence the author was writing a history of the regiment as well as of the war.) (Falls★)

Welch Regiment

Anon
A Short History of the Welch Regiment
Cardiff: Western Mail & Echo, 1938
The Somme, pp. 25–7
This is a small book.

Marden, Maj.-Gen. Sir Thomas O., Colonel of the Welch Regiment
The History of the Welch Regiment
Part II: 1914–18
Cardiff: Western Mail & Echo, 1932
The Somme, pp. 380–98
The book provides good maps and VC citations.

West Yorkshire Regiment

Barker, A.L.
The West Yorkshire Regiment (The XIVth Regiment of Foot)
Leo Cooper, 1974 (Famous Regiments series)
The Somme, p. 54

Phillips, Lt.-Col. C.G., DSO, MC
The West Yorkshire Regiment (The Prince of Wales's Own) 1685–1935: 250th anniversary souvenir
Aldershot: Gale & Polden, 1935
The book has unnumbered pages; the Somme is mentioned in the Great War section.

Tempest, Capt. E.V., DSO, MC
History of the West Yorkshire Regiment
Bradford: Lund Humphries, 1941
The Somme, pp. 45 & 46
The book includes descriptions of actions that won the VC.

Wyrall, Everard
The West Yorkshire Regiment in the War, 1914–1918: A history of the 14th the Prince of Wales's Own (West Yorkshire) Regiment, and of its special reserve, Territorial and Service Battalions in the Great War, 1914–1918
Vol. 1: 1914–16
John Lane, Bodley Head, 1924–7
The Somme, pp. 189–290
This illustrated book has a Somme map and a list of casualties from August 1914 to December 1916.

Tempest, Capt. E.V., DSO, MC
History of the Sixth Battalion West Yorkshire Regiment
Vol. 1: 1/6th Battalion
London & Bradford: Lund Humphries, 1921
The Somme, pp. 88–129
This book includes a roll of honour, pictures of officers and a good map.

Gregory, Capt. E.C.
History of the Sixth Battalion West Yorkshire Regiment
Vol. 2: *2/6th Battalion*
London & Bradford: Lund Humphries, 1923
The Somme, pp. 60–89
The book includes very detailed rolls of honour and some good illustrations.

Milner, L.
Leeds Pals: A history of the 15th (Service) Battalion (1st Leeds) The Prince of Wales's Own (West Yorkshire Regiment) 1914–1918
Leo Cooper, 1991
The Somme, pp. 135–74
This fully illustrated book includes a roll of honour, and a Somme map.

Hudson, R.N.
The Bradford Pals: A history of the 16th & 18th Battalions the West Yorkshire Regiment
Private publication, 1977
The Somme, pp. 19–39 & 47–9
This illustrated book has maps.

Hudson, R.N.
The Bradford Pals
Bradford: Bradford Libraries, 1993, 2nd edn
The Somme, pp. 25–56
This new edition is illustrated and has two Somme maps. The book is not one of the large format Pals books.

Wiltshire Regiment

Gibson, T.
The Wiltshire Regiment (The 62nd and 99th Regiment of Foot)
Leo Cooper, 1969 (Famous Regiments series)
The Somme, p. 109

Gillson, Lt.-Col. R.M.T., DSO
A Short History of the Wiltshire Regiment (Duke of Edinburgh's) (62nd and 99th Foot)
Aldershot: Gale & Polden, 1921
The Somme, pp. 23, 24, 30, 38 & 39
This small book also includes rolls of honour by number of men in each battalion.

Kenrick, Col. N.C.E., DSO
The Story of the Wiltshire Regiment (Duke of Edinburgh's) the 62nd and 99th Foot (1756–1959), the Militia and the Territorials, the Service Battalions and all those others who have been affiliated with The Moonrakers
Aldershot: Gale & Polden, 1963
The Somme, 1st Bn., pp. 116–17; 2nd Bn., pp. 133–5; Territorial, Service, Depot & Volunteer Bns. & 6th Bn., p. 147

Shepherd, Maj. W.S., MC (Adj. 1915–1916, Second in Command 1917–1918)
The 2nd Battalion, The Wiltshire Regiment (99th): A record of their fighting in the Great War, 1914–1918
Aldershot: Gale & Polden, 1927
The Somme, pp. 79–96 & 99–104

Worcester Regiment

Gale, R.
The Worcestershire Regiment (The 29th and 36th Regiment of Foot)
Leo Cooper, 1970 (Famous Regiments series)
The Somme, p. 87
With two good illustrations.

Stacke, Capt. H. Fitzmaurice, MC
The Worcestershire Regiment in the Great War
Kidderminster: Cheshire, 1928
The Somme, pp. 161–213
This detailed book is probably the very

best regimental history of the First World War ever published. No expense was spared in its preparation and the book includes excellent maps, illustrations and rolls of honour.

York & Lancaster Regiment

Payne, A.A., LRCP, MRCS, MBNS
A Concise History of the York and Lancaster Regiment
Bristol: J.W. Arrowsmith, [n.d.]
The Somme (briefly), p. 26
This is a small book.

Wylly, Col. H.C., CB
The York and Lancaster Regiment, the Territorial and Service Battalions, 1758–1919
Frome & London: Butler & Tanner (printer), 1930, 2 vols
The Somme, Vol. 1: pp. 352–62; Vol. 2: 1/4th Hallamshire Bn., pp. 10–15; 1/5th, York and Lancaster Regt., pp. 77–84; 7th Bn., pp. 148–9; 8th Bn., pp. 172–8; 9th Bn., pp. 201–6; 10th Bn., pp. 220–5; 12th Bn., pp. 235–9; 14th Bn., pp. 268–71
The book includes some excellent photographs of sectors of the battlefield.

Grant, Capt. D.P., MC, MA
The 1/4th Hallamshire Battalion York and Lancaster Regiment 1914–1919
Arden Press, 1931?
The Somme, pp. 35–50

Gilvary, M.T.
History of the 7th (Service) Battalion, the York and Lancaster Regiment (Pioneers), 1914–1919
Talbot Press, 1921

The Somme, pp. 21–35
The book includes a roll of honour and maps.

Montagu, J.B.
The History of the 9th (Service) Battalion, the York and Lancaster Regiment
[n.p., n.d.], War Office Library reference A242–65
The Somme, pp. 19–36
Typescript

Gibson, Ralph & Oldfield, Paul
Sheffield City Battalion: The 12th (Service) Battalion York and Lancaster Regiment
Barnsley: Wharncliffe, 1988
The Somme, pp. 145–70 & 177–9
The book is profusely illustrated and also has good maps and a biographical listing. It lists the names of those who took part in the assault on the Somme on 1 July 1916 and the place of burial or commemoration of those killed. It is one of the large format Pals volumes.

Sparling, R.A.
History of the 12th (Service) Battalion, York and Lancaster Regiment
[n.p.], 1920, War Office Library reference A242–65
The Somme, pp. 47–74 & 78–87
The book includes a roll of honour and some illustrations of the Ancre and Serre taken by Germans. It also has a picture of the *sucrerie* at Serre.

Haigh, R.H. & Turner, P.W.
The Battle of the Somme: The experience of the 13th (Service) Battalion of the York and Lancaster Regiment
Sheffield: Pavic Publications, [n.d.]
This A4 booklet gives a brief history of the battalion.

Cooksey, J.

Pals. The 13th and 14th Battalions York and Lancaster Regiment: A history of the two battalions raised by Barnsley in World War 1

Barnsley: Wharncliffe, 1986.

The Somme, pp. 176–239

The book includes illustrations, maps and a roll of honour. It is one of the large format Pals volumes.

AUSTRALIA: GENERAL AND UNIT HISTORIES

Australia had no previous history of army service, being such a young country, and sent its army to Gallipoli, where the men served with distinction and then journeyed to Egypt before arriving in France in the first part of 1916. They supplied four divisions that took part in the Battle of the Somme, the 1st, 2nd, 4th and 5th, allocated to British Army Corps. No fewer than 37 Australian regiments were awarded Pozières as a battle honour. Its capture was planned for 23 July 1916, but it was several weeks before the Germans were finally driven out.

The many unit histories published reflect the interest in the First World War when Australia came to maturity as a nation.

AUSTRALIAN IMPERIAL FORCE

General Histories

Bean, C.E.W.
The Official History of Australia in the War of 1914–1918
Vol. III
Sydney: Angus & Robertson, 1929
The Somme, pp. 448–950
As a correspondent Bean was uniquely placed to write the Australian history of the war. He was actually on the spot when the fighting took place and was able to interview participants and gather material to use later in his writings. His whole project became a major achievement and was a unique official history. (Falls★★)

Bean, C.E.W.
Official History of Australia in the War of 1914–1918
Vol. XII
Sydney: Angus & Robertson, 1943
This book contains some photographs of the Somme battlefield, including a picture of a British trench, La Boisselle, pp. 119 and 201, Pozières, pp. 203–5, the spire of the Basilique in Albert, p. 206, and Mouquet Farm, pp. 236–9.

Bean, C.E.W. (formerly Australian Official War Historian)
Anzac to Amiens: A shorter history of the Australian Fighting Services in the First World War
Canberra: Australian War Memorial, 1946
The Somme, pp. 217–69
This illustrated book has maps.

Butler, Col. A.G., DSO, VD, BA, MB, ChB (Camb.)
The Australian Army Medical Services in the War of 1914–1918
Vol. II
Canberra: Australian War Memorial, 1943
The Somme, pp. 49–103
This excellent book is part of a three-volume history. It includes illustrations and maps, and a list of casualty numbers for the period. Vol. III has a roll of honour.

Lucas, Sir Charles (ed.)
The Empire at War
Vol. 3 (1924): *The Australian Forces in the War*

Section 2: 'The Australians in France, Pozières and Fromelles' by C.E.W. Bean and others
Oxford University Press, 1921–6, 5 vols
The Somme, pp. 113–26

DIVISIONS

Ellis, Capt. A.D., MC (29th Battalion AIF)
The Story of the Fifth Australian Division
Hodder & Stoughton, 1920
The Somme, Ch.7, pp. 135–74
This book includes accounts of VC actions with citations and rolls of honour shown by unit.

ARTILLERY

Anon
The War Service Record of the First Australian Field Artillery Brigade 1914–1919
Adelaide: W.K. Thomas, n.d.
This is a complete service record of personnel, including a roll of honour of those who served. It contains a few maps and illustrations.

Cubis, Richard
History of 'A' Battery New South Wales Artillery (1871–1899) Royal Australian Artillery (1899–1971)
Sydney: Elizabethan Press, 1978
The Somme, pp. 138–41

INFANTRY AND ENGINEERS

Anon
The History of the First Battalion, A.I.F. 1914–19
Sydney: 1st Bn. A.I.F. History Committee, 1931
The Somme, pp. 52–9

This book includes casualty figures by numbers, and a nominal roll of the battalion with casualties noted against a name where appropriate.

Taylor, F.W. & Cusak, T.A. (comps)
Nulli Secundus: A history of the Second Battalion, A.I.F., 1914–1919
Sydney: New Century Press, 1942
The Somme, pp. 177–92, 194 & 200–4
This book includes some good pictures of Pozières.

Wren, Eric
Randwick to Hargicourt: History of the 3rd Battalion A.I.F.
Sydney: Ronald G. McDonald, 1935
The Somme, pp. 155–85 & 192–221
This book includes photographs of men who served.

Keown, A.W.
Forward with the Fifth: The story of five years' war service. Fifth Infantry Battalion A.I.F.
Melbourne: Speciality Press (for the Regimental Association), 1921
The Somme, Book 3, pp. 165–74, 176–7, 185–6, 187–96, 197–206 & 207–16
This is divided into three books and includes some very good photographs.

Speed, Brig. F.W., OBE (ed.)
Esprit de Corps: The history of the Victorian Scottish Regiment and the 5th Infantry Battalion
Sydney: Allen & Unwin, 1988
The Somme, pp. 61–75 & 77–9, for early winter 1916
This illustrated book includes maps.

Austin, Ronald J., RFD (ed.)
As Rough as Bags: The history of the 6th Battalion 1st A.I.F. 1914–1919

McCrae, Australia: R.J. & S.P. Austin, 1992
The Somme, pp. 158–75
This book includes many location photographs, some maps and a roll of honour.

Austin, Ron
Bold Steady Faithful: The history of the 6th Bn. the Royal Melbourne Regiment 1854–1993
Melbourne: R. & S. Austin, 1993
The Somme, pp. 81 & 82
This book is illustrated.

Dean, Arthur & Gutteridge, Eric W.
The Seventh Battalion A.I.F.: Résumé of activities of the Seventh Battalion in the Great War 1914–1918
Melbourne: W. & K. Purbrick, 1933
The Somme, pp. 39–54, 61–9 & 70–3
This book includes a battalion nominal roll of those men killed.

Harvey, Norman K.
From Anzac to the Hindenburg Line: The history of the 9th Battalion A.I.F.
Brisbane: William Brooks, 1941
The Somme, pp. 123, 135, 137–43, 149–54, 159 & 167

Wrench, C.M., MC
Campaigning with the Fighting Ninth: In and out of the line with the 9th Bn A.I.F., 1914–1919
Brisbane: Boolarong Publications, 1985
The Somme, pp. 125–43
This book includes a list of casualties and some illustrations of Pozières and of battalion officers.

Limb, A.
History of the 10th Battalion, A.I.F.
Cassell, 1919
The Somme, pp. 28–35

This book includes a roll of honour of those men killed in France.

Lock, C.B.L.
The Fighting Tenth: A South Australian centenary souvenir of the 10th Bn. A.I.F.
Adelaide: Webb, 1936
The Somme, pp. 56–65 & 67
The Somme pages are written in the form of a war diary named Battalion Chronology. This very detailed book includes a roll of honour.

Belford, Capt. Walter C.
'Legs-Eleven': Being the story of the 11th Battalion (A.I.F.) in the Great War of 1914–1918
Perth: Imperial Printing Company, 1940
The Somme, pp. 259–98 & 306–23
This book includes maps, illustrations and a foreword by Maj.-Gen. E.G. Sinclair Maclagan.

Newton, L.M. (late Lt. & Adj. 12th Bn. AIF)
The Story of the Twelfth: A record of the 12th Battalion A.I.F during the Great War of 1914–1918
Hobart: J. Walch, 1925
The Somme, pp. 211–300
This illustrated book gives a list of casualty figures.

White, T.A.
The Fighting Thirteenth: The history of the Thirteenth Battalion A.I.F.
Sydney: Tyrrells, 1924
The Somme, pp. 64–71 & 72–6
The book includes pictures of company commanders.

Wanliss, N.
The History of the 14th Battalion A.I.F.: Being the story of the vicissitudes of an Australian unit during the Great War

Melbourne: Arrow Printery, 1929
The Somme, pp. 134, 150, 151–7 & 162
The book includes a roll of honour, and some good maps.

Chataway, Lt. T.P.
History of the 15th Battalion Australian Imperial Forces 1914–1918
Brisbane: William Brooks, 1948
The Somme, Ch.7, pp. 115–58
This book has a roll of honour and good pictures of men and officers in the battalion.

Knyvett, Capt. R. Hugh (Anzac Scout Intelligence Officer)
'Over There' with the Australians
New York: Charles Scribner's, 1918
The Somme, pp. 186–96 & 213–17
This illustrated book is a history of the 15th Bn. AIF.

Longmore, Capt. C.
The Old Sixteenth: Being a record of the 16th Battalion A.I.F. during the Great War 1914–1918
Perth: History Committee of the 16th Battalion Association, 1929
The Somme, pp. 115–20 & 125–32
This illustrated book includes a list of casualty figures.

Mackenzie, Lt.-Col. K.W., MC
Story of the Seventeenth Battalion A.I.F. in the Great War, 1914–1918
Sydney: Shipping Newspapers, 1946
The Somme, pp. 110–27
This book includes a roll of honour, some good maps and photographs of men.

McNeil, A.R.
Story of the Twenty-first: Being the official history of the 21st Battalion A.I.F.

Melbourne: 21st Battalion Association, 1939
The Somme, Vol. 1: pp. 4, 7 & 8; Vol. 2: p. 3
This is a journal called *The Red & Black Diamond*, which was the official organ of the 21st Battalion AIF Association.

Gorman, Capt. E., MC
'With the Twenty-second': A history of the 22nd Battalion, A.I.F.
Melbourne: H.H. Champion, Australasian Authors' Agency, 1919
The Somme, pp. 33–41 & 44–5, includes early winter
This book has an introduction by Gen. Sir W.R. Birdwood GCMG, KCB, KCSI, LIE, DSO, ADC and a frontispiece illustration by the artist Lt. Will Dyson.

Harvey, Sgt. W.J.
The Red and White Diamond: The official history of the 24th Battalion A.I.F.
Melbourne: Alexander McCubbin, 1920
The Somme, pp. 91–113, 120–5 & 133–6
This book includes a roll of the fallen.

Dollman, Lt.-Col. W., VD, & Skinner, Sgt. H.M., MM
The Blue and Brown Diamond: A history of the 27th Battalion A.I.F. 1915–1919
Adelaide: Lonnen & Cope, 1921
The Somme, pp. 41–56, 59, 63–7 & 69–76
This book has some good illustrations and a roll of honour.

Kahan, Henry K.
The 28th Battalion Australian Imperial Force: A record of war service
South Perth: Henry Kahan, 1969
The Somme, pp. 23–42
This comb-bound book includes a nominal roll of the men who served in the field.

Sloan, Lt.-Col. H.
The Purple and the Gold: A history of the 30th Battalion
Sydney: Halstead Press (printer), 1938
The Somme, Ch. 9, pp. 106–24, including early winter
This book is illustrated mainly with portraits.

Colliver, Capt. E.J., MC & Richardson, Lt. B.H.
The Forty-third: The story of the official history of the 43rd Battalion A.I.F.
Adelaide: Rigby, 1920
The Somme, pp. 73–4 & 103–6

Lee, Maj. J.E., DSO, MC
The Chronicle of the 45th Battalion A.I.F.
Sydney: Mortons (printers), date in foreword 1924 (private printing)
The Somme, pp. 24–32 & 33–40
The appendices include a nominal roll and details of casualties.

Lee, Maj. J.E., DSO, MC (Australian Service Corps, formerly of the 45th Bn.)
A Brief History of the 45th Battalion A.I.F. 1916–1919
45th Battalion Reunion Association, 1962
The Somme, pp. 4–5

Devine, W.
The Story of a Battalion (48th Battalion, A.I.F.)
Melbourne: Melville & Mullen, 1919
The Somme, pp. 27–57 & pp. 62–70, for early winter
This book includes maps and drawings.

Cranston, F.
Always Faithful: A history of the 49th Infantry Battalion, 1916–1982
Brisbane: Boolarong Publications, 1983

The Somme, pp. 5–13, 16, 18 & 19
This illustrated book has a roll of honour.

Kennedy, J.J., DSO, CF
The Whale Oil Guards
No place: James Dufry, 1919
The Somme, pp. 83–99, includes early winter
This book, written by a padre, is about the experiences of the 53rd Bn. AIF.

Barker, T.
Signals: A history of the Royal Australian Corps of Signals, 1788–1947
Glenroy, Australia: Book Generation, 1987
The Somme, pp. 88–9

Broinowski, L. (ed.)
Tasmania's War Record 1914–1918
Hobart: J. Walch, 1921
The Somme, pp. 43–5
This illustrated book has maps and an introduction by Maj.-Gen. Sir J. Gellibrand, KCB, DSO.

Chatto, R.
The Seventh Company (Field Engineers) Australian Imperial Force 1915–1918
Sydney: Smiths' Newspapers, 1936
The Somme, pp. 25–34, 40–50
The book includes a roll of honour and is illustrated with drawings of the unit.

McNicoll, Maj.-Gen. R.R. [Robert], CBE
History of the Royal Australian Engineers
Vol. 2: *The Royal Australian Engineers 1902–1919: Making and Breaking*
Canberra: Corps Committee of the Royal Australian Engineers, n.d.
The Somme, pp. 68–78
The book lists short biographies of officers.

1. *Wyn Griffith,* author of Up to Mametz, *while an officer with the Royal Welch Fusiliers*

2. *Charles Carrington,* author of Soldier from the Wars Returning

3. *'The Iron Harvest' (Peter Batchelor)*

4. Sir Philip Gibbs, doyen of the war correspondents in the Great War and prolific author

5. FM Earl Haig in the Peace Procession, London, 19 July 1919

6. Australian historian C.E.W. Bean at work on his Official History *in about 1920*

7. Capt. J.C. Dunn, compiler of The War the Infantry Knew, *1938*

8. John Terraine at the Dedication Service of the Butte de Warlencourt (Peter Batchelor)

9. Reggie Glen, the last of the Sheffield Pals, at one of the annual services at Lochnagar Crater (Peter Batchelor)

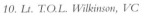

10. Lt. T.O.L. Wilkinson, VC   *11. Pte. F.J. Edwards, VC*   *12. Cpl. J. Davies, VC*

*13. Left to right: Revd A. Proctor, R.E. Ryder, J. Hutchinson, A.C.T. White, T. Adlam and T. Veale at Thiepval Memorial, July 1966 (*Soldier *magazine)*

14. Capt. Brian Brooke of the 2nd Gordon Highlanders was wounded on 1 July 1916 and died on the 25th

15. Capt. John M. Charlton of the 2nd Tyneside Scottish, killed on 1 July 1916

16. Sgt. Leslie Coulson of the Royal Fusiliers was wounded at Guedecourt and died on 7 October 1916

17. Capt. Richard Dennys of the Loyal North Lancashires was wounded on the Somme on 12 July 1916. He died on the 24th

18. Ivor Gurney, a private in the 2/5th Gloucestershires

19. Lt. W.N. Hodgson, MC, of the Devonshire Regt. He was killed on 1 July 1916

20. David Jones was a private in the 15th Royal Welch Fusiliers who was wounded at Mametz Wood in July 1916. He later wrote 'In Parenthesis'

21. Lt. Thomas M. Kettle of the 9th Dublin Fusiliers was killed at Ginchy on 9 September 1916 and has no known grave. His name is one of those listed on the Thiepval Memorial

22. Lt. Ewart A. Mackintosh, MC, of the 5th Seaforth Highlanders, gassed at High Wood and killed at Cambrai on 21 November 1917

23. Cpl. Alexander Robertson of the 12th York & Lancaster Regt., killed on 1 July 1916

24. Lt. (later Capt.) Siegfried Sassoon of the Royal Welch Fusiliers. He won the MC on the Somme

25. Alan Seeger, an American serving with the French Foreign Legion, who was killed on 1 July 1916. His death caused a sensation in the US press

26. Sgt. John W. Streets of the York &
Lancaster Regt., a former miner who was
wounded on 1 July 1916 and died later

27. The Hon. E. Wyndham Tennant, a
lieutenant in the Grenadier Guards, was killed on
22 September 1916 and is buried near his friend
Raymond Asquith at Guillemont Road Cemetery

28. Lt. R.E. Vernède of the 3rd Rifle Brigade,
who served on the Somme in August 1916

29. 2/Lt. Max Plowman of the 10th West Yorkshires
with his son Tim in June 1917

AUSTRALIA: MEMOIRS AND UNOFFICIAL HISTORIES

Adam-Smith, Patsy
The Anzacs
Hamish Hamilton, 1978
The Somme, pp. 190–206
This illustrated book was written as a popular history of the Australian contribution to the Allied war effort.

Andrews, E.M.
The Anzac Illusion: Anglo-Australian relations during World War I
Cambridge University Press, 1983
The Somme, pp. 96–9
This illustrated book includes a picture of 'Gibraltar', a headquarters bunker at Pozières.

Bean, C.E.W.
Letters from France
Cassell, 1917
The Somme, pp. 71–91 & 101–74
This illustrated book has one map.

Bean, C.E.W.
Two Men I Knew: William Bridges and Brudenell White. Founders of the A.I.F.
Sydney: Angus & Robertson, 1957
The Somme, pp. 131–50
These pages include a section on White's career. He became the first Australian to rise to the rank of full general in wartime. He was recalled in the Second World War, but was killed in a plane crash. The book is illustrated.

Beaumont, Joan (ed.)
Australia's War 1914–18
St Leonards, New South Wales: Allen & Unwin, 1985
The Somme, pp. 16–20
This illustrated book is a collection of six essays, three of which are written by the editor. It has a Somme map.

Charlton, Peter
Australians on the Somme: Pozières 1916
Leo Cooper/Secker & Warburg, 1986
This illustrated book is an account of the Australian divisions on the Somme, seen very much from the Australian point of view. The 1st Australian Division took 23 days and 23,000 casualties to capture the village of Pozières. The foreword is by John Terraine and there are eight maps.

Denny, Capt. W.J., MC, MP
The Diggers
Hodder & Stoughton, 1919
The Somme, pp. 151–66

Duffell, W.J.
Soldier Boy: The letters and memoirs of Gunner W.J. Duffell
Stevenage: Spa Books, 1992
The Somme, pp. 33, 47–64, 69–72 & 77–8
Duffell served with the Australian Field Artillery Brigade, AIF. The book is edited by Gilbert Mant, who also provides an introduction.

Dyson, Will
Australia at War: A winter record made on the Somme and at Ypres during the campaigns of 1916 and 1917
Cecil Palmer & Hayward, 1918
This is a book of drawings by the official artist to the AIF. The introduction is by G.K. Chesterton.

Fallon, Capt. David, MC
The Big Fight: Gallipoli to the Somme
Cassell, 1918
The Somme, pp. 144–67
The author was a tank commander.

Gammage, Bill
The Broken Years: Australian soldiers in the Great War
Canberra: Australian National University Press, 1974
The Somme, pp. 156–7 & 162–74
This illustrated book includes maps. It was based on the records of 272 soldiers and a thousand diaries and letters from the Australian War Memorial.

Grant, Ian
Jacka VC: Australia's finest fighting soldier
Macmillan (in association with the Australian War Memorial), 1989
The Somme, pp. 73–90
Jacka became a considerable hero to the Australian people, and was the first Australian member of the AIF to win the VC in the First World War. He also won an MC at Pozières and a bar for it later in the war.

Harney, W.
Bill Harney's War
Victoria: Currey O'Neill Ross Pty Ltd, 1983

The Somme, p. 22
Introduction by Manning Clark, drawings by Will Dyson, Official War Artist.

Laffin, John
Anzacs at War
Abelard-Schuman, 1965
The Somme, pp. 61–74
Anzac VC awards are listed in an appendix.

Laffin, John
Guide to Australian Battlefields of the Western Front 1916–1918
New South Wales: Kangaroo Press and the Australian War Memorial, 1992
A second edition was issued in 1994 with two additional chapters, one on the 75th anniversary commemorations. This fully illustrated paperback has maps, including one of the Somme.

McCarthy, Dudley
Gallipoli to the Somme: The story of C.E.W. Bean
Leo Cooper, 1983
The Somme, pp. 230–43, 246–8, 253–5 & 256
This is an illustrated biography of the famous war historian (1879–1968). It has maps, including one of the Somme.

McKernan, M.
Padre: Australian chaplains in Gallipoli and France
Allen & Unwin, 1986
The Somme, pp. 43, 142–5, 153–4, 164, 166–7, 169–70, 172–3 & 185
This illustrated book consists mainly of material from diaries and letters by individual chaplains.

Matthews, Tony
Crosses: Australian Soldiers in the Great War
Brisbane: Boolarong Publications, 1987

The Somme, pp. 50–65
This illustrated book has a Somme map. Written by a television researcher who was looking for material for a documentary, it was based on interviews with 'Diggers' who by then were in their eighties or nineties.

Maxwell, J., VC, MC, DCM
Hell's Bells and Mademoiselles
Sydney: Angus & Robertson, 1936
The Somme, pp. 62–9
Maxwell was a member of the 18th Bn. AIF and won his VC in October 1918. The foreword is by Lt.-Col. G.F. Murphy, CMG, DSO.

Nixon, Allan M.
Somewhere in France: Letters to home – the war years of Sgt. Roy Whitelaw 1st A.I.F.
Victoria: Five Mile Press, 1989
The Somme, pp. 63–103
This is a good description of life in the AIF in the Somme area of 1916 and is profusely illustrated with photographs and drawings.

Raws, Alec & Goldy (edited by Margaret Young & Bill Gammage)
Hail and Farewell: Letters from two brothers killed in France in 1916
Kenthurst, New South Wales: Kangaroo Press, 1994
The Somme, 98–9 & 144–72
This paperback is a collection of letters written home to their family by two brothers

who were killed on the Somme. They were both members of the 23rd Battalion AIF. It is illustrated with family photographs.

Robson, L.L.
The First A.I.F.: A study of its recruitment 1914–1918
Carlton, Victoria: Melbourne University Press, 1970
The Somme, pp. 83–4, 88, 123, 158 & 191

Rule, E.J., MC, MM
Jacka's Mob
Sydney: Angus & Robertson, 1933
The Somme, pp. 57–86, 89 & 110

Smithers, A.J.
Sir John Monash
Leo Cooper, 1973
The Somme, p 152 & 157
This is a biography of one of Australia's leading soldiers, who after the war gave his name to a university.

Thorp, C. Hampton, AIF
A Handful of Ausseys
John Lane, Bodley Head, 1919
The Somme, pp. 235–44
The illustrations are by James F. Scott.

Williams, H.R.
The Gallant Company: An Australian soldier's story of 1915–1918
Sydney: Angus & Robertson, 1933
The Somme, pp. 69–111

Canada: Official and General Histories

The Canadian Army was established in 1871. At the outbreak of war in 1914 it was deemed that militia regiments would not be allowed to go overseas as a single unit. Instead recruits had to be re-attested into what was called the Canadian Expeditionary Force and units were given numerical ciphers. Personnel for these battalions therefore came from the original regiments. Not surprisingly, this decision caused a lot of heartache, as friends and colleagues could often no longer serve together. Four Canadian divisions served on the Somme with the British Army.

The standard of Canadian Unit histories is generally very good and the following bibliography provides a very useful listing:

Cooke, O.A.
The Canadian Military Experience 1867–1983: A bibliography
Ottawa: Directorate of History, Department of National Defence, 1984, 2nd edn

GENERAL

Canada in the Great War
Vol. IV: *The Turn of the Tide*
Toronto: United Publishers of Canada, 1920
The Somme, pp. 10–94

Goodspeed, D.J.
The Road Past Vimy
The Canadian Corps 1914–1918

Toronto: Macmillan of Canada, 1969
The Somme, pp. 64–79

Grafton, Lt.-Col. C.S., VD
The Canadian 'Emma Gees': A history of the Canadian Machine-gun Corps
London, Ontario: Hunter Printing (for the CMGC Association), 1938
The Somme, pp. 48–57
This illustrated book has one drawing and some maps.

Lucas, Sir Charles (ed.)
The Empire at War
Vol. 2: *The Canadian Forces in the War* by Prof. F.H. Underhill, MA
Oxford University Press, 1921–6, 5 vols
The Somme, pp. 130–52

Nasmith, Col. George G., CMG (C.E.F.)
Canada's Sons in the World War: A complete and authentic history of the commanding part played by Canada and the British Empire in the World's Greatest War
Introduction by Gen. Sir Arthur W. Currie, KCB, KCMG, Commander of the Canadian Army Corps
Toronto: J.C. Winston Co. Ltd, 1919, 2 vols
The Somme, pp. 293–308
This book is illustrated and includes maps.

OFFICIAL

MacPhail, Sir A., KT, OBE, BA, MD, CM, LLD, MRCS, LRCP, FRCS

The Official History of the Canadian Forces in the Great War 1914–1919: The medical services
Ottawa: F.A. Acland (for the Canadian Government), 1925
The Somme, pp. 74–92
This book includes a roll of honour and one map. (Falls★)

Nicholson, Col. G.W.L., CD
Official History of the Canadian Army in the First World War – Canadian Expeditionary Force 1914–1919
Ottawa: Roger Duhamel, FRCS, Queen's Printer & Controller of Stationery, 1962
The Somme, pp. 160–200
The book has superb maps, a list of senior officers and a listing of battalions and casualty figures by month for 1914–20.

Roberts, Maj. Charles G.D.
The Official Story of the Canadian Expeditionary Force
Vol. III
Hodder & Stoughton, 1918
The Somme, pp. 21–121
This book gives a very detailed account of the Somme battle.

OTHER HISTORIES

Sheldon-Williams, R.F.L., MM
The Canadian Front in France and Flanders
Black, 1920
The Somme, pp. 5, 31–7, 133 & 197
This book includes some excellent paintings by Inglis Sheldon-Williams, including one of Mametz village.

Steele, Capt. Harwood, MC
The Canadians in France 1915–1918
Fisher Unwin, 1920

The Somme, pp. 65–87
The appendix has a list of the units of the Canadian Army Corps by divisions.

Swettenham, J.
To Seize the Victory: The Canadian Corps in World War One
Toronto: Ryerson Press, 1965
The Somme, pp. 115–23
This illustrated book has maps.

Swettenham, J.
Canada and the First World War
Canadian War Museum, 1967 (no further details)
The Somme, pp. 15–17
This illustrated booklet in French and English has a map of the Western Front.

Swettenham, J.
Canada and the First World War
Toronto: Ryerson Press, 1967
The Somme: pp. 55–60
This book is based on the 50th Anniversary Armistice Display at the Canadian War Museum, Ottawa.

Worthington, Larry
Amid the Guns Below: The story of the Canadian Corps 1914–1919
Toronto & Montreal: McClelland & Stewart, 1965
The Somme, pp. 53–60
This book is illustrated.

ARTILLERY

Jackson, Lt.-Col. H.M., MBE (ed.)
The Royal Regiment of Artillery, Ottawa 1855–1952: A history
Published by the regiment, [n.d.]

The Somme, pp. 105–12
The book includes one portrait and a list of casualties by year for the 1st Bde. CFA.

Kay, H.R., McGee, G. & MacLennan, F.A.
Battery Action: The story of the 43rd Battery, C.F.A.
Toronto: Warwick Brothers & Rutter, [n.d.]
The Somme is not included in the main text, but is in the appendices. The book has a roll of honour.

Macdonald, J.A.
Gunfire: An historical narrative of the 4th Brigade C.F.A. in the Great War (1914–18)
Toronto: Greenway Press, 1929
The Somme, pp. 53–63
The book has skeleton histories of each battery and comprehensive honour and nominal rolls.

Mitchell, Maj. G.D., MC, CD
R.C.H.A. – Right of the Line: An anecdotal history of the Royal Canadian Horse Artillery from 1871
Ottawa: RCHA History Committee, 1986
The Somme, pp. 45–6
This illustrated book has maps and a roll of honour.

Nicholson, Col. G.W.L., CD
Gunners of Canada: (The history of the Royal Regiment of Canadian Artillery)
Vol. 1: 1534–1919
Toronto: McClelland & Stewart (for the Royal Canadian Artillery Association), 1967
The Somme, pp. 258–72
This illustrated book also has some sketches.

CAVALRY INCLUDING DISMOUNTED

Bennett, Capt. S.G., MC
The 4th Canadian Mounted Rifles
Toronto: Murray, 1926
The Somme, pp. 26–43
This illustrated book has maps and a very detailed roll of honour.

Chalmers, Lt.-Col. G., DSO, MC
The 2nd Canadian Mounted Rifles (British Columbia Horse) in France and Flanders
Vernon, British Columbia: Vernon News, 1933
The Somme, pp. 30–5
The well-illustrated book includes a roll of honour and details of when and where men were killed or wounded.

The above two mounted rifle regiments were in effect infantry battalions and became part of the 8th Canadian Infantry Brigade of the 3rd Canadian Infantry Division.

Fetherstonhaugh, R.C.
A Short History of the Royal Canadian Dragoons
Toronto: Southam Press, 1932
The Somme, pp. 27–9

Fraser, W.B.
Always a Strathcona
Calgary: Comprint, 1976
The Somme, pp. 77 & 78
The book includes a roll of honour.

Greenhous, B.
Dragoon: The centennial history of the Royal Canadian Dragoons, 1883–1983
Ottawa: 1983
The Somme, p. 201
The book is illustrated.

Roy, R.H.
Sinews of Steel: The history of the British Columbia Dragoons
Kelowna, British Columbia: British Columbia Dragoons (1550 Richter St.), 1965
The Somme, Ch. 2, pp. 52–5

Williams, Capt. S.H., MC
Stand to your Horse: Through the First Great War with the Lord Strathcona Horse (R.C.)
Altona, Manitoba: D.W. Friesen, 1961
The Somme, pp. 91–6 & 100–3
This very comprehensive work includes a roll of honour of officers and men as well as some good photographs.

INFANTRY AND ENGINEERS

Anon
A Brief History of the Royal Regiment of Canada (Allied with the Kings Regiment) (Liverpool)
Published by the regiment, 1948
The Somme, pp. 35–6
This is a small booklet.

Barnard, Lt.-Col. W.I., ED, CD
The Queen's Own Rifles of Canada, 1860–1960
Ontario: T.H. Best Printing (for Ontario Publishing), 1960
The Somme, p. 120
This illustrated book has maps.

Duguid, Col. A. Fortescue, DSO, OBE, CD, BSc (Royal Canadian Artillery)
History of the Canadian Grenadier Guards 1760–1964
Montreal: Gazette Printing Company, 1965
The Somme, pp. 109–32

The book gives a list of casualties by number, and rolls of honour for both officers and men.

Fetherstonhaugh, R.C.
The Royal Canadian Regiment 1883–1933
Montreal: Gazette Printing Company, 1936
The Somme, pp. 243–58
The book has some good maps, a list of CEF battalion officers and a listing of casualties.

Goodspeed, Maj. D.J., CD
Battle Royal: A history of the Royal Regiment of Canada 1862–1962
Toronto?: Royal Regiment of Canada Association, 1962
The Somme, pp. 153–66
The book has a small map, some good illustrations and a roll of honour.

Harker, D.E.
The Dukes: The story of the men who have served in peace and war with the British Columbia Regiment (D.C.O.) 1883–1973
Private publication by the regiment, 1974
The Somme, pp. 99–101

Hodder-Williams, R.
Princess Patricia's Canadian Light Infantry 1914–1919
Hodder & Stoughton, 1923, 2 vols
Vol. I: The Somme, pp. 149–188, with a superb map
Vol. II: This book includes a record of service for every officer who served in the regiment, and therefore must be a unique volume.
The books are illustrated.

Hutchinson, P.P.
Canada's Black Watch: The first hundred years 1862–1962
Montreal: private printing, 1962
The Somme, pp. 86–90
The book is illustrated with drawings and maps.

Kerry, Col. A.J., OBE & McDill, Maj. W.E., CD
The History of the Corps of Royal Engineers
Vol. 1: 1749–1939
Toronto: Thornton Press (printer; for the Military Engineers Association of Canada), 1962
The Somme, pp. 114–20
The book is illustrated.

Moir, J.S.
History of the Royal Canadian Corps of Signals, 1903–61
Ottawa: private printing, 1962
The Somme, pp. 16–17
The book is illustrated and has maps.

Rannie, William F.
To the Thunderer his Arms: The Royal Canadian Ordnance Corps
Ontario: Lincoln, 1984
The Somme, p. 42
This illustrated book has one map.

Rogers, R.L.
History of the (Canadian) Lincoln and Welland Regiment
Ottawa: Lincoln & Welland Regiment, 1949
The Somme, pp. 60–2

Stevens, G.R.
A City Goes to War

Brampton, Ontario: Charters Pub. Co. Ltd, 1964
The Somme, pp. 52–69
This book is the history of the Loyal Edmonton Regiment (3rd P.P.C.L.I.), and includes illustrations, maps and a roll of honour.

Tascona, Bruce & Wells, Eric
Little Black Devils: A history of the Royal Winnipeg Rifles
Winnipeg, Manitoba: Frye Publishing (for Royal Winnipeg Rifles), 1983
The Somme, pp. 97–101
This illustrated book has a map of Thiepval Ridge.

Warren, Arnold
Wait for the Waggon: The story of the Royal Canadian Army Service Corps
Toronto: McClelland & Stewart, 1961
The Somme, pp. 103–7

Weatherbee, K. (formerly Maj., 6th Bn., CE)
From the Rideau to the Rhine and Back: The 6th Field Company and Battalion, Canadian Engineers in the Great War
Toronto: Hunter-Rose, 1928
The Somme, pp. 153–71
The book is profusely illustrated and has some maps including a Somme one.

Whitton, Lt.-Col. F.E., CMG
The History of the Prince of Wales's Leinster Regiment (Royal Canadians)
Vol. 2
Aldershot: Gale & Polden, 1924
The Somme, 2nd Bn., pp. 228–49; 7th Bn., pp. 306–18
This illustrated book contains excellent maps.

Williams, J.
Princess Patricia's Canadian Light Infantry
Leo Cooper, 1972
The Somme, pp. 20–1
The book is illustrated.

INFANTRY UNITS WITH NUMBERS INSTEAD OF TITLES (LISTED IN NUMERICAL ORDER)

Murray, W.W.
The History of the 2nd Canadian Battalion (East Ontario Regiment) Canadian Expeditionary Force in the Great War, 1914–1919
Ottawa: Historical Committee, 1947
The Somme, Ch. 6., pp. 115–43

Gibson, Capt. W.L. (comp.)
Records of the Fourth Canadian Infantry Battalion in the Great War 1914–1918
Toronto: Maclean, 1924
The Somme, pp. 14 & 18–329
The book is extremely detailed.

Scudamore, T.V.
The Short History of the 7th Battalion C.E.F.
Vancouver: Anderson & Odlum, 1930
The book has unnumbered pages and only a brief mention of the Somme. It does list casualties by name and date.

Dancocks, Daniel G.
Gallant Canadians: The Story of the Tenth Canadian Infantry Battalion 1914–1919
Calgary: Calgary Highlanders Regimental Funds Association, 1990
The Somme, pp. 87–95
This illustrated book gives casualties by numbers and includes maps.

Holland, J.A.
The Story of the Tenth Canadian Battalion, 1914–1917
Charles (for the Canadian War Records Office), 1918
The Somme, pp. 25–7

Fetherstonhaugh, R.C.
The 13th Battalion Royal Highlanders of Canada 1914–1919
Toronto: Warwick Brothers & Rutter, 1925
The Somme, pp. 122–41
The book has some good maps and illustrations, and a roll of honour of officers and men.

Martin, S.
The Story of the Thirteenth Battalion (The Royal Highlanders of Canada) 1914–1917
Charles (for the Canadian War Records Office), [1918?]
The Somme, pp. 11–15

Fetherstonhaugh, R.C.
The Royal Montreal Regiment, 14th Battalion, C.E.F. 1914–1925
Montreal: Gazette Printing Company (for the Royal Montreal Regiment), 1927
The Somme, pp. 106–23
This illustrated book has some maps, honour rolls and other statistical information.

Urquhart, Lt.-Col. H.M., DSO, MC, ADC
The History of the 16th Battalion (The Canadian Scottish) Canadian Expeditionary Force in the Great War 1914–1919
Toronto: Macmillan of Canada, 1933
The Somme, pp. 161–87

The book was published for the Trustees and Regimental Committee of the 16th Bn. (Canadian Scottish) CEF. It is exceptional in its detailed analysis of casualties suffered by the battalion, and has maps and illustrations including one map of the Somme.

Corrigall, Maj. D.L., DSO, MC
The History of the Twentieth Battalion (Central Ontario Regiment) Canadian Expeditionary Force in the Great War, 1914–1918
Toronto: Stone, 1936
The Somme, pp. 75–97
The author served with the 20th Bn. CEF. The book contains some very good maps and excellent pictures of the battalion in November 1914.

Anon
Historical Calendar; 21st Canadian Infantry Battalion (Eastern Ontario Regiment) Belgium–France–Germany 1915–1919
Aldershot: Gale & Polden, 1919
The Somme, pp. 30 & 31
This book has a list of officers who served with the 21st in France, and a roll of honour for all ranks.

McBride, Capt. Herbert W.
A Rifleman Went to War
Marines, Onslow Co., North Carolina, USA: Small-arms Technical Publishing, 1935
The Somme, pp. 232–45
The author served with the 21st Bn. CEF and in the United States Army.

Chaballe, J.
Histoire du 22e Bataillon Canadien–Français
Vol. 1: 1914–19
Montreal: Les Editions Chantecler, 1952
The Somme, pp. 125–240

Fetherstonhaugh, R.C.
The 24th Battalion, CEF, Victoria Rifles of Canada, 1914–1919
Montreal: Gazette Printing Co., 1930
The Somme, pp. 76–103
The book includes a honour roll and other statistical information.

Calder, Maj. D.G.S. (ed. & comp.)
The History of the 28th (Northwest) Battalion, C.E.F. (October 1914 – June 1919) from the Memoirs of Brigadier General Alexander Ross CMG, DSO, VD
Regina: private printing, 1961
The Somme, pp. 86–101
The book includes some sketch maps, the Official War Diary, the Regimental Part II Orders, the list of officers from 1907 to 1920 and rolls of honour for officers and men.

Hewitt, G.E.
The Story of the Twenty-eighth (North-west) Battalion 1914–1917
Charles (for the Canadian War Records Office), 1918
The Somme, pp. 10–16

Clyne, H.R.N., MC
Perpetuating the 29th (Vancouver) Battalion C.E.F, the Irish Fusiliers of Canada Vancouver Regiment CA (M): A chronicle of the 29th in Flanders fields
Vancouver, British Columbia: Tobin's Tigers Association, 1964
The Somme, pp. 16–23

Singer, H.C. & Peebles, A.A.
History of the Thirty-first Battalion CEF from its organization November 1914 to its demobilization June 1919
Calgary: private printing, 1939

The Somme, pp. 138–74
This illustrated book includes maps.

Topp, Lt.-Col. C. Beresford, DSO, MC
(late Maj. 42nd R.H.C.)
*The 42nd Battalion C.E.F., Royal
Highlanders of Canada in the Great War*
Montreal: Gazette Printing Company, 1931
The Somme, pp. 61–96
This book has some excellent maps, a roll
of honour, a list of casualties at various
periods and an itinerary of the battalion.

Russenholt, E.S.
*Six Thousand Canadian Men: Being the
history of the 44th Battalion Canadian Infantry
1914–1919*
Winnipeg: De Montford Press (for the
Battalion Association), 1932 (private printing)
The Somme, pp. 41–61
This book is illustrated with sketches and
maps.

McWilliams, James L. & Steel, R. James
The Suicide Battalion
Ontario: Vanwell, 1978
The Somme, pp. 43–68
This is the story of the 46th Canadian
Infantry Bn. (South Saskatchewan). In the
appendix is a pen picture of some of the
men who appear in the text.

Beattie, Kim
48th Highlanders of Canada 1891–1928
Toronto: Southam Press, 1932
The Somme, pp. 160–8
This illustrated book has some good maps.

Wheeler, V.W.
No Man's Land
Calgary, Alberta: Comprint (for Alberta
Historical Resources Foundation), 1980

This book includes material about the
battle for the Ancre Heights and
provides a very detailed account of the
daily life of the infantrymen of the 50th
Bn. CEF.

Stanley, G.F.G.
*In the Face of Danger: The history of the
Lake Superior Regiment (52nd Battalion
C.E.F.)*
Ontario: Lake Superior Scottish
Regiment, 1960
The Somme, pp. 18–20

'One Of Them'
*Cinquante-quatre, being a short history of the
54th Canadian Infantry Battalion*
Private publication, 1919
The Somme, pp. 11–12

McEvoy, B. & Finlay, Capt. A.H.
*History of the 72nd Canadian Infantry
Battalion Seaforth Highlanders of Canada*
Vancouver, British Columbia: Cowan &
Brookhouse, 1920
The Somme, pp. 26–31
This book is illustrated.

Gould, L. McLeod, MSM, Croix de
Guerre (BA Cantab.) (late Sgt. HQ Staff
102nd Canadian Infantry Bn.)
*From B.C. to Baisieux: Being the narrative
history of the 102nd Canadian Infantry
Battalion*
Victoria, British Columbia: Thomas R.
Cusack, 1919
The Somme, pp. 28–40
This very comprehensive work contains a
nominal roll of officers and men, with their
home addresses and where they were
wounded or killed. It covers the period
from October to December 1916.

Miscellaneous

Bird, W.R.
Thirteen Years After: The story of the old front revisited (reprinted from Macleans magazine)
Toronto: Maclean Pub. Co., 1932
'Bapaume and Courcelette', pp. 119–26, and 'the old Somme', pp. 127–34
This book tells the story of a return to the battlefields where the Canadians fought. It was first published in *Maclean's Magazine*. The illustrations were taken in 1931.

Bull, W.P.
From Brook to Currie: The military development and the exploits of Canadians in general and the Men of Peel in particular 1791–1930
Toronto: G.J. McLeod, 1935
The Somme, pp. 412–15

Cranston, F.
Thirty Canadian VCs: 23rd April 1915 to 30th March 1918
Skeffington, 1918
The Somme, Leo Clarke, VC, pp. 13–15; J.C. Kerr, VC, pp. 15–19
This book was compiled by the Canadian War Records Office.

Ellis, W.D.
Saga of the Cyclists in the Great War 1914–1918
Toronto: Canadian Corps Cyclist Battalion Association, 1965
The Somme, pp. 53–7
Casualties are listed by numbers.

Gardam, Col. J., OMN, CD
Seventy Years After 1914–1918
Stittsville, Ontario: Canada's Wings (printer), 1983
The Somme, pp. 23–8

Hunt, Capt. M. Stuart (RO)
Nova Scotia's Part in the Great War
Halifax, Nova Scotia: Nova Scotia Veteran, 1920
6th Canadian Mounted Rifles, pp. 16–17; 17th Bty. (6th Bty. CFA), pp. 36–7; Royal Canadian Regt., pp. 61–3; 25th Canadian Infantry Bn., pp. 76–8
This book gives service on the Somme by regiment and battalion and, where applicable, for artillery units or particular corps.

Jackson, Lt.-Col. H.M., MBE (ed.)
The 127th Battalion, C.E.F. 2nd Bn. Canadian Railway Troops
Montreal: Industrial Shops for the Deaf (printer), n.d.
The Somme, pp. 5–24

Fetherstonhaugh, R.C.
No. 3 Canadian General Hospital (McGill) 1914–1919
Montreal: Gazette Printing Company, 1928
The Somme, pp. 56–72
This book includes some excellent photographs of the hospital and its staff.

Gunn, Lt.-Col. J.N. & Dutton, S.Sgt. E.E.
Historical Records of No. 8 Canadian Field Ambulance, Canada, England, France, Belgium 1915–1919
Toronto: Ryerson, 1920
The Somme, pp. 24–9
This illustrated book has two maps and a roll of honour.

Noyes, F.W.
Stretcher Bearers at the Double: History of the Fifth Canadian Field Ambulance 1914–1918

Toronto: Hunter-Rose, 1936
The Somme, pp. 119–44
This book has superb illustrations and a roll of honour.

Biographies

Dancocks, D.G.
Sir Arthur Currie: A biography 1903–1963
Methuen, 1985
The Somme, pp. 71–80
This illustrated biography is the life of one of Canada's most senior soldiers.

Defoe, J.W.
Over the Canadian Battlefields: Notes of a little journey in France in March 1919
Toronto: Thomas Allen, 1919
The Somme, pp. 16–17, 47 & 55
This is a short book.

[Fraser, Pte.]
The Journal of Private Fraser 1914–1918, Canadian Expeditionary Force
Victoria, Canada: Sono Nis Press, 1985
The Somme, pp. 154–233
Fraser served with the 31st Bn. and then with the 6th Bde. Machine-Gun Coy. This journal is one of the most descriptive books about fighting in the war. Fraser had a tremendous eye for detail and the book is illustrated, including maps. It was edited by Reginald H. Roy.

Mathieson, William D.
My Grandfather's War: Canadians remember the First World War 1914–1918
Toronto: Macmillan of Canada, 1981
The Somme, pp. 111–15
This book includes photographs of many places in France and Belgium.

Reid, G.
Poor Bloody Murder; Personal memoirs of the First World War
Ontario: Mosaic Press, 1980
The Somme, pp. 112–32
This book is a collection of accounts written by British and Canadian participants.

Scott, F.G.
The Great War as I Saw It
Vancouver: Clarke & Stuart, 1934
The Somme, pp. 134–48
The author was a Canadian chaplain. This book includes an extraordinary account of his search for the body of his dead son.

Stanley, G.F.G.
Canada's Soldiers: The military history of an unmilitary people
Toronto: Macmillan of Canada, 1960, revised edn
The Somme, pp. 320–2

Steel, R. James
The Men Who Marched Away: Canadian infantry in World War 1 1914–1918
Ontario: Vanwell, 1989
The Somme, pp. 35–44
Appendix A lists battalions under brigades and divisions.

Urquhart, Hugh, CVO, DSO, MC
Arthur Currie: The biography of a great Canadian
Vancouver: J.M. Dent, 1950

The Somme, pp. 132–5
This illustrated book includes some maps. Currie succeeded General Byng as Canadian Corps Commander.

Wells, C.A.
From Montreal to Vimy Ridge and Beyond
McClelland, Goodchild & Stewart, 1917
The Somme, pp. 206–43
Wells was a member of the 8th Bn. CEF. His correspondence was edited by O.C.S. Wallace.

Williams, J.
Byng of Vimy: General and Governor General

Leo Cooper, 1983
The Somme, pp. 134–41
This is an illustrated biography of the British-born Canadian Corps commander at the time of the Somme. Currie was to become the most famous Canadian soldier of the Great War. The book includes a Somme map.

Worthington, Larry
Worthy: A biography of Major-General F.F. Worthington CB, MC and MM
Toronto: Macmillan of Canada, 1961
The Somme, pp. 64–71

INDIA

Unlike the younger Empire countries, India possessed an army whose origins reached back to the East India Company. One of the reasons as to why unit histories are rather 'thin on the ground' was the lack of familiarity with the English language, since only former officers and their friends and families would be interested in such volumes. The Gurkha and the Garhwali have been served better than other units. As far as the Indian Army's involvement in the Battle of the Somme is concerned, the part that it played was a cavalry one, waiting for that elusive breakthrough in the German lines to allow them to burst through. However, as is widely known, this never happened.

The following Indian Cavalry Regiments took part in the Somme battle, mainly in the area of Delville Wood, High Wood and the Bazentin villages: 2nd, 4th, 6th, 18th, 19th, 34th, 36th, and 38th. Some of them received the Battle Honour of Delville Wood and Bazentin.

GENERAL

Lucas, Sir Charles (ed.)
The Empire at War
Pt 4: 'India'. Operations in France 1915 and after by Sir Francis Younghusband, K.C.S.I., KC, I.E.
Oxford University Press, 1921
Indian cavalry on the Somme, pp. 233–4

CAVALRY

Anon
Hodsons Horse: Late 9th Hodsons Horse and 10th D.C.O. Lancers (Hodsons Horse 1857–1928)
Lahore: Civil & Military Gazette Press, 1929
This book was reprinted from the official army lists and includes a nominal roll of officers who served with the regiment.

Hudson, Gen. Sir H., GCB
History of the 19th King George's Own Lancers 1858–1921: formerly 18th King George's Own Lancers (Fanes Horse), amalgamated in 1921
Aldershot: Gale & Polden, 1937
The Somme, pp. 156–63
This illustrated book includes a list of honours awarded and a roll of officers who served with the Lancers between 1860 and 1921.

Maunsell, Col. E.B. (late Comdt.)
Prince of Wales's Own, the Scinde Horse
Regimental Committee, 1926
The Somme, pp. 75–85
This book is well illustrated throughout and includes a list of casualties by location and service number.

Sandhu, Maj. Gen. Gurcharn Singh, PVSM (retd)
The Indian Cavalry: History of the Indian Armoured Corps
Vol. 1

New Delhi: Vision Books, 1981
The Somme, pp. 305–8
This book includes battle honours.

Tennant, Lt.-Col. E.(late 20th Deccan Horse)
The Royal Deccan Horse in the Great War
Aldershot: Gale & Polden, 1939
The Somme, pp. 46–52
This book gives a good account of the action at Delville Wood, in which the Deccan Horse took part in July 1916. It also contains maps.

Watson, Maj.-Gen. W.A., CB, CMG, CIE
King George's Own Central India Horse: The story of a local Corps
Edinburgh & London: William Blackwood, 1930

The Somme, pp. 336–8
This illustrated book has maps.

Whitworth, Capt. D.E., MC
History of the 2nd Lancers (Gardners Horse) from 1809–1922
Sifton Praed, 1924
The Somme, pp. 78, 79 & 86–9
This book lists the war service of officers from the 2nd Lancers.

Wylly, Col. H.C., CB
The Poona Horse (17th Queen Victoria's Own Cavalry)
Vol. 11: 1914–31
Royal United Service Institution, 1933
The Somme, pp. 112–17
This book includes a list of serving officers.

NEWFOUNDLAND

The Newfoundland Regiment was formed as a result of popular feeling and its first contingent of men sailed from the Dominion as early as October 1914. The battalion arrived at Gallipoli and joined the 29th Division late on in that campaign. They then journeyed to France via Egypt and arrived on the Somme in time for the disastrous attack on Beaumont-Hamel where they suffered 715 casualties. The regiment was awarded the Battle Honour of Albert (Beaumont-Hamel) 1916 for this. They later fought at Guillemont, Ginchy and Gueudecourt.

GENERAL

Lucas, Sir Charles
The Empire at War
Vol. 2: *Newfoundland* by McGrath, P.T.
Oxford University Press, 1923
The Somme, Pt. 2, pp. 314–15

HISTORIES AND MEMOIRS

Cave, Joy B.
What Became of Corporal Pittman?
Portugal Cove, Newfoundland: Breakwater Books, 1976
This book covers the Battle of the Somme at Beaumont-Hamel. It has a roll of honour and some good maps.

Cramm, R.
The First Five Hundred: Being a historical sketch of the military operations of the Royal Newfoundland Regiment in Gallipoli and on the Western Front during the Great War (1914–1918), together with
the individual military records and photographs where obtainable of the men of the first contingent, known as the 'First Five Hundred' or 'The Blue Puttees'
Albany, New York: C.F. Williams [n.d.]
The Somme, pp. 55–76
This illustrated book has maps.

Nicholson, Col. G.W.L., CD
The Fighting Newfoundlanders: A history of the Royal Newfoundland Regiment
Government of Newfoundland, 1964
The Somme, pp. 232–323
This illustrated book has rolls of honour and fold-out colour maps.

Parsons, W. D.
Pilgrimage: A guide to the Royal Newfoundland Regiment in World War One
St Johns, Newfoundland: Creative Publishers, 1994
The Somme, pp. 29–45, 49–60; guide book section pp. 169–71 & 174–7
This paperback also provides a guide to the section of the Western Front where the Regiment was involved. It includes 14 maps and 16 illustrations, and is the history and guide to the only regiment to receive the title 'Royal' during any war.

Tait, Maj. R.H., MC
Trail of the Caribou
Boston: Newfoundland Pub. Co. Inc., 1933
The Somme, pp. 1–43
Much of this book is written in verse and tells the story of the Newfoundland contingent. Readers are referred to notes for the Somme on pp. 54–5.

NEW ZEALAND

New Zealand organized an expeditionary force similar to those of other countries in the British Empire, and their infantry division went first to the Middle East before transferring to France. This small country sent 100,444 men overseas during the war and 17,202 of them died. Their casualties on the Somme were particularly high.

Many of the First World War histories were paid for by the Army and were therefore under a certain amount of constraint. Most of them were produced in the 1950s and 1960s. The Auckland firm of Whitcombe & Tombs was the contracted printer for many of the books.

GENERAL

Burton, O.E., MM, Médaille d'Honneur
The Silent Division: New Zealanders at the front, 1914–1919
Sydney: Angus & Robertson, 1935
The Somme, pp. 160–80
This book covers the New Zealanders' involvement in the Somme battle for the period September–October 1916. The foreword is by Maj.-Gen. Sir Andrew Russell KCB, KC, MG. The author also wrote *The Auckland Regiment, a Study in Creative History*.

King, Michael
New Zealanders at War
Auckland: Heinemann, 1981
The Somme, pp. 128–36
This is a fully illustrated book.

Lucas, Sir Charles (ed.)
The Empire at War
Vol. 3
Oxford University Press, 1924
The New Zealand involvement in the Battle of the Somme by Malcolm Ross, pp. 322–33

Phillips, Jock, Boyack, Nicholas & Malone, E.P. (eds.)
'The Great Adventure': The letters of Randolph Norman Gray in the great adventure. New Zealand soldiers describe the First World War
Wellington: Allen & Unwin, 1988
The Somme, pp. 88–98
This paperback book is illustrated.

Pugsley, Christopher
On the Fringe of Hell: New Zealanders and military discipline in the First World War
Hodder & Stoughton, 1991
The Somme, pp. 122–31
The book covers cases of courts martial and of subsequent executions of New Zealand troops.

UNIT HISTORIES AND MEMOIRS

Aitken, Alexander
Gallipoli to the Somme: Recollections of a New Zealand infantryman of the 1st Bt. Otago
Oxford University Press, 1963
The Somme, pp. 126–76

The book has maps and an introduction by Sir Bernard Fergusson, Governor-General of New Zealand. After the war the author became a professor of mathematics.

Annabell, N.
Official History of the New Zealand Engineers during the Great War, 1914–1919
Wanganui, New Zealand: Evans, Cobb & Sharpe, 1927
The Somme, pp. 85–98

Austin, Lt.-Col. W.S.
The Official History of the New Zealand Rifle Brigade (The Earl of Liverpool's Own) in the Great War from 1915–1919
Wellington: L.T. Watkins, 1924
The Somme, pp. 113–46
This illustrated book has maps.

Brereton, Maj. C.B.
Tales of Three Campaigns
Selwyn & Blount, 1926
The Somme, pp. 193–207
This illustrated book was written by the unit commander of the 12th (Nelson) Coy. NZEF.

Burton, 2/Lt. O.E., MM, Médaille d'Honneur
The Auckland Regiment: Being an account of the doings on active service of the First, Second and Third Battalions of the Auckland Regiment
Auckland: Whitcombe & Tombs, 1922
The Somme, pp. 104–17 & 118–28, early winter
This book includes maps and portraits.

Byrne, Lt. A.E., MC
Official History of the Otago Regiment NZEF in the Great War 1914–1918

Dunedin: J. Wilkie, 1921 (2nd edn, 1933)
The Somme, Ch. 2, pp. 111–41
This illustrated book has some good maps.

Byrne, Lt. J.R.
New Zealand Artillery in the Field, 1914–18
Auckland: Whitcombe & Tombs, 1922
The Somme, Pt 2, pp. 121–51
This superb book contains some very good maps and illustrations.

Carbery, Lt.-Col. A.D., CBE, (D), NZMC (res.)
The New Zealand Medical Service in the Great War 1914–1918: Based on official documents
Auckland: Whitcombe & Tombs, 1924
The Somme, pp. 189–226
This book is illustrated.

Cowan, J.
The Maoris in the Great War
Auckland: Whitcombe & Tombs, 1926
The Somme, pp. 88–102
This illustrated book has maps and a detailed roll of honour.

Cunningham, W.H., DSO, Treadwell, C.A.L., OBE, & Hanna, J.S.
The Wellington Regiment NZEF 1914–1919
Wellington: Ferguson & Osborn, 1928
The Somme, pp. 111–26
This book is illustrated with pictures of people and places, and includes a Somme map and a roll of honour.

Ellis, Roy F., MM
By Wires to Victory
Auckland: Batley, 1968
The Somme, pp. 44–8

Ferguson, D.
The History of the Canterbury Regiment
Auckland: Whitcombe & Tombs, 1921
The Somme, pp. 108–27
This illustrated book has maps.

Haigh, J. Bryant
Men of Faith and Courage: The official history of New Zealand's army chaplains
Auckland: World Publishers, 1983
The Somme, p. 65
This book tells the stories of individual chaplains.

Lea, Peter A.
Sunday Soldiers: A brief history of the Wellington Regiment – City of Wellington's Own
Wellington: Bryce Francis, 1982
The Somme, pp. 39–41
This book is illustrated.

Luxford, Maj. J.H.
With the Machine Gunners in France and Palestine: The official history of the New Zealand Machine-Gun Corps in the Great World War 1914–1918
Auckland: Whitcombe & Tombs, 1923

The Somme, pp. 38–58
This illustrated book has maps.

Stewart, Col. H., CMG, DSO, MC (late Commanding 2nd Bn. Canterbury Regt.)
The New Zealand Division 1916–1919: A popular history based on official records
Auckland: Whitcombe & Tombs, 1921
The Somme, pp. 61–123
This illustrated book includes maps. (Falls★)

Weston, Lt.-Col., DSO, LLB (NZ)
Three Years with the New Zealanders
Skeffington, 1918
The Somme, pp. 91 & 115
This book includes some good small photographs.

Wilson, Maj. R.A., DSO, RGA
A Two Years' Interlude: France, 1916–1918
Palmerston North, New Zealand: Keeling & Mundy (printer), n.d.
The Somme battle is included. The author was with the Grenadier Guards before joining the Artillery. The book is illustrated, including some of the Somme.

SOUTH AFRICA

GENERAL

Although South Africa did not have an army prepared for overseas service, it was decided to help Great Britain by raising an expeditionary force similar to those from other countries in the Empire. Some of the first men to join had recently been serving in South West Africa. The brigade that was subsequently raised served in Egypt and the Western Front.

Four South African regiments made up the South African Brigade. On the Somme in 1916 they served with the 9th (Scottish) Division along with the British 26th and 27th Brigades. Some men who served had fought against the British in the Boer War, a decade or so earlier. The brigade suffered very high casualties and was awarded the Battle Honour of Delville Wood.

Other units who served on the Somme were the following six Artillery Batteries: 71st to 75th and 125th. Three of these received the Battle Honour as well.

Anon
Union of South Africa and the Great War 1914–1918: Official history
Pretoria: Government Printing & Stationery Office, 1924
The Somme, pp. 99–120
This illustrated book has maps. An appendix gives the number of South Africans killed in action or deceased by unit as a result of active service.

Lucas, Sir Charles (ed.)
The Empire at War
Vol. 4: *The South Africans on the Western Front*
Section 3: 'The Union of South Africa' by Maj. A.N. Colville MA
Oxford University Press, 1925
The Somme, pp. 474–79

HISTORIES AND MEMOIRS

Anon
A History of the Seventy First Siege Battery South African Heavy Artillery
J. Miles, n.d.
The Somme, pp. 11–16
This book has excellent illustrations and a list of battery positions, as well as a list of casualties.

Anon
The Story of Delville Wood Told in Letters from the Front
Cape Town: Cape Times, n.d.
The Somme, pp. 27–40
The book includes some drawings and a roll of honour.

Bailey, H., MC
A Short History of the 72nd (South African) Siege Battery
Hastings: F.J. Parsons, 1924
The Somme, pp. 6–7
This small book contains a list of casualties, and a roll of officers and senior NCOs.

Buchan, John
The History of the South African forces in France
Thomas Nelson, 1920
The Somme, pp. 43–103
Buchan was asked to write this book by Jan Smuts, the South African soldier and statesman. It has illustrations, maps and a roll of honour, and was reissued in 1992 by the Imperial War Museum/Battery Press. (Falls★)

Curson, Dr H.H., FRCVS
The History of the Kimberley Regiment 1876–1962
Kimberley: Northern Cape Printers, 1963
The Somme, p. 162

Digby, P.K.A.
Pyramids and Poppies: The 1st South African Brigade in Libya, France and Flanders 1915–1919
Rivonia, South Africa: Ashanti, 1993
The Somme, pp. 112–48 & 155–75

Johnston, R.E.
Ulundi to Delville Wood
Cape Town: Lukin, 1930
The Somme, pp. 141–56
This book is a life of Sir H.T. Lukin, a prominent South African who was gassed at Delville Wood, which possibly led to his premature death in 1925.

Orpen, Neil
The Capetown Highlanders 1885–1970
Cape Town: Cape & Transvaal Printers, 1970
The Somme, pp. 85–8
This illustrated book has maps and a roll of honour.

Orpen, Neil
The 'Dukes'
A history of the Cape Town Rifles 'Dukes'

Cape Town: Cape Town Rifles Dukes Association, 1984
The Somme, pp. 82–3

Uys, Ian
The Delville Wood Story
Rensbury, South Africa: Uys Publishers, 1983
This book gives a very full description of the South African Infantry Brigade's fight for possession of Delville Wood, told through the memories of men who were there. It is illustrated and has a roll of honour which includes dates of death. The conditions in Delville Wood were possibly the very worst on the Somme battlefield.

Uys, Ian
Longueval
Germiston, South Africa: Uys Publishers, 1983
Although this is a slim paperback of 62 pages, it is a little gem of a book. It tells the story of the battle and has many superb illustrations, both German and Allied.

Uys, Ian
Roll-Call: The Delville Wood Story
Germiston, South Africa: Uys Publishers, 1991
This illustrated book is a companion to the author's *Delville Wood* and is a day-by-day account of the South African Brigade and its fight for the wood in July 1916. It includes a roll of honour and tidies up any errors in the previous book. It also has more useful information about the brigade.

Warwick, George G.
We Band of Brothers
Cape Town: Howard Timmins, 1962
The Somme, pp. 69–87
The author was a lance-corporal in the 4th South African Infantry during the Battle of the Somme.

Biographies, Autobiographies and Memoirs

The first section contains general biographical works and those that cover more than one person. They are arranged in alphabetical order of author.

Anon
The Medical Victoria Crosses
Aldershot: Royal Army Medical Corps Historical Museum, n.d.
The Somme, pp. 55–60
This booklet has brief portraits of three soldiers who gained the VC during the Battle of the Somme: Maj. W.B. Allen, Capt. Noel Chavasse & Capt. J.L. Green.

Bridger, G.
Valiant Hearts of Ringmer: The men behind the names of Ringmer's War Memorial
Lewes: Ammonite Press, 1994
The Somme, pp. 34–8 & 41–6
This paperback book is fully illustrated.

Buchan, John
These for Remembrance
Private publication, 1919
The Somme, p. 82
This is the memoir of six of Buchan's friends who were killed in the First World War. It includes an essay on Raymond Asquith (Grenadier Guards) who fell in the fighting at Ginchy in mid-September 1916 and is buried at Guillemont Road Cemetery. The book is addressed to the author's children, in order that they should understand the sacrifice made by these six men. The book was reissued by Buchan & Enright in 1987 with an introduction by Peter Vansittart.

Clarke, David A.
Great War Memories: Soldiers' experiences 1914–1918
Blackburn: T.H.C.L. Books, 1987
The Somme, pp. 47–8 & 52 (Royal Army Medical Corps)
The author compiled a number of reminiscences into a booklet.

Davies, Frank & Maddocks, Graham
Bloody Red Tabs: General officer casualties of the Great War, 1914–1918
Leo Cooper, 1995
This book sets out to destroy the myth that general officers never went near the front line, by giving short biographies of over two hundred of them who were killed in the war. Forty-six of these men were killed in 1916. References to the Somme are scattered throughout the text.

Gliddon, Gerald
VCs of the Somme: A biographical portrait
Norwich: Gliddon Books, 1991
This book consists of short biographies of the fifty-one men who won the Victoria Cross during the Battle of the Somme. It is profusely illustrated and includes maps.

Kirby, H.L. & Walsh, R.R.
The Seven VCs of Stonyhurst College
T.H.C.L., 1987
The Somme, (pp. 88–103)
This book contains a chapter on the life of 2/Lt. George Gabriel Coury, VC, a member of the South Lancashire Regt., who gained his medal in the Battle of the Somme. The book is illustrated with photographs and maps.

Laffin, John (ed.)
Letters from the Front 1914–1918
Dent, 1973
The Somme, on pp. 6, 54, 67, 68, 69, 71 & 86
This is a series of letters by different correspondents.

Laffin, John (ed.)
On the Western Front: Soldiers' stories from France and Flanders 1914–1918
Gloucester: Alan Sutton Publishing, 1985
The Somme, pp. 112, 114, 117–21, 123–4, 126, 128–36, 138, 141–52 & 154
This book includes maps and illustrations.

Liddle, Peter H.
The Soldier's War 1914–1918
Blandford Press, 1988
The Somme, pp. 92, 94–110, 111, 113, 118 & 163
This book is one of several based on Liddle's First World War archive held at the University of Leeds. It is fully illustrated.

Liddle, Peter H.
Voices of War: Front Line and Home Front, 1914–1918
Leo Cooper, 1988
References to the Somme are scattered throughout the text.

This book was accompanied by a television series and was based on the First World War archive kept in the Liddle Collection at the University of Leeds.

McCrery, Nigel
For Conspicuous Gallantry: A brief history of the recipients of the Victoria Cross from Nottinghamshire and Derbyshire
Derby: Hall, 1990
The Somme, pp. 50–3
This booklet contains brief biographies of Capt. J.L. Green and Cpl. Robert Ryder, who both gained the VC during the Battle of the Somme.

Macdonald, Lyn
The Roses of No Man's Land
Michael Joseph, 1980
The Somme, pp. 125, 147, 158, 159–70, 171, 172–82, 184–5, 226, 254, 257, 266, 281 & 282
This is another of Lyn Macdonald's works of vernacular history, based on the recollections of members of the nursing and medical profession. The book is illustrated.

Macdonald, Lyn
1914–1918: Voices and Images of the Great War
Joseph, 1988
The Somme, pp. 143, 152–90, 196, 210 & 215
This book is profusely illustrated.

Moynihan, Michael (ed.)
People at War 1914–1918: Their own account of the conflict in the trenches, in the air and at sea
Newton Abbot: David & Charles, 1973

The Somme, pp. 69–84 & 134
Moynihan has assembled a book of recollections by nine individual combatants. The chapter on the Somme includes a very moving account of Casualty Clearing Stations by the Revd J.M.S. Walker. It contains an account by William Pressey, a gunner in the RFA.

Moynihan, Michael (ed.)
A Place Called Armageddon
Newton Abbot: David & Charles, 1975
References to the Somme occur throughout the text.

Moynihan, Michael (ed.)
Greater Love: Letters home 1914–1918
Allen, 1980
The Somme, pp. 77–83
The book is based on letters written home by six different writers from contrasting backgrounds.

Moynihan, Michael (ed.)
God on Our Side: The British Padre in World War I
Leo Cooper, 1983
The Somme, pp. 60–7 & 187–92
The book is based on letters and diaries and devotes separate chapters to individual padres.

Panichas, George A. (ed.)
Promise of Greatness: The war of 1914–1918
Cassell, 1968
The Somme, pp. 43–6, 105–10 & 195–7
This book consists of forty-two essays commissioned by the editor. A few have been published elsewhere (the pieces by Gerald Brenan, Liddell Hart and Geoffrey Keynes), but not necessarily in the same form. In a review of this book in the *Daily*

Telegraph, 14 November 1968, the writer Ernest Raymond mentioned that he still had total recall of his experiences of the war, but no such detailed memory from 1919 to 1968.

Pearson, I.C.
Sheffield Soldiers killed in action 1st July 1916: The opening day of the Somme offensive
Sheffield: I.C. Pearson, 1991
This booklet lists the men from Sheffield who were killed on the Somme's opening day and lists where they met their deaths.

Purdom, C.B.
Everyman at War: Sixty personal narratives of war
Dent, 1930
The Somme, pp. 77–81, 82–8, 89–94 & 98–106
The book deals with accounts by different contributors. (Falls★)

Quinn, Tom (ed.)
Tales of the Old Soldiers: Ten veterans of the First World War remember life and death in the trenches
Stroud: Alan Sutton Publishing, 1993
The Somme, pp. xii–xviii, 1, 5, 7, 17, 20, 21, 29, 31, 54, 76, 77, 82, 87, 102, 105, 136, & 144

Richards, J. (ed.)
Wales on the Western Front
Cardiff: University of Wales, 1994
This anthology of Welsh writers and men who served in Welsh units is a series of extracts of work by twenty-six writers. The pieces that deal with the Somme are: Llewellyn Wyn Griffith, pp. 84–91, David Jones, pp. 104–13, Aneurin Williams, pp. 184–6

Richardson, Sue (ed.)
The Recollections of Three Manchesters in the Great War: Mike Lally of the Old Contemptibles, Joe Horgan of the Territorials, John Hallows of the Pals
Manchester: Neil Richardson, 1985
The Somme, pp. 23–4, 51–3 & 63–73
The editor compiled this booklet from conversations with the above three veterans.

Sanger, E. (ed.)
Letters from Two World Wars
Stroud: Alan Sutton Publishing, 1993
The Somme, pp. 56–61
This is an anthology of letters.

Southwell, E. & White, M.
Two Men: A Memoir
Oxford University Press, 1919
The Somme, pp. 147–302
This is a memoir of two schoolteachers from Shrewsbury who were both killed in the Somme battle. E.H.L. Southwell of the 9th Bn. Rifle Brigade was killed in action on 15 September 1916, and M.G. White of the 6th Bn. Rifle Brigade was killed on 1 July 1916. The book has seven illustrations.

Tapert, Annette
Despatches from the Heart
Hamish Hamilton, 1984
The Somme, pp. 38–51
This is a well-illustrated collection of letters written home by soldiers from the front and includes one very long one from Pte. D.J. Sweeney of the 1st Lincolnshire Regt.

Vansittart, P.E. (ed.)
Voices from the Great War
Cape, 1981

The Somme, pp. 114, 118, 123, 124, 125, 126 & 127
This is a collection of material drawn from letters, poems and newspapers, etc.

Wolff, Anne
Subalterns of the Foot: Three World War I diaries of officers of the Cheshire Regiment
Worcester: Square One Publications, 1992
The Somme, pp. 155–222

The second section contains works on named individual people or families, and is ordered by their names.

Ackerley, J.R.
My Father and Myself
Bodley Head, 1968
The Somme, pp. 56–60
This is an autobiography written by Ackerley and is dedicated to Tulip, his dog. The book is illustrated with family photographs. His material on the Somme is expanded in Peter Parker's biography, see below.

Parker, Peter
Ackerley: The Life of J.R. Ackerley
Constable, 1989
The Somme, pp. 22–9
Ackerley was a 2/Lt. (Temporary) in the 8th East Surrey Regt. (55th Bde./18th Eastern Div.). During his training he was billeted with 'Billie' Nevill and in April 1915 Ackerley was promoted to lieutenant. On 1 July 1916 the divisional objective was the village of Montauban. In order to encourage the men to advance Nevill had dreamt up the scheme of issuing several footballs to the men in his unit. Nevill was subsequently killed in

the advance, and Ackerley was wounded. Later in the war he became a prisoner of war. The biography is illustrated with pictures of Ackerley's family and friends.

Adams, Bernard
Nothing of Importance: A record of eight months at the front with a Welsh Battalion, October 1915 to June 1916
Methuen, 1917
Although this book deals with the period of the war before the Battle of the Somme, the detail that it provides is of very great use to researchers of the battlefield. The author, who died of wounds on 27 February 1917, was a member of the 1st Royal Welch Fusiliers (7th Div.). The book was reissued by Strong Oak Press with Tom Donovan Publishing in 1988, adding some very useful information put together by Peter T. Scott. There is a new introduction, notes to each chapter and a section on dramatis personae.

Nicolson, Nigel
Alex: The life of Field Marshal Earl Alexander of Tunis
Weidenfeld & Nicolson, 1973
Alexander served as a regimental officer with the 2nd Irish Guards in the First World War and rose to the highest rank in the Second World War.

James, Lawrence
Imperial Warrior: The life and times of Field Marshal Viscount Allenby 1861–1936
Weidenfeld & Nicolson, 1993
The Somme, pp. 88–91

Richardson, Sue (ed.)
Orders are Orders – A Manchester Pal on the Somme: From the account of Albert William Andrews of the 19th Manchesters, written in 1917

Manchester: Neil Richardson, 1987
This is a small paperback.

Andrews, William Linton
Haunting Years: The commentaries of a war Territorial
Hutchinson, 1920
The Somme, pp. 194–205
The author was a member of the 4th/5th Black Watch.

Arnold, C. (ed. by S. Royle)
From Mons to Messines and Beyond: The Great War experiences of Sgt. Charles Arnold
Studley: Bredon Books, 1985
The Somme, pp. 40–5
The author was a member of the 6th Border Regt. 33rd Bde./11th Div.

Ashley, R.S.
War Diary of Private R.S. (Jack) Ashley 2472: 7th London Regiment 1914–1918
South Woodford: Philipa Stone, 1982
The Somme, pp. 53–68
The author was captured by the German Naval Division.

Ashurst, George (ed. by Dr Richard Holmes)
My Bit: A Lancashire Fusilier at war 1914–1918
Marlborough: Crowood, 1987
The Somme, Ch. 5, pp. 87–109
The author served with the Lancashire Fusiliers, firstly with the 2nd Bn. (12th Bde./4th Div.), then 1st Bn. (86th Bde./29th Div.) and lastly with the 16th Bn. (96 Bde./32nd Div.).

Asquith, H.
Moments of Memory: Recollections and impressions

National Book Association/Hutchinson, [n.d.]
The Somme, pp. 258–66
Herbert Asquith's second son, a captain in the RFA, was the author of this memoir.

Jolliffe, John (ed.)
Raymond Asquith: Life and letters
Collins, 1980
The Somme, pp. 281–98
Asquith, who served with the Grenadier Guards, was the eldest son of Herbert Asquith, the Liberal Prime Minister of Britain in the first months of the war. He was also a great friend of John Buchan (with whom he had been at Oxford), a Fellow of All Souls and a prospective parliamentary candidate. He was mortally wounded in the advance towards Les Boeufs, close to what is now the Guards Memorial on the Ginchy–Les Boeufs Road. He is buried at Guillemont Road Cemetery.

Bayly, Hugh Wansey
Triple Challenge: Or war, whirligigs and windmills. A doctor's memoirs of the years 1914–1929
Hutchinson, 1935
The Somme, pp. 109–30
Bayly was Medical Officer to 2nd Guards Bde. and treated Raymond Asquith when he was mortally wounded.

The War Diary of the Master of Belhaven 1914–1918
John Murray, 1924
The Somme, pp. 220–65
This is the diary of the only son of the 10th Lord Belhaven and Stenton, an artilleryman who served as battery and later brigade commander in France with the 24th Div. from September 1915 until his death on 31 March 1918, when in command of the 106th Bde. RFA 24th Div. It is one of the classic books of the First World War and includes maps and sketches. (Falls ★★)

Bell, Douglas H. (ed. & intro. by Henry Williamson)
A Soldier's Diary of the Great War
Faber & Gwyer, 1929
The Somme, pp. 161–8
Bell and Williamson – along with Victor Yeates, author of 'Winged Victory' (a superb book about the RFC in the First World War) – attended the same school before the war. Bell and Williamson also both joined the London Rifle Brigade and the former joined the 1st Queen's Own Cameron Highlanders, becoming a captain before transferring to the RFC in 1916.

Biscoe, Julian Tyndale
Gunner Subaltern
Leo Cooper, 1971
The Somme, pp. 91–101
Letters written by a young man who was a subaltern in the RHA to his father during the First World War. The book contains maps and illustrations.

Blunden, Edmund
Minds Eye
Cape, 1934
This is a series of essays under the general heading of Flanders and includes a postscript to Blunden's *Undertones of War*. The chapter 'The Somme Still Flows', pp. 36–43, was written in 1929.

Blunden, Edmund
Undertones of War
Cobden Sanderson, 1928
The Somme, pp. 86–148
Blunden (1896–1974) was commissioned

with the 11th Royal Sussex Regt. (116th Bde./39th Div.) and was discharged on health grounds in March 1918. He suffered from the effects of gas poisoning for the rest of his life. He began to write the first draft of this memoir soon after the war finished, but put the manuscript to one side in 1924. This was fortunate, as its publication in 1928 coincided with the boom in war books. The first half of the book describes the everyday life on the Western Front, and the second half is a poetic response to the same experience. It is one of the very best memoirs of the war. Of her late husband, Claire Blunden said, 'No days passed in which he did not refer to that war. He was obsessed with it.' He spent more time in the trenches than other poets, and Claire Blunden became 'wearied with the wretched war'. Blunden suffered from the nervous strain of the trenches in his last four years when he had become an invalid. (Falls ★★★)

Webb, Barry
Edmund Blunden: A biography
Yale University Press, 1990
The Somme, pp. 59, 60–6, 82–3, 93, 98 & 99. Visits after the war was over, pp. 205 & 318
This book is the first biography of the poet and author of *Undertones of War*, published sixteen years after the poet's death.

Bone, Muirhead
The Western Front
Pts I & II
Country Life, 1917
This is a collection of drawings by Muirhead Bone (1876–1953), who was a second lieutenant with the staff attached to GHQ in France. He was given a temporary appointment as an official War Office artist and went to the Front on 12 July 1916.

The Somme battlefield is well represented in this book. (Falls ★)

Assher, Ben (pseud.)
A Nomad under Arms: The chronicle of an artilleryman from 1914 to the Armistice
Witherby, 1931
The Somme, pp. 104–208
The author's name was a pseudonym for Capt. Colin Borradaile, MC, who served with 115th Heavy Bty., 2nd Corps and was attached to other batteries. He ended the war as a battery commander and after it wrote several travel books. This book has some illustrations by the author and seven maps.

Slater, Guy (ed.)
My Warrior Sons: The Borton Family diary 1914–1918
Peter Davies, 1973
The Somme, pp. 83, 92, 103, 163 & 167
This is the diary of Col. Borton, along with letters from his soldier sons 'Biffy' and 'Bosky'. The sons real names were Amyas, who joined the Black Watch as a subaltern before transferring to the RFC, and Arthur, who joined the RFC. The book includes an introduction written by the editor.

Boyd, Donald
Salute of Guns
Cape, 1930
The Somme, pp. 109–50 (summer) & p. 151 (winter)
A memoir which was very highly thought of by Robert Graves.

Bradford, R.B.
A memoir written by relatives and friends of Brigadier-General R.B. Bradford, V.C., M.C. and his brothers
Private publication, [n.d.]

The Somme, pp. 32 & 64–82
Bradford was with the 9th Durham Light Infantry. This memoir was reissued by Ray Westlake Military Books of Newport in 1994.

Brenan, Gerald
A Life of One's Own
Cape, 1962
The Somme, pp. 202–7
The author (1894–1987) first joined the 5th Gloucesters and was then seconded to the 48th Divisional Cyclists Company, with whom he was serving when the Somme battle began. During the war he won the MC, and for his liaison work with the French 120th Div. he was awarded the Croix de Guerre. For a time after the war he was a member of the Bloomsbury Group before taking up writing and living in Spain.

Brittain, Harry E.
To Verdun from the Somme: An Anglo-American glimpse of the great advance
John Lane/Bodley Head, 1917
The Somme, pp. 17–61

Fraser, David
Alan Brooke
Collins, 1982
The Somme, pp. 69–75 & 80
Alan Brooke served as a regimental officer with the Royal Horse Artillery, and on the Somme served with the 18th Div. He was an early supporter of the 'creeping barrage' in which the artillery moved forward with its targets and destroyed selected enemy strong points. He became the CIGS in the Second World War. A map of the situation of the 18th Div. is included.

Brown, M.
Tommy Goes to War
Dent, 1978
The Somme, pp. 12, 13, 35, 45, 56, 97, 104, 126, 128, 130, 137–74, 176–82, 185, 209, 251, 252 & 260
The text is illustrated by stills from the Battle of the Somme film. Much of the text material was sent in by survivors who wrote in response to the author's request for reminiscences.

Middlebrook, Martin (ed.)
The Diaries of Private Horace Bruckshaw 1915–1916
Scolar Press, 1979
Bruckshaw was a member of the 2nd Royal Marine Light Infantry. He fought in Gallipoli and took part in the Ancre battle which began on 13 November 1916. He was killed in action near Gavrelle Windmill on 28 April 1917. Martin Middlebrook also wrote an introduction to the book.

Buckley, Francis
Q 6 A and other Places: Recollections of 1916, 1917 and 1918
Spottiswoode & Ballantyre, 1920
The Somme, pp. 68–96
The author served with the 7th Northumberland Fusiliers (149th Bde./50th Div.)

Copley, Ian
George Butterworth and his Music: A centennial tribute
Thames Publishing, 1985
The Somme, pp. 45–51
Butterworth was an officer in the 13th Durham Light Infantry who won the MC and was shot dead near Pozières on 5

August 1916 when in charge of a bombing party. He was a talented musical composer and arranger and a great loss to English music. He was particularly well known as the arranger of two folk-songs into the idyllic 'By the Banks of Green Willow' and as the composer of 'The Shropshire Lad'. In 1985 BBC Radio 3 devoted a three-part centenary programme to his memory.

Woods, Edward S., MA, CF (ed.)
Andrew Buxton: The Rifle Brigade. A memoir
Robert Scott, 1918
The Somme, pp. 198–216
Buxton was with the 3rd Rifle Bde. as a company commander. He was a colleague of second lieutenant Vernède, the writer. Buxton was killed near Oostaverne on 7 June 1917. The memoir is illustrated with family photographs. It is based on letters that he wrote home, and those dealing with the Somme include coverage of the battle for Guillemont. The editor was also the author of *Knights in Armour*.

Cave, J.B. (ed.)
I Survived, Didn't I?: The Great War reminiscences of Private 'Ginger' Byrne
Leo Cooper, 1993
The Somme, pp. 37–52
The author was connected with the 2nd Hampshire Bn. (88 Bde./29th Div.) from March 1916 until transferring to the Machine Gun Corps in August. He was temporarily attached to the Newfoundland Regt. on 1 July 1916 and then served with the 29 (Div.) MG Bn. for the rest of the war.

Edmonds, Charles (pseud.)
A Subaltern's War
Peter Davies, 1929

The Somme, pp. 37–96
Edmonds later expanded this book as *Soldier from the Wars Returning*, written under his real name, Charles Carrington, see below. (Falls ★★)

Carrington, Charles
Soldier from the Wars Returning
Hutchinson, 1965
The Somme, pp. 109–34
Charles Carrington (1897–1990) became the adjutant with the 5th Royal Warwicks (143rd Bde./48th Div.). This is an expanded version of his earlier book *A Subaltern's War* written under his pseudonym, Charles Edmonds (see above). The author won the MC and the book is a very articulate expression of the First World War generation. Both of these two books are perceptive and humane, and an antidote to the postwar view, as he tries to explain just why it was that so many young men were willing to give their lives for their country. Carrington wrote several other books including a standard life of Rudyard Kipling.

Carstairs, Carroll, MC
A Generation Missing
Heinemann, 1930
The Somme, pp. 63–8
Carstairs was an American who served with the Allied troops before the Americans entered the war. He was a member of the 3rd Grenadier Guards on the Somme at the end of September 1916. In 1989 Strong Oak Press/Tom Donovan Publishing reissued the book with a new introduction and additional chapter notes compiled by Peter T. Scott.

Lyttelton, Oliver (Viscount Chandos), PC, DSO, MC, LLD
From Peace to War: A study in contrast 1857–1918
Bodley Head, 1968
The Somme, pp. 163–74
Chandos (1893–1972) joined up in December 1914 as Oliver Lyttelton. He served with the 4th Bn. the Bedfordshire Regt. (Militia) before being gazetted with the 2nd Gren. Gds. (4th Gds. Bde./2nd Div.), followed by the 1st Gds. Bde. (Gds. Div.) and then 3rd Gren. Gds. (2nd Gds. Bde. Gds. Div.) as adjutant. As for so many others, the war for Lyttelton 'was a great formative experience'. In April 1918, when a brigade major with the 4th Gds. Bde., he was wounded. Not only did he win the DSO and MC, but he was mentioned three times in despatches. This illustrated book includes maps and is divided into two sections: the second part is based on Chandos' letters home from the front to his mother.

Lyttelton, Oliver (Viscount Chandos), PC, DSO, MC, LLD
Memoirs of Lord Chandos
Bodley Head, 1962
The Somme, pp. 57–70
After the war the author served the British Government in various posts and was a friend of three prime ministers: Winston Churchill, Anthony Eden and Harold Macmillan.

Chapman, Guy
A Passionate Prodigality: Fragments of autobiography
MacGibbon & Kee, 1965, 2nd edn
The Somme, pp. 92–139
The author served as an officer with the 13th Royal Fusiliers (111 Bde./37th Div.). He was awarded the MC and later the OBE, and became a prominent historian of French history after the war.

Chapman, Guy
A Kind of a Survivor
Victor Gollancz, 1975
The Somme, pp. 57–85
This is virtually an autobiography which partly reworks the above book. It was edited by Storm Jameson, his widow.

Charteris, Brig.-Gen. J., CMG, DSO
At G.H.Q.
Cassell, 1931
The Somme, pp. 129–50, 151–60, 161–7 & 168–82
The author was Chief of Intelligence at GHQ from 3 January 1916 until 23 January 1918, when he was relieved of his job because of political and military pressure. His 'crime' had been to pander to Haig's optimistic assessments of German reserve strength. The book covers the whole war, and is based on letters written home which were then turned into diary form.

Clayton, Ann
Chavasse Double VC
Leo Cooper, 1992
The Somme, pp. 156–8, 167, 189 & 200
This is an illustrated biography of Noel Chavasse, the only man to win two VCs in the First World War. He was MO with the 10th King's (Liverpool) Bn.

Gilbert, M.
Winston S. Churchill
Vol. III. 1914–1916
Heinemann, 1971
The Somme, pp. 774 & 791–4

Clayton, C.P.
The Hungry One
Llandysul: Gomer Press, 1978
The Somme (Mametz Wood), pp. 138–84
Clayton served with the 1st Welch Regt.
(84th Bde./28th Div.) and ended the war as
the CO of the 2nd Bn. (3rd Bde./1st Div.).

Cliff, Norman D.
To Hell and Back with the Guards
Braunton: Merlin Books, 1988
The Somme, pp. 74–8
The author served with the Grenadier
Guards, joining the 1st Bn. in 1915, and
was with them until the occupation of
Germany. He was awarded the MM and
after the war worked as a newspaper
foreign editor.

Cloete, Stuart
*A Victorian Son: An autobiography
1897–1922*
Collins, 1972
The Somme, pp. 227–44
The author admits that this autobiography
overlaps with his novel *How Young They
Died*, in which he covers his own
experiences during the war, but 'worked
up' the love interest. Cloete was gazetted as
a temporary officer with the 9th King's
Own Yorkshire Light Infantry and went to
France with them on 12 January 1916. He
was wounded in September 1916 and was
sent home to recuperate. He was later a
regular officer with the 2nd Coldstream
Guards (4th Gds. Bde./2nd Div.) and 1st
Gds. Bde. (Guards Div.). He was wounded
for the second time at St Léger.

*Comrades in Arms: The letters of Frank
Cocker, a soldier in the Great War*
Brighton: Tressell, 1988

The Somme, pp. 30–4
Cocker was a member of the Duke of
Wellington's (West Riding) Regt. This is
an illustrated A4 booklet.

Norman, Terry (ed.)
Armageddon Road: A VC's diary 1914–1916
Kimber, 1982
The Somme, pp. 191–7
This book is the diary of Billy Congreve,
who was a brevet major with the Rifle
Brigade when he was killed on the
Somme in July 1916. He is buried at
Corbie.

Thornton, Lt.-Col. L.H., CMG, DSO &
Fraser, Pamela
*The Congreves: Father and Son: General Sir
Walter Norris Congreve, VC BT.-Major
William La Touche Congreve, VC*
John Murray, 1930
The Somme, pp. 154–61 & 206–7
The book is illustrated.

Cook, Arthur Henry, DCM, MM, BEM
(ed. by Lt.-Gen. G.N. Molesworth)
A Soldier's War
Taunton: E. Goodman (printer), 1957
The Somme, pp. 44–57
The author served in the 1st Somerset
Light Infantry and kept this diary.

Coppard, George
*With a Machine Gun to Cambrai: The tale of
a young Tommy in Kitchener's Army
1914–1918*
Imperial War Museum, 1980
The Somme, pp. 78–93
The author enlisted with the 6th Queen's
Royal West Surreys as a Kitchener
volunteer and later served with the
Machine Gun Corps.

Croney, Percy
Soldier's Luck: Memoirs of a soldier of the Great War
Arthur H. Stockwell, 1965
The Somme (Ancre Valley), pp. 82–134
The author served with the 2nd Cambridgeshire Regt. (23rd Bde/8th Div.) and 59th Bde./20th Div. after Gallipoli, and later the Essex Regt.

Crozier, Brig.-Gen. F.P. CB, CMG, DSO
A Brass-Hat in No Man's Land
Cape, 1930
The Somme, pp. 88–112
The author was CO of the 9th Royal Irish Rifles (107th Bde./36th (Ulster) Div.) at the beginning of the Battle of the Somme, before being appointed commander of 119th Bde./40th Div. In this memoir Crozier 'pulls no punches'. Between the wars he served in Ireland until resigning, and became Inspector General of the Lithuanian Army. In 1989 the book was reissued by Gliddon Books, with a new introduction by Philip Orr.

Crozier, Brig.-Gen. F.P., CB, CMG, DSO
Impressions and Recollections
T. Werner Laurie, 1930
The Somme, pp. 173–5 & 178–80

Cuddeford, D.W.J.
And All For What?: Some war-time experiences
Heath Cranton, 1933
The Somme, pp. 44–81
The author was in the Scots Guards.

Davis, R.J. (ed. by Sir Ernest Hodder-Williams)
One Young Man
Private publication, 1917
The Somme, pp. 158–69

This book tells the story of a young man wounded in the Battle of the Somme. His division was on the left of the left flank of the British attack at Gommecourt. Davis later became a director of the publishing firm Hodder & Stoughton.

Davson, Lt.-Col. H.M., CMG, DSO
Memoirs of the Great War
Gale & Polden, 1964
The Somme, pp. 46–57
At the time of the Somme the writer was an artilleryman with the 35th Div. The book has a portrait of the author.

Devas, D.
From Cloister to Camp: Being the reminiscences of a priest in France, 1915–1918
Edinburgh: Sands, 1919
The Somme, pp. 44–76, including winter 1916

Dillon, Brig. Viscount, CMG, DSO
Memories of Three Wars
Allan Wingate, 1951
The Somme, pp. 53–72
This illustrated book was based on the author's diary. He was a liaison officer with Gen. Foch. Later he was HM Bodyguard of the Honourable Corps of Gentlemen at Arms.

Dolden, A. Stuart
Cannon Fodder: An infantryman's life on the Western Front 1914–18
Blandford, 1980
The Somme, pp. 71–92
The author was a member of the 1st London Scottish Regt.

Douie, Charles
The Weary Road: Recollections of a subaltern of infantry
Murray, 1929

The Somme, pp. 130–53 & 154–76

Douie served with the 1st Dorsetshire Regt. (14th Bde./32nd Div.). The book has an introduction by Maj.-Gen. Sir Ernest Swinton. In 1988 the book was reissued by Strong Oak Press/Tom Donovan Publishing, with an additional introduction and chapter notes compiled by Peter T. Scott. (Falls ★★)

Dundas, Henry
Henry Dundas, Scots Guards
Edinburgh: Blackwood, 1921
The Somme (Les Boeufs), pp. 77–128
Dundas served with the 1st Scots Gds. (2nd Gds. Bde/Guards Div.) from May 1916 to 27 September 1918. He was killed in an attack against the Hindenberg Line. The book has a small map.

Dyer, Geoff
The Missing on the Somme
Hamish Hamilton, 1994
Dyer is a journalist and appears to be much under the influence of Paul Fussell's *The Great War and Modern Memory*. This illustrated book is a journey of enquiry to the Western Front and it relies more on personal impressions than on systematic analysis.

Ebelhauser, G.A. (ed. by Richard Baumgartner)
The Passage: A tragedy of the First World War
Huntingdon, WV, USA: Griffin, 1984
This is a well-illustrated account of a German soldier, including his participation in the Somme battle.

Eberle, Lt.-Col. V.F., MC
My Sapper Venture: Four years in Belgium, France and Italy with RE Field Company of 48th South Midland (Territorial) Division

Pitman, 1973
The Somme, pp. 56–108
This memoir deals with the build-up to the Somme battle, and covers the period from autumn 1915 to January 1917. The author was deeply involved with the development of the Bangalore Torpedo.

Eden, Anthony, Earl of Avon, KG, PC, MC
Another World 1897–1917
Allen Lane, 1976
The Somme, pp. 95–120
Eden served on the Somme with the 21st King's Royal Rifle Corps (Yeoman Rifles) (124th Bde./41st Div.) and later won the MC. At the end of the war he was one of the British Army's youngest brigade majors. He later became British Prime Minister. The book includes two small drawings by André Dunoyer Segonzac.

Empey, Arthur Guy
From the Fire Step: The experiences of an American soldier in the British Army
New York: Burt, 1917
The Somme, pp. 242–61
Empey was a machine-gunner, serving in France. This illustrated book was issued in London by Putnam in 1917 under the title of *Over the Top*.

Ewart, Wilfrid
Scots Guard
Rich & Cowan, 1934
The Somme, pp. 109–28
The author (1897–1922) served with the 2nd Scots Guards (3rd Gds. Bde./Gds. Div.) as a captain, and after the war became a well-known writer until his premature accidental death in Mexico. His biography was written by his friend Stephen Graham, who was also in the

Scots Guards and who found him shot dead. Graham had helped Ewart to make a career out of writing.

Eyre, C.E.M.
Somme Harvest: Memories of a P.B.I. in the summer of 1916
Jarrold, 1936
The Somme, pp. 99–249
The author was a member of the 2nd King's Royal Rifle Corps (2nd Bde./1st Div.). The book covers two months of intensive fighting between May and July 1916 before he was taken prisoner. In the same year he was a witness to the death of William Mariner, VC. The book was reissued by the London Stamp Exchange in 1991.

von Falkenhayn, Erich
General Headquarters 1914–16 and its critical decisions
Hutchinson, 1919
The Somme, pp. 261–9

Fallon, Capt. David, MC
The Big Fight
Cassell, 1918
The Somme, pp. 144–67
Includes tank action at Beaumont-Hamel and the attack against Mouquet Farm.

Feilding, Rowland
War Letters to a Wife: France and Flanders, 1915–1919
Medici Society, 1919
The Somme, pp. 81–129
Before the First World War Feilding was a regular officer in the Coldstream Guards. He became CO of the 6th Connaught Rangers and later transferred to the 1st/15th Bn. Prince of Wales's Own Civil Service Rifles. The letters were addressed to his wife. (Falls ★★)

Aston, Maj.-Gen. Sir George, KCB
The Biography of the Late Marshal Foch
Hutchinson, 1929
The Somme, pp. 165–73, 174–9 & 180–8
There are many Foch portraits in the book.

Atteridge, A. Hilliard
Marshal Ferdinand Foch: his life and theory of modern war
Skeffington, 1918
The Somme, pp. 201–5
This book includes a preface by John Buchan.

Foch, Marshal (trans. by Col. Bentley Mott)
The Memoirs of Marshal Foch
Heinemann, 1931
The Somme, pp. 85–8, 246–51 & 319–21
This is a description of the French involvement in the battle.

Liddell Hart, B.H.
Foch: The man of Orleans
Eyre & Spottiswoode, 1931
The Somme, pp. 224–7

Foley, Henry Arthur
Three Years on Active Service and Eight Months as Prisoner-of-War
Bridgwater: Walter Belcher, 1920 (private publication)
The Somme, pp. 85–8
The book contains 13 plates by W. Cecil Dunford and three sketch maps. Foley was a member of the 6th Somerset Light Infantry and was wounded in September 1916. He died in his 95th year, in Stoke Mandeville Hospital.

Foot, Stephen, DSO, MA (later Brev. Maj. RE)
Three Lives – and Now
Heinemann, 1934

Foot was a major in the Royal Engineers who transferred to the Tank Corps in 1916 and became a Staff Officer. At the time of the beginning of the Somme he was adjutant with the 21st Div. in their attack against Fricourt.

Fraser-Tytler, Lt.-Col. Neil (ed. by Maj. F.N. Baker RGA)
Field Guns in France
Hutchinson, 1929
The Somme, pp. 36–133
This excellent book was based on letters written home by a Gunner officer to his parents from November 1915 to August 1918. The above section includes the six months prior to the start of the Somme battle. Fraser-Tytler was officer commanding 'D' Bty. (151) (HOW) Bde. 30th Div. and in May 1916 he switched to 150th Bde. in the same division. Later in the war Fraser-Tytler was badly gassed, and was nursed by his wife Christian until he died in 1937. His wife died in June 1995 shortly before this book was reissued by Tom Donovan Publishing with the subtitle 'A Howitzer Battery in the Battles of the Somme, Arras, Messines, Passchendaele, 1915–1918, by the Battery Commander'.

French, A.
Gone for a Soldier
Kineton, Warwickshire: Roundwood, 1972
The Somme, pp. 59–86
French served with 1/15th Prince of Wales's Own Civil Service Rifles at High Wood.

Fuller, Maj.-Gen. J.F.C., CB, CBE, DSO
Memoirs of an Unconventional Soldier
Ivor Nicholson & Watson, 1936
The Somme, pp. 69, 236 & 245
The references are brief and the book is illustrated. Fuller was Chief of General Staff of the Tank Corps.

Gale, Gen. Sir Richard
Call to Arms
Hutchinson, 1968
The Somme, pp. 10–22, 56 & 59

Gibbs, Philip
The Pageant of the Years: An Autobiography
Heinemann, 1946
The Somme, pp. 180–94
This was the fourth occasion that Gibbs covered the war in his writings; this time he spoke of the Somme from a point of view thirty years on.

Gladden, N.
The Somme 1916: A personal account
Kimber, 1974
The Somme, pp. 87–90
This is a personal account of the Somme battle and of being wounded. The author was in the 7th Northumberland Fusiliers 149th Bde. 50th (Northumbrian) Div. The book includes a Somme map.

Glubb, J.
Into Battle: A soldier's diary of the Great War
Cassell, 1978
The Somme, pp. 57–78
On the Somme Glubb served in the 7th Field Coy. Royal Engineers 50th Territorial Div. from August 1916 to January 1917. He later became Commander of the Arab Legion until he was sacked.

Royle, Trevor
Glubb Pasha: The life and times of Sir John Bagot Glubb, Commander of the Arab Legion
Little Brown, 1992
The Somme, pp. 44–6

Gosse, Philip
Memoirs of a Camp Follower: (Adventures and impressions of a doctor in the Great War)
Longmans Green, 1934
The Somme, pp. 90–122
The author was son of Sir Edmund Gosse and served with the 69th Field Ambulance (Royal Army Medical Corps) in France until autumn 1917 before being sent to India. The book was later reissued under the main title of *A Naturalist Goes to War*.

Farrar-Hockley, Anthony
Goughie: The life of General Sir Hubert Gough CGB, GCMG and KCVO
Hart-Davis McGibbon, 1975
The Somme, pp. 178–204
Gough was in command of the Fifth Army when he was sent home in spring 1918.

Graham, Stephen
Challenge of the Dead
Cassell, 1921
The Somme, pp. 86–106
A retrospective account of the First World War battlefields. Graham was a great friend of Wilfrid Ewart.

Grant, Capt. W. & Newman, B.
Tunnellers
Jenkins, 1936
The Somme, pp. 112–38
The book includes maps and two Somme pictures.

Graves, Robert
Goodbye to All That: An autobiography
Jonathan Cape, 1929
The Somme, pp. 261–80
The first issue of this book was withdrawn as Siegfried Sassoon objected to the use of a poem he had written that Graves had included without his permission. It appeared between pp. 341–3 and began, 'Dear Roberto, I'd timed my death in action to the minute'. Fewer than a hundred copies of this first issue were distributed before being recalled, and they are now collector's items that are worth several hundred pounds. The book was revised and reissued by Cassell in 1957.

Graves made no secret of the fact that he wrote his autobiography in order to help cover the costs of his growing domestic responsibilities. Although the book is a classic and a *tour de force* it should still be treated with a certain amount of caution over some of its factual statements. Graves served as a young officer with the regular battalion the 2nd Royal Welch Fusiliers from 1915 and was seriously wounded in the fighting for High Wood in July 1916. He was left for dead at one point. After the war Graves was the model for one of the figures in the 24th Divisional memorial in Battersea Park.

In 1995 Berghahn Books reissued the book in its original edition with a biographical essay by Richard Perceval Graves, who also had access to Sassoon's annotated copy and included this material in the new text as well. (Falls ★)

Graves, Robert (ed. by P. O'Prey)
In Broken Images: Selected letters of Robert Graves 1914–1916
Hutchinson, 1982
The Somme, pp. 54–5

Greenwell, Graham
An Infant in Arms: War letters of a company officer 1914–1918
Allen Lane, Penguin Press, 1972
The Somme, pp. 108–49
This was first published by Lovat Dickson

& Thompson in 1935. Greenwell was a member of the 4th Oxfordshire & Buckinghamshire Light Infantry (145th Bde./48th South Midland). The reissue has an introduction by John Terraine.

Griffith, Ll. Wyn
Up to Mametz
Faber & Faber, 1931
The Somme, pp. 207–60
Griffith was an officer in the 15th Royal Welch Fusiliers (113th Bde.). In this book he describes the experiences of the 38th (Welsh) Div. and in particular its involvement in the struggle to capture Mametz Wood. Griffiths became a captain and a staff officer. In 1988 the book was reissued by Gliddon Books with a new introduction by Colin Hughes, together with a map.

Gwynne, H.A. (comp. & ed. by Keith Wilson)
The Rasp of War: The letters of H.A. Gwynne to the Countess of Bathurst 1914–1918
Sidgwick & Jackson, 1988
The Somme, pp. 98, 189–90, 199–201 & 238

Charteris, John
Field-Marshal Earl Haig
Cassell, 1929
The Somme, pp. 214–29
The book has half-tone plates, line engravings, a map and a foreword by John Buchan.

Duff Cooper, A.
Haig
Vol. I
Faber, 1935
The Somme, pp. 331–69
This book fails to tackle the more controversial aspects of Haig's career.

Duncan, G.S.
Douglas Haig as I Knew Him
Allen & Unwin, 1966
The Somme, pp. 42–50
Duncan was Haig's chaplain from early 1916.

de Groot, G.J.
Douglas Haig 1861–1928
Unwin Hyman, 1988
The Somme, pp. 247–77
The book is a modern study of the man in charge of the BEF at the time of the Battle of the Somme.

Haig, Douglas (ed. by Robert Blake)
The Private Papers of Douglas Haig 1914–1919
Eyre & Spottiswoode, 1952
The Somme, pp. 132–51 (preparations), pp. 152–77, p. 215 (Haig's reflections on the Somme)
The book is a collection of extracts, mainly from Haig's diaries. Appendix A 'Operations of 1916' (pp. 365–8) gives selections from a memorandum on the Western Front Operations 1916–1918, deposited at the British Museum, and closed until 1940. This document, written under Haig's supervision, gives a summary of Haig's motives for launching the offensive.

Johnston, C.H.L.
Famous Generals of the Great War
Boston: Page, 1919
Sir Douglas Haig, pp. 115–32

Liddell Hart, B.H.
Reputations
Murray, 1928
The Somme, pp. 99–105
This is a study of military leaders of the

First World War and includes a chapter on Haig and his handling of the Somme battle. (Falls ★)

Marshall-Cornwall, Gen. Sir James, KCB, CBE, DSO, MC
Haig: As military commander
Batsford, 1973
The Somme, pp. 184–208
The author was on Haig's intelligence staff during 1916 and 1917. The book includes two Somme maps and it is illustrated, but not within the Somme section.

Terraine, John
Douglas Haig: the educated soldier
Hutchinson, 1963
The Somme, pp. 173–236
Terraine firmly defended Haig's reputation in this biography which is still in print, but is in need of revision. The American edition is called *Ordeal of Victory*.

Warner, Philip
Field Marshal Earl Haig
Bodley Head, 1991
The Somme, pp. 197–215

Winter, Denis
Haig's Command: A reassessment
Viking, 1991
The Somme, pp. 45–67
When this book was published it was widely reviewed as yet another book attacking the posthumous reputation of FM Haig. In turn it was attacked, in particular by John Terraine and by Correlli Barnet in the pages of the *Times Literary Supplement*. The fire-power of the anti-Winter faction was equal to Winter's diatribe against Haig's reputation.

Haigh, R.H. & Turner, P.W.
Not for Glory: A personal history of the 1914–18 war
Robert Maxwell, 1969
The Somme, pp. 39–61
This book was based on the memoirs of Gilbert Hall, a private who volunteered with the 13th (1st Barnsley) Yorkshire & Lancashire Regt. and who was later commissioned in the 2/4th King's Own Yorkshire Light Infantry. It has maps and illustrations.

Hall, Michael
Sacrifice on the Somme
Belfast: Farset Publications, [1989]
This was the first publication in magazine form of the Farset Association of Northern Ireland, promoting interest in the role of the province in the Battle of the Somme, in particular. This A4 booklet was reissued by Island Publications of Belfast as an A5 pamphlet in 1993.

Harbottle, George
Civilian Soldiers 1914–1919: A period relived
Newcastle-upon-Tyne, n.d.
The Somme, pp. 59–63
This illustrated book includes a portrait. The author was a member of the 6th Northumberland Fusiliers.

Hawkings, Frank (ed. by Arthur Taylor)
From Ypres to Cambrai: The 1914–1919 diary of an infantryman
Morley: Elmfield Press, 1974
The Somme, pp. 91–3, 96–105 & 108
This illustrated book has some good maps. The author served with the Queen Victoria's Rifles (9th London Regt.) and was commissioned in the Royal Naval Div.

Head, Lt.-Col. Charles O., DSO
No Great Shakes: An autobiography
Hale, 1943
The Somme, pp. 174–9
The author raised a battery and a brigade (and later a regiment of the New Army). The book is illustrated.

Hitchcock, F.C.
'Stand To': A diary of the trenches 1915–1918
Hurst & Blackett, 1937
The Somme, pp. 135–85
The author was a regular officer and became a captain in the 2nd Leinster Regt. (serving with the 17th, 73rd and 47th Bdes. of 6th, 24th and 16th Divs.) At one time in August 1916 his front-line sector was opposite that of Ernst Junger of 73rd Hanoverian Fusiliers at Guillemont. In 1988 the book was reissued by Gliddon Books with a new introduction by Anthony Spagnoly.

Holloway, S.M.
From Trench and Turret: Royal Marines' letters and diaries 1914–1918
The Somme, pp. 49–63
This small paperback is illustrated and includes maps.

Home, A.
The Diary of a World War I Cavalry Officer
Tunbridge Wells: Costello, 1985
The Somme, pp. 120–6
This illustrated book has a Somme battle map. The author served on the cavalry staff during the Somme campaign.

Seton, Graham [Lt.-Col. G.S. Hutchison]
Footslogger: An autobiography
Hutchinson, 1931

The Somme, pp. 158–71
Prior to the war, the author was a regular officer who left the Army and took up various jobs. On the outbreak of war he returned to the Army as an officer with the 2nd Argyll & Sutherland Highlanders. In 1918 he took command of the Machine Gun Corps.

Hutchison, Lt.-Col. Graham Seton
Pilgrimage
Rich & Cowan, 1935
The Somme, pp. 39–102
The book is illustrated, and is a reworking of the author's earlier books.

Hutchison, Lt.-Col. Graham Seton
Warrior
Hutchinson, 1932
The Somme, pp. 123–63
This illustrated book is based on *Footslogger*, one of the author's earlier books. As a soldier, Hutchison was obsessed with combat.

Huxtable, Charles
From the Somme to Singapore: A medical officer in two World Wars
Tunbridge Wells: Costello, 1987
The Somme, pp. 22, 24, 25 & 26
This book was first published in Australia. Huxtable served with the 9th Royal Sussex and 2nd Lancashire Fusiliers.

Jack, James Lockhead (ed. & intro. by John Terraine)
General Jack's Diary: The trench diary of Brigadier-General J.L. Jack DSO
Eyre & Spottiswoode, 1964
The Somme, pp. 135–52 & 161–87
The author was a regular officer, second-in-command 2nd Cameronians from August 1915 to August 1916. He was

promoted to commander of the 2nd West Yorkshire Regt. from August 1916 to July 1917, and later was commander of 28th Bde. 9th (Scottish) Div.

Jerrold, Douglas
Georgian Adventure
The Right Book Club, 1937
The Somme, pp. 181–95
This book was written by a historian for the Royal Naval Div. who later became a publisher. He lost an arm during the Battle of the Ancre in November 1916.

Jones, N.H.
The War Walk: A journey along the Western Front
Robert Hale, 1983
The Somme, pp. 94–110
This is an illustrated personal account of a trip to the former Western Front. It has a foreword by Alistair Horne, but unfortunately no maps.

Jones, Paul
War Letters of a Public School Boy
Cassell, 1918
The Somme, pp. 202–12
During the Battle of the Somme, Jones was in charge of an ammunition working party at an advanced railhead. The book is illustrated with portraits of Jones, who was killed near Zonnebeke on 31 July 1917.

Junger, Ernst
The Storm of Steel
From the diary of a German storm-troop officer on the Western Front
Chatto & Windus, 1929
The Somme, pp. 64–110
This is an English translation of one of the most famous German memoirs of the war. It is based on the diary of a German storm trooper officer who joined the 73rd Hanoverian Fusiliers in 1914. He was made an officer in November 1915 and served for the rest of the war. In August 1916 at Guillemont he was in the German front line opposite Capt. F.C. Hitchcock of the 2nd Leinster Regt. This is a classic memoir and pulls no punches; Junger seems to have actually enjoyed his war, despite being wounded fourteen times. He was awarded the Pour le Mérite. At the time of writing Junger is still alive, a great survivor who has reached his 102nd year. (Falls ★★)

Kelly, R.B. Talbert
A Subaltern's Odyssey: Memoir of the Great War 1915–1917
Kimber, 1980
The Somme, pp. 85–105
In August 1914 Kelly left Rugby to join the army. He was commissioned with the RHA and served with 'A' Bty, 52nd Bde. RFA 9th (Scottish) Division between May 1915 and August 1917. He won the MC and was mentioned in despatches. He was a water-colour artist and some of his work appears in this book.

Kennedy, Sir Alexander B.W.
Ypres to Verdun
Country Life & George Newnes, 1921
The Somme, pp. 38–51
This book is well illustrated.

Keynes, Geoffrey
Gates of Memory
Oxford University Press, 1981
The Somme, pp. 139–42
Keynes was a great friend of Rupert Brooke before the war, and in 1914 was already a qualified surgeon. In 1916 he was a captain in the Royal Army Medical

Corps, and was able to practise his skills on casualties on the Western Front. During the war he won the MC, rose to the rank of major and was mentioned in despatches. He was a brother of the economist Maynard Keynes and a considerable bibliophile who lived to the age of ninety-five, dying in 1982. The book is illustrated.

Lascelles, Sir Alan (ed. by Duff Hart-Davis)
End of an Era: Letters & journals of Sir Alan Lascelles from 1887–1920
Hamish Hamilton, 1986
The Somme, pp. 201–13
Lascelles was a cavalry officer with the Bedfordshire Yeomanry during the First World War. Later he was on the staff of the Prince of Wales, who became Edward VIII.

Law, F.
A Man at Arms: Memoirs of two World Wars
Collins, 1983
The Somme, pp. 72–6
Law was with the Irish Guards. The book is illustrated with pictures of the author.

Fletcher, Ian (ed.)
Letters from the Front: The Great War correspondence of Lieutenant Brian Lawrence, 1916–17
Tunbridge Wells: Parapress, 1993
The Somme, pp. 15–43
Lawrence was with the 1st Grenadier Guards.

Bond, Brian
Liddell Hart: A study of his military thought
Cassell, 1977
The Somme, pp. 16–18

Liddell Hart, B.H.
Memoirs
Vol. 1

Cassell, 1965
The author was an officer with the 9th King's Own Yorkshire Light Infantry and was wounded on the Somme in July 1916. He later became a stimulating writer on military matters, and some of his ideas were taken up by the German Army and used in the Second World War.

Mearsheimer, J.J.
Liddell Hart and the Weight of History
Brasseys, 1989
The Somme, pp. 23–4, 53–4 & 65
This is a critical work on Liddell Hart's reputation. There is a footnote on p. 68 about Somme casualties.

Linzell, Harold Harding (ed. by M.A. Argyle)
Fallen on the Somme: The war diary of 2nd Lt. Harold Harding Linzell M.C. 7th Border Regiment
Barnstaple, Devon: M.A. Argyle, 1981
This short booklet is based on the diary of a 2/Lt. who was killed on 3 July 1916, and subsequently covers the war prior to the start of the battle. It is illustrated and has maps.

Liveing, Edward G.D.
Attack on the Somme: An infantry subaltern's impressions of July 1st 1916
Stevenage: Spa Books/Tom Donovan, 1986
This book was first published under the title *Battle* by Macmillan, New York, in 1918. Liveing was an officer with the 1/12th London (Rangers) 16th Bde., (56th Div.) and was wounded on the first day of the Battle of the Somme in the diversionary attack against the village of Gommecourt. The book is short, but very detailed and includes a roll of honour. The

introduction is by John Masefield. The artwork for the original cover design was offered for sale in 1991.

Lloyd, R.A.
Trooper in Tins
Hurst & Blackett, 1938
The Somme, pp. 228–45
Lloyd served with the 1st Life Guards and was a regular soldier both before and during the war.

Lloyd George, David
War Memoirs of David Lloyd George
Odhams Press, 1938, 2 vols
The Somme, pp. 3l9, 321–3, 326, 337, 358, 389–92, 472, 514, 521, 536–7, 546, 585-6, 652, 825, 834, 868, 1205, 1247, 1259, & 2036
One of the great controversies of the First World War was the conflict between Lloyd George, the British Prime Minister from December 1916, and the General Staff. It was said that Lloyd George wanted to sack Sir Douglas Haig, but did not have the courage to do so, nor did he have a suitable replacement. It was also known that Haig was on friendly terms with King George V, whose support he could rely upon. Liddell Hart, who was also anti-Haig, helped Lloyd George with the writing and research for his memoirs, which made the former premier a lot of money from newspaper and book rights. The book was very critical of Haig, who did not live long enough to read the attacks on his reputation.

Goodspeed, D.J.
Ludendorff: soldier: dictator: revolutionary
Hart-Davis, 1966
The Somme, pp. 166–8
This book is about Erich von Ludendorff

who became joint commander-in-chief of all German forces.

Severn, Mark (pseud.)
The Gambadier
Benn, 1930
The Somme, pp. 91–109
This illustrated book gives a good account of training and of work with a heavy and siege artillery in France. The author's real name was Frank Lushington, who was Edward Thomas' field officer at the time of his death in April 1917.

Lytton, Neville
The Press and the General Staff
Collins, 1921
The Somme, pp. 40, 41, 42, 45–6, 64, 65 & 81–4
This book includes some beautiful drawings by the author, who was at one point in the 11th Royal Sussex Regt., the same unit as his friend, Edmund Blunden.

Macmillan, Harold
The Winds of Change
Macmillan, 1966
The Somme, p. 85
The author, who was later to become the British Prime Minister, was a 2/Lt. with the King's Royal Rifle Corps before being transferred to the 4th Grenadier Guards as a temporary officer. He was severely wounded at Ginchy.

Malins, Geoffrey
How I filmed the war
Herbert Jenkins, 1920
The Somme, pp. 176–8 & 183–223
Malins was one of a small band of official photographers who was heavily involved in the filming of the Battle of the Somme.

His memoirs tend to exaggerate his experiences and achievements but nevertheless he must have been brave to be on the battlefield unarmed except for a camera. This book was reissued by the Imperial War Museum with a new introduction by Dr N.P. Hiley in 1993.

Martin, B.
Poor Bloody Infantry: A subaltern on the Western Front 1916–1917
Murray, 1987
The Somme, pp. 82–96
The author was commissioned with the North Staffordshire Regt.

Masefield, John (ed. by Peter Vansittart)
John Masefield's Letters from the Front 1915–17
Constable, 1984
Masefield visited the Somme battlefield from October 1916 to spring 1917, in order to carry out research for a book, later published as *The Old Front Line*. There are many references to the Somme battle in these letters.

Matthews, E.C.
A Subaltern in the Field
Heath Cranston, 1920
The Somme, pp. 31–7
The author was an officer in the Duke of Cornwall's Light Infantry.

Baynes, John
Far from a Donkey: The life of General Sir Ivor Maxse KCB, CVO, DSO
Brasseys, 1995
The Somme, pp. 135–65
Maxse was in command of the 18th Div. This illustrated book includes three Somme maps.

Maxwell, Charlotte (ed.)
Frank Maxwell Brigadier General VC, CSI, DSO: A memoir and some letters
Murray, 1921
The Somme, pp. 147–59
Maxwell was CO of the 12th Middlesex. (Falls ★)

Maxwell, W.B.
Time Gathered: An autobiography
Hutchinson, 1937
The Somme, pp. 234–42
The author was a transport officer on the Somme.

Maze, Paul
A Frenchman in Khaki
Heinemann, 1934
The Somme, pp. 134–96
Sgt. Maze was an artist, interpreter and liaison officer who served throughout the war. He won the DCM, MM and Bar, and the Croix de Guerre, and was encouraged to take up painting by Winston Churchill.

Mellersh, H.E.L.
Schoolboy into War
Kimber, 1978
The Somme, pp. 84–94
Mellersh was a temporary Special Reserve Officer commissioned as a second lieutenant in the 2nd East Lancashire Regt.

Woodall, D.
The Mobbs' Own: The 7th Battalion the Northamptonshire Regiment 1914–1918
Spratton: Roger Frisby (in association with David Woodall), 1995
The Somme, pp. 87–91
Edgar Mobbs (1882–1918) was a well-known rugby player who played for Northamptonshire Saints as well as for

England. Mobbs's battalion was in 73rd Bde./24th Div. He won the DSO in 1917. There is still an annual Mobbs Memorial match played in Northampton between East Midlands and the Barbarians in his memory. A battalion roll of honour is included in the book.

Elton, O.
C.E. Montague – A Memoir
Chatto & Windus, 1929
The Somme, pp. 132–47
Montague became an intelligence officer in July 1916 and one of his duties was to show famous visitors around the battlefield. Montague was also a novelist and critic.

Montague, C.E.
Disenchantment
Chatto & Windus, 1922
The author was an intelligence officer on the Somme. References to the Somme are scattered throughout the text. (Falls ★★)

Hamilton, Nigel
Monty: The making of a General 1887–1942
Hamish Hamilton, 1981
The Somme, pp. 107–18
Montgomery was a regimental officer with the Royal Warwickshire Regt. and on the staff of 104th Bde. The book includes letters home and observations on the actions.

Moran, Lord
Anatomy of Courage
Constable, 1945
The Somme, pp. 125–41
The author was medical officer with the 1st Royal Fusiliers and later became Winston Churchill's physician.

Mottram, Ralph Hale
Journey to the Western Front Twenty Years After
Bell, 1936
The Somme, pp. 217–54

Bond, Brian & Robbins, Simon (eds.)
Staff Officer: The diaries of Walter Guinness (First Lord Moyne) 1914–1918
Leo Cooper, 1987
The Somme, pp. 101–30
Moyne served with the 11th Cheshires at the time of the Somme battle.

Murray, J.
Call to Arms
Kimber, 1980
The Somme, pp. 100–34
The author was a rating with the Hood Bn. (RND). The book is illustrated.

Nash, Capt. T.A.M.
The Diary of an Unprofessional Soldier
Chippenham: Picton Publishing, 1991
The Somme, pp. 44–97
This book is edited by the author's son and has some portraits of officers. Nash was in 'B' Coy of the 16th Bn. Manchester Regt.

Neame, P.
Playing with Strife: The autobiography of a soldier
Harrap, 1947
The Somme, pp. 60–5
The author served with the Royal Engineers and won the VC in 1914. In the Somme campaign he was brigade major with 168th Bde. (56th London Div.) in time for the diversionary attack against the village of Gommecourt. He later took part in battles for the possession of Ginchy, Combles and Les Boeufs. The book is illustrated.

Harris, Ruth Elwin
Billie: The Nevill Letters 1914–1916
Julia MacRae, 1991
The book consists of letters written by Capt. Wilfred Nevill, attached to the 8th East Surrey Regt. Nevill died on 1 July 1916 and was the instigator of the famous 'football incident' at Carnoy on that day, where his body is now buried. The Somme material deals therefore with the preliminary period before the battle began and reveals a man typical of his class and time, but he lacks the depth of feeling of many of those who wrote later in the war.

O'Connor, V.C. Scott
The Scene of War
William Blackwood, 1917
The Somme, pp. 183–205. The French Army, pp. 215–36

O.E.
Iron Times with the Guards
John Murray, 1918
The Somme, pp. 218–33, 234–41 & 265–6

Glover, Michael (ed. & intro.)
The Fateful Battle Line: The Great War journals and sketches of Captain Henry Ogle, MC
Leo Cooper, 1993
The Somme, pp. 91–148
Capt. Ogle was a member of the 7th Royal Warwickshire Regt. TF, 48th (South Midland) Div., and served with them for two years. He was later commissioned in the King's Own. This outstanding book is illustrated with Ogle's own drawings, which have the freshness of having been done on the spot. Michael Glover also supplied the book with linking historical notes.

Orpen, Sir William
An Onlooker in France
Williams & Norgate, 1921
The Somme, pp. 36–49
Orpen was an official artist and the book includes many of his paintings and an account of how the battlefield looked in 1917. (Falls ★)

Parker, Ernest
Into Battle 1914–1918: A seventeen-year-old joins Kitchener's army
Longman, 1964
The Somme, pp. 44–61
This is a book of reminiscences written between the wars and describes the life of a volunteer in Kitchener's Army. Parker (1896–1978) was later commissioned and won the MC. After the war he spent most of his working life with Longman publishers and produced several books, including a number of anthologies. This book was reissued in 1994 by Leo Cooper, with an introduction by John Terraine.

Jean de Pierrefeu
French Headquarters 1915–1918
Bles, n.d.
The Somme, pp. 72–84
The author had close contacts with some of the famous French commanders, as he was involved in drawing up communiqués.

Plowman, Max
Bridge into Future: Letters of Max Plowman
Andrew Dakers, 1944
The Somme, pp. 43–58
Plowman was a pacifist who joined the Royal Army Medical Corps before serving as an officer with a line regiment, the 10th West Yorkshire Bn. on the Western Front. Later he resigned his commission and

returned to being a pacifist. He devoted the rest of his life to pacifism and became a leading member of the Peace Pledge Union.

Mark VII (pseud.)
A Subaltern on the Somme in 1916
Dent, 1927
This book is written in diary form and covers the author's experiences from mid-July 1916 to January 1917. The author was Max Plowman of the 10th West Yorkshire Regt. (see above entry). (Falls ★)

Pollard, Capt. A.O., VC, MC, DCM
Fire-eater: The memoirs of a VC
Hutchinson, 1932
The Somme, pp. 148–58
Pollard enlisted in the Honourable Artillery Company in 1914, and won the MC and DCM as well as the VC. From his book he appears to have been a very arrogant man.

Prideaux, Capt. G.A., MC
Soldier's Diary of the Great War 1914–1917
Chiswick Press, 1918 (private publication)
The Somme, pp. 136–72
The author was a lieutenant with the 1st Somerset Light Infantry (11th Bde./4th Div.) and his diary was written in field service notebooks. It was unaltered for publication. Prideaux was killed by shell fire on 19 January 1917.

Bird, Antony (ed.)
Unversed in Arms – A subaltern on the Western Front: The First World War diary of P.D. Ravenscroft MC
Swindon: Crowood, 1990
The Somme, pp. 43–54 & 57–64
Ravenscroft was a 2/Lt. with the King's

Royal Rifle Corps and served with the battalion from November 1915 until the end of the war.

Maurice, Maj.-Gen. Sir Frederick (ed.)
The Life of General Lord Rawlinson of Trent GCB: Journals and letters
Cassell, 1928
The Somme, pp. 153–82
The book describes the role of being commander of the Fourth Army and of the battle planning and progress. The book is illustrated and includes maps. (Falls★)

Read, I.L.
Of Those We Loved
Bishop Auckland: Pentland Press, 1994
The Somme, pp. 129–65 & 178–211
The author was a sergeant with the 17th Leicestershire Regt. and in 1917 he was commissioned in the 35th Royal Sussex Regt. This superb memoir includes drawings and maps.

Repington, Charles à Court
The First World War 1914–1918
Vol. 1: *Personal experiences of Lt. Col. C. à Court Repington*
Constable, 1921
The Somme, pp. 252–73
Repington, a born intriguer, was an officer before the war, but was forced to resign after an affair and took up journalism. (Falls★)

Richards, Frank
Old Soldiers Never Die
Faber, 1933
The Somme, pp. 180–203
Richards had been a reservist before the war before rejoining when war broke out.

He wrote this book with the help of Robert Graves who 'licked it into shape'. They were both former members of the 2nd Royal Welch Fusiliers and were in the same company during the Battle of Loos in September 1915. During the war Richards won the DCM and MM. The book has become a classic written by a ranker, comparing well with John Lucy's *There's a Devil in the Drum,* and was reissued in 1995 by P. Austen of Sleaford, Lincolnshire, but unfortunately without any introductory material.

Bonham-Carter, Victor
Soldier True: The life and times of Field-Marshal Sir William Robertson, 1860–1933
Muller, 1963
The Somme, pp. 142–61
Robertson was CIGS from December 1915 to February 1918.

Robertson, FM Sir William
Soldiers and Statesmen, 1914–1918
Vol. 1
Cassell, 1926
The Somme, pp. 269–73. (Falls★)

Woodward, David R. (ed.)
The Military Correspondence of Field-Marshal Sir William Robertson Chief Imperial General Staff December 1915 – February 1918
Bodley Head (for the Army Records Society), 1989
The Somme, pp. 59–127

Rogerson, Sidney
Twelve Days
Arthur Barker, 1930
Rogerson was an officer in the 2nd West Yorkshire Regt. (23rd Bde./8th Div.) and a colleague of Gen. Jack. His book covers a period of twelve days in November 1916 at the end of the Battle of the Somme. In 1988 the book was reissued by Gliddon Books without its original illustrations, but with an introduction by John Terraine. The work was given the subtitle of 'The Somme November 1916'.

Rorie, David, DSO, TD, MD, DPH
A Medico's Luck in the War: Being reminiscences of R.A.M.C work with the 51st Highland Division
Aberdeen: Milne & Hutchinson, 1929
The Somme, pp. 82–116
Rorie was formerly Officer Commanding 1/2nd Highland Field Ambulance and later ADM 51st (Highland) Division. This illustrated book has two maps.

Russell, A.
The Machine Gunner
Kineton, Warwickshire: Roundwood Press
The Somme, pp. 34–64
The author joined the East Yorkshire Regt. before transferring to the Machine Gun Corps and serving with the 98th Machine Gun Company. This illustrated book has a map of the Somme.

Russell, A.
With the Machine Gun Corps from Grantham to Cologne
Dranes, 1923
The Somme, pp. 24–53

Sansom, A.J.
Letters from France: June 1915 – July 1917
Melrose, 1921
The Somme, pp. 213–22
At the time of the Somme the author was serving as a captain in the Royal Sussex Regt.

Scarisbrick, Diana M. (ed.)
My Dear Ralph: Letters of a family at war 1914–1918
Minerva Press, 1994
This illustrated paperback is a collection of letters written during the First World War from a large family. Two brothers were killed on the Somme and a third was very seriously wounded. They belonged to the Glosters, 20th Middlesex Bn. and the 10th Lincolnshire Regt.

Schuman, Arthur
Memoirs of Arthur Schuman Ex Corporal of the London Rifle Brigade
n.p., n.d.
The Somme, pp. 4–7
This is a very small illustrated booklet with a map.

Seely, Maj.-Gen. Rt Hon. J.E.B., PC, CB, CMG, DSO
Adventure
William Heinemann, 1930
The Somme, pp. 249–54
The author was a Cavalry Brigade Commander at the beginning of the Somme battle.

Shephard, Ernest (ed. by Bruce Rossor & Richard Holmes)
A Sergeant-Major's War: From Hill 60 to the Somme
Marlborough: Crowood (in association with Anthony Bird), 1987
The Somme, pp. 103–15
Shephard was with the 1st Dorset Regt. from 1909, becoming a sergeant-major from February 1916 until commissioned in November 1916 with the 5th Dorsets (33rd Bde./11th Div.). He was killed on 11 January 1917 while leading an attack close

to Beaumont-Hamel. His diary was discovered in a chocolate box sixty years after his death.

Siepmann, Harry
Echo of the Guns: Recollections of an artillery officer 1914–18
Hale, 1987
The Somme, pp. 34, 39 & 40
The author was half-German and half-English.

Simpson, Andy
Hot Blood and Cold Steel
Donovan, 1993
The Somme, pp. 172–98
This book provides a thematic description of life in the trenches, drawn from diaries, memoirs and letters, etc. It is illustrated and has three maps, including two of the Somme.

Slack, Cecil Moorhouse
Grandfather's Adventures in the Great War 1914–1918
Ilfracombe: Arthur H. Stockwell, 1977
The Somme, pp. 84–5, 101 & 117–18
Slack was an officer with the 4th East Yorkshire Regt. and won the MC. This book was made up from letters he wrote home, as well as those he received. The book has an introduction by John Terraine.

Smith, Aubrey
Four Years on the Western Front by a Rifleman: Being the experiences of a ranker in the London Rifle Brigade, 4th, 3rd and 56th Divisions
Odhams Press, 1922
The Somme, pp. 140–89
This is a superbly detailed account from a ranker in the transport (horse) section of 1/5th London Regt., a unit that was part

of 56th (London) Division. It is based on letters that Smith wrote home, but the book reads as a continuous narrative. He was awarded the MM and a Bar for work that he carried out in the very last days of the war. The book was reissued by the London Stamp Exchange in 1987.

Spears, E.L.
Liaison, 1914
Heinemann, 1930
The author was an eyewitness observer of different infantry tactics employed by the French and British during the 1 July 1916 attack.

Spicer, Lancelot Dykes
Letters from France 1915–1918
Robert York, 1979
The Somme, pp. 54–69
Spicer was a temporary officer with the 9th King's Own Yorkshire Light Infantry and these letters were addressed to his mother.

Starr, L.
The War Story of Dillwyn Parrish Starr: By his father Louis Starr
New York & London: Putnam, 1917 (private publication)
The Somme, pp. 71–96
This mainly consists of letters written home. D.P. Starr was an officer with the 2nd Coldstream Guards.

Stokes, Louis (ed. by R.A. Barlow & H.V. Brown)
Dear and Noble Boy: The life and letters of Louis Stokes 1897–1916
Leo Cooper, 1995
The Somme, pp. 167–73
In 1915, fresh from Rugby College, Stokes

joined the Royal Marine Light Infantry with a commission. He was killed at Beaumont-Hamel on 13 November 1916 during the Battle of the Ancre while serving with the 2nd Bn. RMLI (63rd Royal Naval Div.). These letters are representative of the schoolboy generation that was killed in the war. The book is illustrated.

Stone, Christopher (ed. by G.D. Sheffield & G.I.S. Inglis)
From Vimy Ridge to the Rhine: The Great War letters of Christopher Stone DSO MC
Marlborough: Crowood, 1989
The Somme, pp. 58, 59–76, 100 & 132
Stone was an officer with the 22nd Royal Fusiliers (99th Bde./2nd Div). He was a brother-in-law of novelist Compton Mackenzie.

Stormont Gibbs, Capt. (ed. by Richard Devonald-Lewis)
From the Somme to the Armistice: The memoirs of Captain Stormont Gibbs, MC
Kimber, 1986
The Somme, pp. 23–87
Stormont Gibbs was an officer with the 4th Suffolks (98th Bde./33rd Div.) and Pioneer Bn./58th Div. This book was reissued in paperback in 1992 by Gliddon Books with a foreword by the Rt. Hon. Enoch Powell, MBE, MP.

Tait, J.
'Hull to the Somme': The Diary of Pte. James Tait 10th Bn. East Yorkshire Regt.
Hull: Male Lambert School, 1982
The Somme, pp. 31–42
This educational booklet deals with a period of time before the battle of the Somme began.

Tawney, R.H.
The Attack and Other Papers
Allen & Unwin, 1953
In this book of essays the title essay, first published in the *Westminster Gazette*, describes the author's experiences in the Somme battle. Tawney was a member of the 22nd Manchester Regt. and was wounded near Fricourt on 1 July 1916. He became a well-known writer and academic historian after the war.

Powell, Anne
Bim: A tribute to the honourable Edward Wyndham Tennant Lieutenant, 4th Battalion Grenadier Guards 1897–1916
Salisbury: Anne Powell, 1990
The Somme, pp. 45–57
Tennant was a Guards officer and a poet, who was killed on 22 September 1916 and was buried at Guillemont Road Cemetery, close to his great friend Raymond Asquith. The illustrated booklet includes a portrait of the exceedingly good-looking Tennant by John Singer Sargent.

Tennant, N.
Saturday Night Soldiers' War 1913–1918
Waddesdon: Kylin Press, 1983
The Somme, pp. 37–69
These pages cover the period from January to December 1916 based on a diary of the 11th West Riding Howitzer Bty. Included are many superb drawings by the author, who at the time of writing (1995) is still alive.

Thomas, A.
A Life Apart
Gollancz, 1968
The Somme, pp. 47–57
The author was a member of the 6th Royal West Kents (37th Bde./12th Div.).

Trafford, P. (comp.)
Love and War: A London terrier's tale of 1915–16
Bristol: Peter Trafford, 1992
The Somme, pp. 151–6
Trafford, a member of the 20th Bn., the County of London Regt., was wounded at High Wood on 15 September 1916 and sent home. His book is a collection of letters between Edward Henry Trafford and his wife Rose. It is illustrated and has a Somme map.

Tucker, John F.
Johnny Get your Gun: A personal narrative of the Somme, Ypres and Arras
Kimber, 1978
The Somme, pp. 50–90
The author was a member of the London Regt. (13th Kensingtons).

Underhill, Edward Samuel (ed. by Sidney Milledge)
A Year on the Western Front
[Privately published], 1924
The Somme, pp. 75–95 & 106–18
Underhill was a captain with the 8th Loyal North Lancashire Regt. and was killed at Stuff Redoubt on 12 October 1916. The book includes maps and some illustrations. It was reissued in 1988 by the London Stamp Exchange.

Warren, Frank
Honour Satisfied: A Dorset Rifleman at War 1916–1918
Swindon: Crowood, 1990
The Somme, pp. 7–48, including winter 1916
Warren was a second lieutenant with the 20th King's Royal Rifle Corps. The diary was edited by Antony Bird.

Collins, R.J.
Lord Wavell 1883–1941
A military biography
Hodder & Stoughton, 1948
The Somme, pp. 76–7
This is the biography of FM Earl Archibald Wavell, a senior commander in the Second World War.

Wedderburn-Maxwell, J.
Young Contemptible
Croydon: A Tek-Art, 1982
The Somme, pp. 17–20
The author of this booklet served in the Royal Artillery.

White, Lt. Arthur Preston (ed. by Michael Hammerson)
No Easy Hopes or Lies
London Stamp Exchange, 1991
The Somme, pp. 163–221
White was an officer in the Northamptonshire Regt.

White, Revd John, MD
With The Cameronians (Scottish Rifles) in France: Leaves from a chaplain's diary
Glasgow: John Smith, 1917
The Somme, pp. 88–96

Whitehouse, Arch
Epics and Legends of the First World War
Muller, 1964
The Somme, pp. 93–106

de Wiart, Adrian Carton
Happy Odyssey
The memoirs of Lieutenant-General Sir Adrian Carton de Wiart VC, KBE, CB, CMG and DSO
Cape, 1950
The Somme, pp. 56–63

The author was Commanding Officer of the 8th Gloucesters at the beginning of the Somme battle in July 1916.

Williamson, Benedict
'Happy Days'
(47th and 48th Divs)
The Somme, pp. 81–92
Williamson was a brave and well-loved padre with the nickname of 'Happy Days'. This book gives a good account of working in a Casualty Clearing Station and has an introduction by Lt.-Col. R.C. Feilding, DSO.

Williamson, Henry
Days of Wonder
[n.p.], Henry Williamson Society, 1987
The Somme, pp. 5–14
This book consists of a collection of newspaper articles written by Williamson, illustrated by R.A. Williamson and D. Roberts and edited by John Gregory. Two articles on the Somme are included: 'The Somme Just 50 Years After', which were first published in the *Daily Express*, 29 and 30 June 1966.

Williamson, Henry
The Wet Flanders Plain
Beaumont Press, 1928; Faber & Faber, 1929; Gliddon Books, 1987
The Somme, pp. 138–48
Williamson served with the 1/5th London Rifle Bde. and as a temporary officer in the 10th Bedfordshire Regt., later serving with the Machine Gun Corps. In 1927 he returned to the former Western Front on his honeymoon. This book was first published at the price of 25 shillings (£1.25) in a hand press edition of 400 copies by Cyril Beaumont (1891–1976). Beaumont ran his

press in the cellar of his Charing Cross Road bookshop and published books, including fine editions of works of Richard Aldington, Edmund Blunden, John Drinkwater & D.H. Lawrence.

Faber & Faber issued the book in a trade edition and a third version was later issued by Gliddon Books, which included an introduction by the author's son, Richard Williamson, and some photographs from the Williamson archive. It also had some additional material written by Henry Williamson under the title of 'Return to Hell', which first appeared in the *Evening Standard* in 1964.

Collier, Basil
Brasshat
A biography of Field-Marshal Sir Henry Wilson
Secker & Warburg, 1961
The Somme, pp. 235–42

Wilson, R.A.
A Two Year's Interlude
France 1916–1918
Palmerston North, New Zealand: Pelling & Mundy, 1963
The Somme, pp. 12–23
Wilson served with the 116 Siege Bty. RGA.

LITERATURE

ENGLISH LITERATURE AND CRITICISM

Bergonzie, B.
Heroes' Twilight: A study of the literature of the Great War
Macmillan, 1980, 2nd edn

Buitenhuis, P.
The Great War of Words: Literature as propaganda 1914–18 and after
Batsford, 1989
The Somme, pp. xiv, 35, 93–9, 115–16, 127, 132, 149–50, 154, 157–8 & 172
The book is illustrated.

Chapman, Guy (ed.)
Vain Glory: A miscellany of the Great War 1914–1918 written by those who fought in it on each side and all fronts
Cassell, 1937
The Somme, pp. 313–60
Chapman served with the Royal Fusiliers in France.

Eksteins, M.
Rites of Spring: The Great War and the birth of the modern age
Bantam Press, 1989
The Somme, pp. 101, 114, 126, 139, 144–8, 154, 165, 172, 181, 191, 204, 211, 218, 220 & 229

Fussell, P.
The Great War and Modern Memory
Oxford University Press, 1975

This study of the literature of the First World War by an American academic caused a great stir when it was first published. However, it has been dismissed as not only being occasionally inaccurate, but also far too dependent on Robert Graves's autobiography *Goodbye to All That*. The Somme is referred to throughout the text.

Fussell, Paul (ed.)
Sassoon's Long Journey: An illustrated selection from Siegfried Sassoon's memoirs of George Sherston
Faber & Faber, 1983
The Somme, pp. 79–96

Glover, Jon & Silkin, Jon
The Penguin Book of First World War Prose
Viking, 1989
The Somme, pp. 164–5 (Edmund Blunden), pp. 293–301 (Frederic Manning), & pp. 313–15 (Robert Graves)
This is a collection of prose extracts from the work of more than eighty European and American writers. It is similar to Guy Chapman's *Vain Glory*.

Gurney, I. (ed. by R.K.R. Thornton)
Collected Letters
Mid Northumberland Art Group/Carcanet Press, 1991
The Somme, pp. xvi, 160–1 & 162
This is a book of letters by the poet and composer Ivor Gurney.

Hague, Rene (ed.)
Dai Great-Coat: A self-portrait of David Jones in his letters
Faber & Faber, 1980
This book of letters compiled after Jones's death refers throughout to the fight for Mametz Wood.

Hart-Davis, Rupert (ed.)
Siegfried Sassoon Diaries 1915–1918
Faber & Faber, 1983
The Somme, pp. 82–99
Sassoon was posted to France in November 1915 as an officer with the lst Royal Welch Fusiliers and was with them for the build-up to the Somme battle. He won the MC in June and took part in the July fighting, especially that close to Mametz Wood. He was invalided home with trench fever in early August 1916. It is very interesting to compare this diary with Sassoon's fictionalized version of the same events in *The Complete Memoirs of George Sherston*. As a coincidence, Sassoon went to Marlborough, the same school attended by Charles Sorley (1895–1915).

Hughes, Colin
David Jones: The man who was on the field. In Parenthesis as straight reporting
Manchester: David Jones Society, 1979
This 32-page booklet discusses Jones's long poem and compares it with Jones's actual war experiences with the Royal Welch Fusiliers. It is illustrated and includes some very good maps.

Hynes, Samuel
A War Imagined: The First World War and English culture
Bodley Head, 1990
The Somme, pp. 99, 100, 101–5, 106, 110, 111, 113, 115 & 116. The Battle of the Somme film, pp. 122–6
The book is illustrated.

Klein, Holger (ed.)
The First World War in Fiction: A collection of critical essays
Macmillan, 1976
This contains essays on three writers who served on the Somme: Diane DeBell, 'Strategies of Survival', Robert Graves, 'Goodbye to All That', & David Jones, 'In Parenthesis'. It also contains C.N. Smith's 'The Very Plain Song of It' and Frederic Manning's *Her Privates We*.

Newman, Bernard & Evans, I.O. (eds.)
Anthology of Armageddon
Archer: 1935
This anthology of work by 150 writers was reissued in 1989. It is similar to Guy Chapman's *Vain Glory*, in that most of the material was written by participants in the war. The Somme material is by different authors, including work by Richard Blake, F. Britten Austin, Winston Churchill, Robert Graves, Wyn Griffith, Frederic Manning (Pte. 19022), Frank Richards, Sidney Rogerson, Siegfried Sassoon, Frederick Sleath, H.M. Tomlinson and Henry Williamson. Both editors served in the war; Newman was with the 21st Divisional Artillery Group on the Somme and elsewhere.

Parker, Peter
The Old Lie: The Great War and the public school ethos
Constable, 1987
The Somme, pp. 25, 134, 161, 169, 177, 186, 196, 202, 204, 207, 212, 213–14, 225–6, 232, 237, 241 & 261

This book traces the history of an ideal, and examines its workings in the lives of those caught up in the First World War. It is a lively and enthusiastic work.

Powell, Anne
A Deep Cry: A literary pilgrimage to the battlefields and cemeteries of First World War British soldier-poets killed in Northern France and Flanders
Aberporth: Palladour, 1993
This labour of love is set out chronologically, using a selection of work by the poets along with a short biography. The 'Somme Poets' (pp. 69 & 173) are: Raymond Asquith (3rd Grenadier Guards), Robert Becke (12th East Yorkshire Regt.), William Berridge (6th Somerset Light Infantry Bn.), Leslie Coulson (2nd London Regt. (Royal Fusiliers)), Richard Dennys (10th Loyal North Lancashire Regt.), Henry Field (6th Royal Warwickshire Regt.), William Noel Hodgson (9th Devonshire Regt.), Donald Johnson (2nd Manchester Regt.), Thomas Kettle (9th Royal Dublin Fusiliers Bn.), Alfred Ratcliffe (10th West Yorkshire Regt.), Alexander Robertson (12th York & Lancaster Regt.), Hugh Smith (2nd Argyll & Sutherland Bn.), John William Streets (12th York & Lancaster Regt.), Edward Wyndham Tennant (4th Grenadier Guards), Nicholas Todd (1/12 London Regt. (The Rangers)), Gilbert Waterhouse (2nd Essex Regt.), Bernard Charles de Boismaison White (20th Northumberland Fusiliers Bn.), Cyril Winterbotham (1/5th Gloucestershire Regt.).

Quinn, Patrick J.
Great War and the Missing Muse: The early writings of Robert Graves and Siegfried Sassoon
Susquehanna University Press, 1994
This book is not directly about the Somme,

but does cover in depth two of its most famous writers. It offers a useful survey of the lives of the two men up to 1929 and attempts to analyse how they worked the war into their postwar writings.

Roucoux, M. (ed.)
English Literature of the Great War Revisited: Proceedings of the symposium on the British literature of the First World War
Amiens: University of Picardy, 1986
The Somme, pp. 125–58
These papers were given at a conference at the University of Picardy in 1986. Eleven papers were presented, including one by Alan Bishop, 'The Battle of the Somme and Vera Brittain' and Lyn Macdonald, 'The Somme Front'.

Rutherford, A.
The Literature of War: Studies in heroic virtue
Macmillan, 1989, 2nd edn
This literary criticism covers war in general. In the chapter on the Western Front the author discusses Frederic Manning's *Her Privates We*.

Seymour-Smith, Martin
Robert Graves: His life and work
Hutchinson, 1982
The Somme, pp. 45–54
This biography was written when Graves was still alive. It was followed by the publication of selections of letters written by Graves and a further set of biographies by Richard Percival Graves. It was revised and reissued in 1995 by Bloomsbury.

Sinnett, Lt.-Col. R.J.M.
The History and Literature of the Royal Welch Fusiliers
The Regiment, March 1986

It is remarkable that so many writers who served in the First World War belonged to the Royal Welch Fusiliers. The list includes Bernard Adams, Capt. J.C. Dunn, Robert Graves, Ll. Wyn Griffith, David Jones, Frank Richards, Siegfried Sassoon & V. de Sola Pinto. This book contains a checklist of their writings on pp. 1–9.

FICTION

It must be stressed that in the following list of First World War fiction I am only seeking to include those novels which refer at least in part to the Battle of the Somme in 1916. Thus, readers will not find listed here such famous books as Richard Aldington's *Death of a Hero* or Erich Maria Remarque's *All Quiet on the Western Front*.

Nevertheless, the following selection of novels about the First World War does represent, at least in part, what has been published in the English language in the last eighty years. I am also interested in the writers as participants in the conflict, which also applies to the poets within their own section.

The great boom in publications about the war occurred in the period 1928–32 and publishers could barely keep up with the demand. Of course, this was not just for novels, but for all aspects of the subject. It seems that many writers needed to wait for a decade after the armistice before allowing themselves to commit pen to paper.

After this peak, books on the war were still published until the eve of a second world war. However, there was an increasing backlash against war books and what they were deemed to stand for, as people turned against the very real possibility of another war. Unfortunately, this led to a soft line when it came to dealing with the new European dictators, who capitalized on this weakness. It is hardly surprising that the publication of books on what became the First World War almost dried up altogether for twenty years or more.

In 1964, to coincide with the fiftieth anniversary of the war's beginning, the BBC produced a major series of programmes that covered all aspects of the war and included interviews with survivors as well as old newsreel film. Television increasingly influenced public taste and interest in the war. Over the years since the mid-1960s there have been adaptations of R.F. Delderfield's books, Vera Brittain's *Testament of Youth*, Catherine Cookson's *The Cinder Path*, and the very popular *Upstairs Downstairs*. None of these is particularly concerned with the Somme, but the battle and the war were increasingly used by writers and television producers as a backdrop to a story. In other words, the First World War had become box-office material.

Novels by survivors of the First World War dried up completely with the exception of the works of Henry Williamson and Stuart Cloete's *How Young They Died*, and seemingly women began to fill the gap in the market. Thus, in the 1970s and '80s books, which were often 'blockbusters' or family sagas, increasingly appeared on the bookshop and library shelves, almost all written by women. As with television adaptations, the war became part of the background in these novels. Many of them covered a period of sixty or seventy years in the life of one or two families, and described how they became interrelated. For example, Claire Rayner's series of books called *The Poppy Chronicles* covers the period from the end of the Boer War to the 1960s, telling the history of two families. It is hardly surprising that this new batch of novels had heroines who were either nurses or ambulance drivers, for this was as close as women could get to the Western Front.

The novelist Pat Barker is very much an exception to this rule in that she has written three remarkable novels about the war in which her main protagonists were fighting men and not women who became nurses.

The last book to be mentioned is Sebastian Faulks's *Birdsong*. It augurs well for First World War fiction that the last few years have produced the brilliant novels of truth, genuine sympathy and understanding that Barker and Faulks have written.

For this section I have consulted the excellent bibliography compiled by two American academics:

Hager, Philip E. & Taylor, Desmond
The Novels of World War 1: An annotated bibliography
New York: Garland Publishing, 1981
This book tracks down 884 titles in English published before 1980. I have, of course, discarded the 51 published before 1916.

Other useful books to which to refer include:

Cecil, Hugh
The Flower of Battle: British fiction writers of the First World War
Secker & Warburg, 1995
This book is illustrated with portraits of some of the novelists discussed.

Onions, John
English Fiction and Drama of the Great War, 1918–1939
Macmillan, 1990

Parfitt, G.
Fiction of the First World War
Faber & Faber, 1988
The novels are listed here in order of their date of publication.

Dawson, Capt. A.J.
Somme Battle Stories
Hodder & Stoughton (for *The Bystander*), 1916
This is a collection of stories told to Capt. Dawson by men wounded during the Battle of the Somme after they returned to England.

Cable, Boyd (pseud.)
Grapes of Wrath
Smith & Elder, 1917
The author's real name was Ernest Adrian Ewart. The Somme battle provides the background for this book.

Parry, D.H.
With Haig on the Somme
Cassell, 1917
This book tells the story of Archibald Webb of the '2/12 Battalion Royal Reedshires' and contains four colour plates by Archibald Webb.

Herbert, A.P.
Secret Battle
Methuen, 1919
The author served in Gallipoli with the Hawke Bn. of the 63rd (Royal Navy Division) and was mentioned in despatches. He later served in France and

became Adjutant. The main character in this book is a young officer called Harry Penrose, who also serves in Gallipoli and France. He is based on Sub-Lt. Edwin Dyett of the Nelson Bn. of the same division, who was one of three officers to be shot by the British in the First World War. Before the war Herbert had studied law at Oxford, but in the guise of a character called Benson in the novel he curiously makes no real attempt to save Penrose's life. It is obvious that Penrose was 'set up' because he was continuously given all the 'dirty jobs' by his colonel, until his nerve and spirit were broken and he was sentenced to death for cowardice.

The book covers the Somme battle from p. 130, including the November battle of the Ancre. The author does not give much away in the way of historical facts, but his own division was on the Somme from October 1916 until February 1917, which is when the main action of the novel takes place. At the time of publication the book made a considerable impact and Sub-Lt. Dyett's father campaigned to clear his son's name. The book has an introduction by Winston Churchill. It was reissued in paperback in 1982 by OUP, with an introduction by John Terraine. (Falls ★★)

Frankau, Gilbert
Peter Jackson — Cigar Merchant: A romance of married life
Hutchinson, 1920
The Somme, pp. 290–318
The author was with the 9th East Surrey Regt. (72nd Bde./24th Div.) and then with the RFA 107th Bde. and later propaganda officer in Italy. Frankau considered this novel as 'some slight of a history of the 24th Division' from its formation until September

1916, and it is regarded as one of the best descriptions of an artilleryman's war. It tells the stories of three families, with Peter Jackson being transferred from the '10th Chalkshire Battalion' to the 'Fourth Southdown Bde. R.F.A'. He serves on the Headquarters Staff as adjutant before rejoining the artillery with 'Beer Battery'. Jackson is not only wounded but is sent home with pneumonia and nearly dies. (Falls ★★)

Ewart, Wilfrid
Way of Revelation
Putnam, 1921
The Somme, pp. 339–50
The Somme chapter is brief. The author was a captain in the Scots Guards and mentions the names of Ginchy, Morval and Les Boeufs, so readers can assume that he is describing the involvement of the Guards in September 1916. Ewart wrote that his division of 6,000 men was reduced to 2,000 because of the very high casualties. Reinforcements began to arrive in October and the division spent the early part of the winter in the area of Beaumont-Hamel.

Basically, the novel tells the story of Sir Adrian Knoyle and his great friend Eric Sinclair, and of what happened to them on the Home Front and in France and Flanders over a period of five years from 1914 to 1919. The book was highly praised by Henry Williamson when it was published.

Born in 1892, Ewart joined up in 1914 as a private in the Guards along with Stephen Graham who became a good friend of his. Ewart's going overseas was delayed as his eyesight was poor and he had had health problems as a child. He finally went to France in 1915, but was invalided out of the Army in 1917 as a result of a riding accident. In March 1922 he had a nervous breakdown which prevented him from writing, and he died tragically in Mexico City in 1922 when he was accidentally shot dead by a stray bullet from the gun of a new year reveller. (Falls ★)

Hueffer, Ford Madox (1873–1939)
Hueffer wrote four novels under the collective name of *Parades End*, otherwise known as 'The Tietjens Novels'. They dealt with the war and the Home Front, but there is only one reference to the Battle of the Somme. Published between 1924 and 1932 by Gerald Duckworth, they therefore missed the peak of public interest in war literature which was from 1928 to 1930.

The books follow the lives of Capt. Christopher Tietjens, his estranged wife Sylvia and his lover Valentine. In *No More Parades*, the second book in the series, the action mainly takes place in France over a period of three days, where the hero is in charge of a draft battalion being trained to go into the line for the first time. Hueffer was gazetted to the 3rd Welch Regt. in August 1915 at the age of forty-one and joined the 9th Bn. at Bécourt Wood on 16 July 1916. After various positions he ended the war as a captain attached to the 23rd King's Liverpool Regt. He subsequently changed his name to Ford.

Gristwood, A.D.
The Somme
Cape, 1927
The Somme, pp. 15–115
This book has an introduction by H.G. Wells and includes a story called 'The Coward'. The chief character of the book is a Pte. Everitt of the '10th Loamshires', and the main action covers the fighting to take Hazy Trench towards Les Boeufs in September 1916, when he is wounded. I would hazard a guess that the author might have been a member of the 169th Bde of 56th Div. as he mentions Fusiliers and Rifles. This could mean the Queen's Westminster Rifles or Queen Victoria's Rifles.

Sassoon, Siegfried
Memoirs of a Fox-hunting Man
Faber & Faber, 1928
This is the first book of a trilogy *The Complete Memoirs of George Sherston*, in which Sassoon deals with the experiences of George Sherston's life before 1916. Prior to the war Sherston's main preoccupation had been with fox-hunting and when war began he joined the yeomanry, but in order to get to the front more quickly he managed to become transferred to the 'The Royal Flintshire Fusiliers'. Sherston joined the 1st Bn. and reached the Somme region in January 1916, where he was appointed Transport Officer. The book covers the same period as Sassoon's diary and stops in April 1916. (Falls. ★★)

Hodson, James Lansdale
Grey Dawn – Red Night
Victor Gollancz, 1929
The Somme, pp. 246–76
This is the story of John Hardcastle, a reporter in times of peace and war. The book covers the hero's life from boyhood to death by a German shell in France, when he was on his way home to receive a commission. Mametz Valley is identified in July 1916 as is the battle for High Wood. Hardcastle is a member of a Lewis Gun

Team. 'Grey Dawn' stands for his childhood and 'Red Night' for the war itself. The book is dedicated to the 3rd Public Schools Bn. (20th Royal Fusiliers) with whom Hodson served before being commissioned in the Royal Naval Division. The author reissued this book himself in 1954.

Manning, Frederic
The Middle Parts of Fortune
This was first published in 1929 by Peter Davies in a two-volume edition of 520 copies by Private 19022. It was then reissued in 1930 in an expurgated edition as *Her Privates We*. The author's identity was not included on the title page until the 1943 edition.

The book has had introductions by Edmund Blunden and Prof. Michael Howard and was very highly thought of by T.E. Lawrence and Henry Williamson, among others. Lawrence recognized Manning's style in the first anonymous issue of the book.

Manning, who was an Australian, was a minor 'man of letters' before the war. During the war he served as a private with the 7th King's Shropshire Light Infantry. He described this book as a 'record of experience on the Somme and Ancre fronts, with an interval behind the lines, during the latter half of 1916'. The story evokes the life and experiences of the ordinary soldier 'trapped in the inarticulate misery of the Somme'. The book was dramatized for BBC Radio in the 1980s and is, quite simply, a masterpiece. (Falls. ★★★)

Blaker, Richard
Medal Without Bar
Hodder & Stoughton, 1930
This is an extremely vivid and detailed account of the life of an artilleryman in the war and could only have been written by someone who served on the Western Front. The 1916 Somme section runs from p. 178 for around two hundred pages. Place names are mentioned, including a very realistic section on the fight for Thiepval in September. (Falls ★)

Sassoon, Siegfried
Memoirs of an Infantry Officer
Faber & Faber, 1930
The Somme, pp. 73–117
This is the second volume of a trilogy called *The Complete Memoirs of George Sherston*. It opens in April 1916 on the Somme front when active preparations were being made for the Big Push which was due to take place at the end of June. Sherston (Sassoon) was a Transport Officer with the Royal Flintshire Fusiliers (1st Royal Welch Fusiliers) and at one point meets up with David Cromlech (Robert Graves) of the 1st Bn. During this period Sherston (Sassoon) wins a MC and after the battle of the Somme opens he is sent home with trench fever, via Amiens, Rouen and Southampton.

Tomlinson, H.
All Our Yesterdays
Heinemann, 1930
The Somme, pp. 469–96 & 636
Tomlinson served at British GHQ and was also a journalist. He was editor of *The Nation* from 1917 to 1925. (Falls ★★)

Williamson, Henry
The Patriot's Progress: Being the vicissitudes of Pte. John Bullock related by Henry Williamson and drawn by William Kermode
Bles, 1930
The Somme, pp. 92–119
The book tells the story of John Bullock

from his enlistment to the armistice. During a battle where almost everyone is killed, Bullock has a leg amputated and is returned to England. The linocuts, by William Kermode, MC, are very stark. The book was reissued by Macdonald and Jane's in 1968 with additional material by the author.

Tilsley W.V.
Other Ranks
Cobden-Sanderson, 1931
The Somme, pp. 1–30
The author served with the 4th Loyal North Lancashire Regt. (164 Bde./55th Div.).

Seton, Graham (pseud.)
Life Without End
Thornton Butterworth, 1932
Graham Seton Hutchison wrote books under his two names and was founder of the National Workers' Movement in 1933, which three years later became the National Socialist Workers' Party. He was a Scotsman who won the MC and DSO as well as being mentioned in despatches four times.

Unfortunately, he became obsessed with the Nazi regime in Germany and in 1936 claimed that 'all the forces of World Jewry and Freemasonry have been enlisted to form an armed ring round Germany'. Along with Blunden and Williamson he believed that the spirit of the Christmas Truce of 1914 could be used to prevent a second world war. In this belief all three writers were incredibly naïve. Robert Graves, in a private letter, described Hutchison as 'being cracked after High Wood'.

In *Life Without End* the author tells the story of Hugh Richmond, a young vicar who was wounded at Bazentin in 1916 and returns to France in 1923 in order to restore his lost faith.

Brophy, John
World Went Mad
Cape, 1934
The Somme, pp. 111–17
This book is dedicated to Vera Brittain and Winifred Holtby.

Fitzgerald, F. Scott
Tender is the Night
New York: Scribners, 1934
The reference to the war is very short and in the 1986 Penguin edition it is found in pp. 66–8. It is partly taken up by a trip to Newfoundland Park at Beaumont-Hamel, in which there is a discussion as to why the war happened when it did and how it could never be repeated. This is because the Allies and the Central Powers would never again be so finely balanced with 'a whole Empire walking very slowly, dying in front and pushing forward behind. And another Empire walking very slowly backwards a few inches a day, leaving the dead like a million bloody rugs.'

Forester, C.S.
The General
Michael Joseph, 1936
The Somme, pp. 230–42
This satirical novel tells the story of General Sir Hubert Curzon from his early military career in the Boer War to his serious wounding in the March Retreat of 1918, when he was sent home. His career in the Army is meteoric; having commanded a cavalry unit he goes on to command '91st Division' and is then promoted to '42nd Corps' commander. In the book there is a vivid account of the chaos of the Battle of Loos (1915).

Hodson, James Lansdale
Return to the Wood – A Novel
Victor Gollancz, 1955
This is the story of William Hargreaves, a solicitor. The book is mainly concerned with a return to the Somme battlefield by a group of friends who were survivors of the war.

Williamson, Henry
The Golden Virgin
Macdonald, 1957
This is the sixth book of the author's fifteen-volume series *A Chronicle of Ancient Sunlight*. Like the other volumes, it follows the career of Phillip Maddison (Henry Williamson) who is a 2/Lt. with the '8th (Service) The Prince Regent's Own Regiment' and attached to the Machine Gun Corps. The title of the book is taken from the statue of the virgin and baby which was suspended from the top of the spire of the Albert Basilique for much of the war. Part two of the novel is called 'The Somme' and covers the build-up to the battle. Maddison is involved in the initial attack to the north of the Albert–Bapaume road, close to the village of La Boisselle, and is wounded in the attack (pp. 205–314). The book is dedicated to the novelist Richard Aldington who wrote *Death of a Hero* and other books.

Harris, John
Covenant with Death
Hutchinson, 1961
This book was written as a documentary novel based upon a story of a Volunteer City Battalion from its inception to its destruction on 1 July 1916 in trying to capture the fortified village of Serre. The story is told by a ranker and is based on the experiences of the Sheffield City Battalion (12th Bn. York & Lancaster Regt.). The author's father served on the Somme.

Clevely, Hugh
Garland of Valour
Cassell, 1963
John Kelly is a young American who travels to Europe and survives the sinking of the *Lusitania*. He joins the Grenadier Guards and is wounded on the Somme (pp. 103–17).

Cloete, S.
How Young They Died
Collins, 1969
Jim Hilton, the hero of this book, begins the war as a young subaltern in 1916 with the '10th King's Own Wiltshire Light Infantry' which is part of '16th Division'. The unit's original number is the 51st Regiment of Foot, which was the actual number of the King's Own Yorkshire Light Infantry in which Cloete himself served. The author switches the second Ypres battle to 1916, but keeps to the basic facts for the Somme battle including the first use of tanks in September 1916. During the war Hilton is seriously wounded twice and his convalescence is punctuated with a stream of sexual adventures. He ends the novel as a newly married major.

As far as I can establish, Cloete (pronounced Clooty) was the last survivor of the First World War to write a novel about his experience, which included the Battle of the Somme. This is why the description of the war scenes is so authentic. In his autobiography *A Victorian Son* Cloete says that all a person who

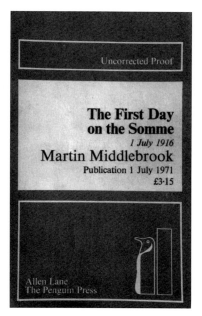

30. *The cover of the first edition of John Buchan's* Battle of the Somme. *The book carries no publication date*

31. *The cover of the uncorrected proof version of Martin Middlebrook's* The First Day on the Somme

32. *Nearly 300 diaries and notebooks were used by C.E.W. Bean for his* Official History

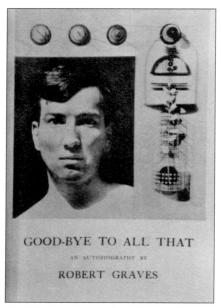

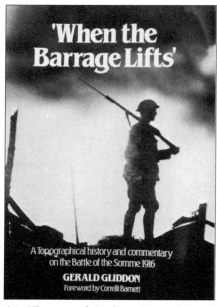

33. *The cover of the first edition of Robert Graves' autobiography*

34. *The cover of the first edition of Gerald Gliddon's* When the Barrage Lifts

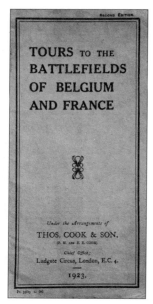

35. *Lynton Lamb's cover design for The World's Classics edition of Blunden's* Undertones of War

36. *Edmund Blunden's grave, Long Melford, Suffolk (Claire Blunden)*

37. *The cover of a Cook's tour to the Western Front battlefields, 1923*

38. Memorial to the 36th (Ulster) Division at Thiepval (Mike Scott)

39. The Memorial to the 38th (Welsh) Division facing the Hammerhead at Mametz Wood (Peter Batchelor)

40. British tank, Mk 1 male, at Thiepval, 26 September 1916

My subject is War, and the pity of War. The Poetry is in the pity

RICHARD
  ALDINGTON
LAURENCE
  BINYON
EDMUND
  BLUNDEN
RUPERT
  BROOKE
WILFRID
  GIBSON
ROBERT
  GRAVES
JULIAN
  GRENFELL
IVOR
  GURNEY
DAVID
  JONES
ROBERT
  NICHOLS
WILFRED
  OWEN
HERBERT
  READ
ISAAC
  ROSENBERG
SIEGFRIED
  SASSOON
CHARLES
  SORLEY
EDWARD
  THOMAS

1914 + 1918

41. *Poets' Corner, Westminster Abbey. The memorial to the First World War poets (Dean & Chapter, Westminster Abbey)*

42. The scene of desolation at Delville Wood, 1916, the worst part of the Somme battlefield

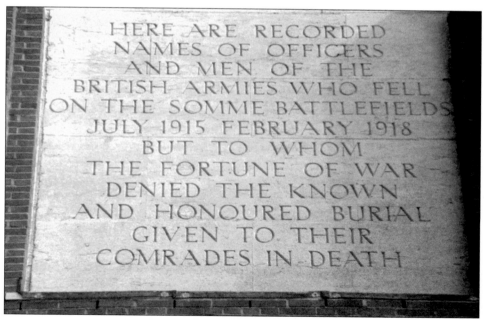

HERE ARE RECORDED
NAMES OF OFFICERS
AND MEN OF THE
BRITISH ARMIES WHO FELL
ON THE SOMME BATTLEFIELDS
JULY 1915 FEBRUARY 1918
BUT TO WHOM
THE FORTUNE OF WAR
DENIED THE KNOWN
AND HONOURED BURIAL
GIVEN TO THEIR
COMRADES IN DEATH

43. The Memorial to the Missing, Thiepval (Peter Batchelor)

44. *Aerial view of the South African memorial and museum at Delville Wood (Lambert Smith)*

45. *Memorial from the Devonshire Cemetery/Mansell Copse Cemetery (Mike Scott)*

46. *The New Zealand Memorial at Longueval (Mike Scott)*

47. *Memorial to the 16th Irish Division at Guillemont (Peter Batchelor)*

48. *Cairn Memorial to the Glasgow Highlanders at High Wood (Ian Alexander)*

49. *Querrieu Military Cemetery, dedicated on 19 March 1918*

50. *The original wooden cross erected to the memory of the 47th (London) Division, High Wood*

51. *The Australian Memorial, the site of the windmill at Pozières (Mike Scott)*

52. *The Canadian Memorial at Courcelette (Mike Scott)*

experienced the war can do when writing a novel about it, is to write about his or her own experience. He admits that the above book is basically the story of his own life in the war, and that he increased the love interest to make the story more widely appealing.

Price, Anthony
Other Paths to Glory
Victor Gollancz, 1974
In a brilliant mystery story the author uses the former Somme battlefield as a backdrop. It is very well researched.

Rock, Philip
The Passing Bells
Hodder & Stoughton, 1979
The Somme, pp. 381–403
The fictional unit that the hero belongs to is the '2nd Royal Windsor Fusiliers'.

Harrison, Sarah
The Flowers of the Field
Macdonald, 1980
The Somme, pp. 527–43
This book tells the stories of three very different women and how their lives were affected by the war.

Masters, John
Heart of War
Michael Joseph, 1980
The Somme, pp. 146–82
This is the second of a trilogy called *Loss of Eden*, written by a former regular soldier. The book covers the lives of the Rowland family and those people bound up with them. The Somme battle is seen through the eyes of a subaltern in the 'Weald Light Infantry' and of an officer in the Royal Flying Corps.

Hennessey, Max (pseud.)
Blunted Lance
Hamish Hamilton, 1983
The Somme, pp. 211–21
Written under John Harris's other name, this book tells the story of the '19th Lancers' and in particular of FM Colby Goff. Harris's father witnessed a mounted cavalry charge on the Somme in 1916, which presumably gave his son the background information. Harris also wrote the excellent *Covenant with Death*.

Hill, Reginald
No Man's Land
Collins, 1985
The Somme, pp. 21–47
For years a myth has persisted that a group of deserters drawn from both sides of the conflict existed on the waste land of the old Somme battlefield. I have never found any documentary proof that this was in fact so, but the author used this particular theme in this work of fiction. The war is seen from the Allied and German points of view.

Goddard, Robert
In Pale Battalions
Bantam Press, 1988
This can be described as a mystery novel and its title is taken from a poem by Charles Sorley. The story opens with a prologue at the Thiepval Memorial to the Missing of the Somme (pp. 11–17) and ends at the Tyne Cot Cemetery in Belgium in an epilogue. The story is told in flashback. The book is dedicated to the memory of Frederick John Goddard, 1st Hampshires 1885–1915.

Hamilton, Julia
The Idle Hill of Summer
Collins, 1988
This novel is dedicated to the Master of Belhaven, the author's brother, and is also in memory of Ralph Gerard Belhaven 1883–1918, an earlier Master of Belhaven who died in the First World War. (See *The War Diary of the Master of Belhaven 1914–1918*.)

Hughesdon, Beverley
Song of Songs
Century, 1988
The Somme, pp. 199–207 & 220
This is a blockbuster of a novel. The heroine is serving as a nurse at the time of the Somme.

Crane, Teresa
Tomorrow, Jerusalem
Collins, 1989
This is another blockbuster of a novel and in the section on the Somme the battle is seen through the eyes of a nurse. Actual Somme place names are mentioned in the book between pages 475 and 493, including that of Gommecourt to the north of the Somme battlefield, on the left flank of the British Army.

Saunders, Jean
The Bannister Girls
Allen, 1990
The Somme, pp. 210–20
The heroine drives an ambulance.

Barker, Pat
Regeneration
Viking, 1991
This book was the first of a trilogy which was completed for publication in September 1995 and mainly concerns the life of Siegfried Sassoon and his relationship with his Royal Army Medical Corps psychiatrist, Dr W.H.R. Rivers. The action takes place between July and November 1917, a year after the Battle of the Somme, but deals with the consequences of that conflict. Thus, the battle and the war, combined with Sassoon's own experiences, provide the background to the novel. The book uses fact and fiction which is interwoven throughout the trilogy and is a triumph for its author. She went on to win the Booker Prize for fiction in November 1995 with the final book called *The Ghost Road*. Barker was formerly a teacher of history and politics who was born in 1943.

Roberts, Ann Victoria
Liam's Story
Chatto & Windus, 1991
The author says in a foreword that this book is based on an actual diary written by a young Australian soldier in 1916. She even includes an uncaptioned photograph of him in the frontispiece.

Faulks, Sebastian
Birdsong
Hutchinson, 1993
The Somme, pp. 168–92
The author was inspired to write this first-rate novel when on a tour of the Western Front that was designed as a promotion for one of Lyn Macdonald's books. The action of the book begins in 1910 in Amiens, takes in the First World War and ends in 1979. The hero of the book, Stephen Wraysford, 'goes through a number of traumatic experiences, from the clandestine love affair that tears apart the family with

whom he lives, to the unprecedented experience of the war itself'. The Somme battle scenes are extremely authentic and Faulks is possibly the only English language non-combatant novelist to succeed in describing what could surely only have been described by one who was there. It is a brilliant novel.

BRITISH POETS AND POETRY

In Catherine Reilly's excellent bibliography *English Poetry of the First World War* she lists no fewer than 2,225 poets from the British Isles who responded to the war in verse, 532 of them being women.

It is hardly surprising that a fair number of these poets took part in the Battle of the Somme, some even lost their lives during the campaign. The most famous British poets who fought in the battle were Edmund Blunden, Robert Graves and Siegfried Sassoon. One of the reasons they are famous is, of course, that they survived to tell the tale and were able to write highly thought-of memoirs as well as verse. They have all become cultural heroes. There can only be speculation as to what the soldier poets who were killed on the battlefield would have produced in the way of poetry in later years.

Poets who wrote about the Somme:

This is a selection of poems written as a response to the Battle of the Somme, which were therefore written in the main between June and December 1916. However, this does not mean to say that they were all published during this period. A separate section lists some other poets

who we know took part in the battle, although they may not have been in a position to respond to it in verse. The poets are listed alphabetically.

Blunden, Edmund (1896–1974)
A member of the Royal Sussex Regt. and author of the classic memoir *Undertones of War*, which has a poetry section at the back.
'At Senlis Once'
'Trench Nomenclature'
'The Ancre at Hamel: afterwards'
'1916 seen from 1921'

Coulson, Leslie (1889–1916)
A sergeant with the 12th London Regt. (The Rangers), killed on 7 October 1916 near Les Boeufs and buried at Grove Town Cemetery. He had been transferred from the 2nd London Regiment (Royal Fusiliers).
'Who Made the Law?'
'From the Somme'

Graves, Robert (1895–1986)
An officer with the Royal Welch Fusiliers, author of a best-selling autobiography *Goodbye to All That*. Graves was one of sixteen First World War poets commemorated in Poets' Corner in Westminster Abbey in 1985 and was the only one then still alive.

In 1988 the poet's son William Graves edited a volume called *Poems About War*, which contains 54 of Graves's war poems, but is far from complete. In his own lifetime Graves wished to suppress most of this early poetical work.
From *Goliath and David*:
'The Bough of Nonsense'
'Goliath and David' (dedicated to David

Thomas 1st Bn. RWF, killed at Fricourt in March 1916)
'The Last Post'
'A Dead Boche'
'Escape' (inspired by an experience that resulted in Graves being left for dead at a disued dressing-station in Mametz Wood. It ends on a note of passionate affirmation for life.)
'Not Dead'
From *Fairies and Fusiliers*:
'Two Fusiliers'
'Familiar Letter to Siegfried Sassoon'
'A Child's Nightmare'
From other sources:
'Died of Wounds'
'The Leveller'
'Bazentin, 1916'

Gurney, Ivor (1890–1937)
Served as a private in the 2/5th Gloucestershire Bn. He had a mental health problem even before the war but, despite this and his subsequent tragic life, he was able to produce poetry, songs and settings of other poets' work, as well as a series of letters that have been critically acclaimed. He prepared two books of his own verse for publication: *Severn & Somme* and *War's Embers*. They were reissued by Carcanet Press in a single volume in 1987 on the 50th anniversary of the poet's death and were edited with very helpful and explanatory notes by R.K.R. Thornton.
From *Severn & Somme*:
'Ballad of the Three Spectres'

Herbert, Alan (1890–1971)
A member of the Royal Naval Division. He had a successful career in law and as a writer of musical comedies.
'Beaucourt Revisited'

Hodgson, William Noel, MC (1893–1916)
A competent officer in the Devonshire Regt. who was killed on the first day of the Battle of the Somme (at Mansell Copse) and was buried in the Devonshire Cemetery overlooking the village of Mametz. He was one of 159 men buried in their front-line trench at the end of 1 July.
'Before Action'

Johnson, Philip
Something of a mystery man; nothing appears to be known about him.
'High Wood'

Jones, David (1895–1974)
A private in 15th (1st London Welsh) Royal Welch Fusiliers. Jones was not only famous for his verse poem *In Parenthesis*, which T.S. Eliot described as a work of genius, but was also a leading water-colourist, painter and engraver.

In *In Parenthesis*, Pt. 7 is based on the attack of the 38th (Welsh) Division on Mametz Wood in July 1916. John Ball tells the story in a combination of verse and prose of his experiences with a New Army Battalion who is wounded at Mametz Wood. Jones's parents were a mixture of Welsh and cockney and he served with the Royal Welch Fusiliers until 1918 when he was wounded and invalided home. As in the cases of Blunden and others, the war loomed over him for the rest of his life. He also later suffered from neurasthenia and had a breakdown which plagued him until he died. *In Parenthesis* won for Jones the Hawthornden Prize in 1938.

Kettle, Thomas Michael (1880–1916)
A member of the Royal Dublin Fusiliers. A lawyer and politician, he was killed in an

attack on the village of Ginchy on 9 September 1916.
'To My Daughter Betty'

Kitchin, Clifford Henry Benn (1895–1967)
A lieutenant in the Royal Warwickshire Regt. He was a writer of fiction as well as verse.
'Somme Film'

Mackintosh, Ewart Alan MC (1893–1917)
An officer in the Seaforth Highlanders. He was gassed and wounded in High Wood in August 1916 and later killed in the Battle of Cambrai on 21 November 1917. He is buried at Orival Wood British Cemetery, Flesquières.
'In Memoriam'

Sassoon, Siegfried Loraine (1886–1967)
An officer with the Royal Welch Fusiliers. Arguably the most famous writer to serve on the Somme battlefield. He was a poet and a writer of a masterly but fictionalized autobiography, and after his death his diaries were published.
'Counter Attack'
'The Death-bed'
'At Carnoy'
'A Subaltern'
'The Last Meeting'
'A Letter Home'
'France'
'Before the Battle'
'Died of Wounds'
'A Night Attack'
'To His Dead Body'
'Christ and the Soldier'
'The Hero'
'The Road'
'A Ballad'

Stewart, John E.
A major in the Staffordshire Bn., killed on 26 April 1918.
'Before Action'

Streets, John William
Formerly a miner who became a sergeant with the 12th York & Lancaster Regt., he was mortally wounded in the attack against Serre on 1 July 1916. He is buried at Euston Road Cemetery, Colincamps.
'Mathew Copse (June 1916)'

Vernède, Robert Ernest
An officer attached to the 3rd Rifle Bde., who was killed on 9 April 1917 in an attack on Havrincourt Wood. His body lies in La Bucucquière Communal Cemetery.
'Before the Assault'

Other poets who took part in the Battle of the Somme:

Berridge, William Eric
Served with the Somerset Light Infantry and was killed on 20 August 1916.

Brooke, Brian
An officer in the Gordon Highlanders who was wounded on 1 July 1916 at Mametz and died three weeks later.

Brown, David Westcott (1892–1916)
An officer in the Leicestershire Regt. who was killed in the fighting at Bazentin-le-Petit on 14 July 1916.

Dartford, Richard Charles Gordon
Born in 1895, he served in the London Regt. at Loos and on the Somme, and was later a liaison officer with the Portuguese troops. He survived the war.

Dennys, Richard Molesworth (1884–1916)
An officer with the Loyal North Lancashire Regt. who was wounded on the Somme in July 1916 and subsequently died. He is buried in the St Sever Cemetery, Rouen.

Field, Henry Lionel
A lieutenant in the Royal Warwickshire Regt. who was killed on the first day of the Battle of the Somme and is buried at Serre Road Cemetery No. 2.

Heath, Roger Meyrick (1889–1916)
An officer in the Somerset Light Infantry who was killed by a shell at Delville Wood on 16 September 1916. His name is one of the missing listed on the Thiepval Memorial.

Johnson, Donald Frederic Goold (1890–1916)
An officer in the 2nd Manchester Regt. who was killed on 15 July 1916 when leading his men. He is buried at Bouzincourt Communal Cemetery.

Kennedy, Geoffrey Anketell Studdert (1883–1929)
Served as an Army padre and became known by the troops as 'Woodbine Willie' owing to his habit of handing out cigarettes to the troops.

Mann, Arthur James (1896–1917)
Served on the Somme in the Black Watch and was mortally wounded on 9 April at the Battle of Arras, dying the next day. He is buried in Aubigny Communal Cemetery Extension.

Plowman, Max (1883–1941)
An officer in the West Yorkshire Regt. who is mostly famous for his book *A Subaltern on the Somme*, he also published four volumes of verse.

Prewett, Frank (1893–1962)
Served in France from 1916 as a second lieutenant in the Royal Field Artillery. He was a friend of Siegfried Sassoon, who nicknamed him 'Toronto'.

Ratcliffe, Alfred Victor
A lieutenant with the West Yorkshire Regt. who was killed at Fricourt on 1 July 1916. His grave is at Fricourt New Military Cemetery.

Robertson, Alexander (1882–1916)
A corporal with the York & Lancaster Regt. who was killed at Serre on 1 July 1916. His name is listed among the missing on the Thiepval Memorial.

Seeger, Alan (1888–1916)
Born in New York, he served with the French Foreign Legion and was killed at Belloy-en-Santerre on 4 July when his party was enfiladed by German machine-gunners. His death caused a minor sensation in the American press at the time.

Smith, Geoffrey Bache
A lieutenant with the 19th Lancashire Fusiliers who died of wounds on 3 December 1916. He is buried at Warlincourt Halte British Cemetery, Saulty, France.

Smith, Hugh Stewart
A captain with 'D' Coy. 2nd Bn. Argyll & Sutherland Highlanders who was killed on

18 August 1916. He is buried at Caterpillar Valley Cemetery, Longueval, France.

Tennant, Edward Wyndham (1897–1916)
An officer in the Grenadier Guards who was killed in action on 22 September 1916 and is buried at Guillemont Road Cemetery.

Todd, Herbert Nicholls (1878–1916)
A rifleman with the Queen's Westminsters who was killed in action on 7 October 1916. His name is listed among the missing on the Thiepval Memorial.

Waterhouse, Gilbert
A second lieutenant with the 2nd Essex Regt. who was killed on the Somme on 1 July 1916, south of Serre. His body is buried at Serre Road Cemetery No. 2.

White, Bernard Charles de Boismaison (1886–1916)
An officer with the Northumberland Fusiliers who was killed on 1 July 1916.

Winterbotham, Cyril William (1887–1916)
An officer with the Gloucestershire Regt. who met his death at Skyline Trench, south-west of Pozières on 27 August 1916. His name is listed among the missing on the Thiepval Memorial.

DRAMA

Four plays have been written in recent years concerning the Battle of the Somme:

Chilton, Charles, Theatre Workshop and the members of the original cast
Oh! What a Lovely War
Methuen, 1965
This famous musical play was presented at the Theatre Royal, Stratford, London, under the direction of Joan Littlewood. Its major strength was its timing, in as much as it caught the mood of the young and the anti-war sentiments of the 1960s. It is a satire directed against war in general and the First World War in particular. It had an enormous influence and the film that followed it even more so. It took several years before serious study of the war and its consequences returned more to the centre ground.

Macdonald, Stephen
Not About Heroes
This play does not directly relate to the Battle of the Somme as it is based on the relationship between the two poets Siegfried Sassoon and Wilfred Owen, and the latter did not reach the Western Front until after the Battle of the Somme was over. The play was first performed at the Edinburgh Festival in 1982 and was later performed on BBC Radio 4.

McGuinness, Frank
Observe the Sons of Ulster Marching Towards the Somme
This play was first performed at the Peacock Theatre, Dublin in February 1985. It is based on the experiences of the 36th (Ulster) Division who were involved in an heroic attempt to capture the German-held village of Thiepval on 1 July 1916. The dramatist is a Catholic from Ulster who sets out to dissect the Protestant community of Northern Ireland in the play. The first day of the Battle of the Somme, like the Battle of the Boyne of 1690, has come to have a sacred place in the Loyalist Protestant mind. It was always said that the Protestants put on their orange

sashes before going over the top, but this seems to be doubtful. The play was performed on BBC Radio 3 on 4 November 1990.

Whelan, Peter
The Accrington Pals
This play was first performed at the Warehouse Theatre, London, by the Royal Shakespeare Company in April 1981. It was also broadcast on BBC Radio. The play is about the experiences of two groups: a band of recruits, and the women they leave behind. The play aims to offer a reconstruction of working-class Lancashire life.

BIBLIOGRAPHIES

Baker, Anthony
Battle Honours of the British and Commonwealth Armies
Ian Allan Ltd, 1986
This book includes a brief history of the Somme campaign (pp. 114–16) and brings together the achievements of the British and Commonwealth Armies over the past 300 years.

Beckett, Ian F.W. & Simpson, Keith
A Nation in Arms: A social study of the British Army in the First World War
Manchester University Press, 1985
The last chapter of 28 pages is called 'An Annotated Bibliography of the British Army'. It was compiled by Keith Simpson and was based on the British Army and the First World War, also the subject of a symposium that took place at the Royal Military Academy, Sandhurst in 1978.

Bond, Brian (ed.)
The First World War and British Military History
Clarendon Press/Oxford University Press, 1991
This is a collection of essays by a group of British military historians who set out to describe how the First World War has been 'written up' over the years since the war ended.

Bray, Arthur T.E.
The Battle of the Somme 1916: A bibliography
University Microfilms, 1967

This was a thesis produced for the Library Association, and was never commercially published. It was a pioneering work which I found extremely useful when researching my book *When the Barrage Lifts*. Bray made a distinct selection of those subjects which he chose to cover, which included paintings and aircraft types. However, in his selection of military units he left out the role of the artillery and the cavalry.

Cooke, O.A.
The Canadian Military Experience 1867–1983: A bibliography
Ottawa: Directorate of History Department of National Defence, 1984, 2nd edn

Enser, A.G.S.
A Subject Bibliography of the First World War: Books in English 1914–1978
Deutsch, 1979
This book was the first general bibliography of books on the First World War in English to be published for many years. Unfortunately, Mr Enser was not a sufficient expert in the subject and his listing under animals of Alan Clark's *Donkeys*, a book about the Western Front generals and the role they played in 1915, destroyed his credibility. The book was also arranged in a very confusing manner and there was much duplication of title listings. Mr Enser revised his book up to the end of 1986, but died before seeing the new edition, which was published in 1990 by Gower Publishing. I have to report that

several hundred books were left out from the subjects that he chose to cover and he often omitted second authors' names. In his section on the Battle of the Somme he has thirty-one books listed. Therefore, the First World War is still in need of a bibliography of books in English and, if published, it would run to several volumes.

European War: Subject index of the books relating to the European War, 1914–1918, acquired by the British Museum, 1914–1920
British Museum, 1922

Falls, Cyril
War Books: A critical guide
Peter Davies, 1930
In the late 1920s and early '30s the British reading public had an insatiable appetite for books on the First World War, which had then been over for ten years or more. Cyril Falls, an ex-serving officer, compiled his bibliography which he divided into seven sections, including fiction. He not only wrote a short paragraph about each book selected, but also gave them a one to four star rating. Amazingly, many of his 'best books' are still highly thought of today. Falls's wonderful book was updated by R.J. Wyatt in a reissue by Greenhill Books in 1989. The new edition is called *War Books. An annotated bibliography of books about the Great War*. The additional material runs to 37 pages.

Haythornthwaite, Philip J.
The World War One Source Book
Arms & Armour, 1992
The Somme pp. 32–3, 35, 79–80, 216, 267, 329 & 369
This book is fully illustrated.

Higham, Robin (ed.)
A Guide to the Sources of British Military History
Routledge & Kegan Paul, 1972
This book is made up of work by a dozen military historians who cover other periods of British history as well as the First World War.

James, Brig. E.A., OBE, TD
British Regiments 1914–18
Samson Books, 1978
This book gives a comprehensive listing of units which served in the First World War.

Laird, J.Y.
A Checklist of Australian Literature of the First World War
St Lucia, Queensland: Australian Literary Studies, 1985

Mayer, S.L. & Koenig, W.J.
The Two World Wars: A guide to the manuscript collections in the United Kingdom
Bowker, 1976
This book is a selection of material held in local government offices and at regimental museums. It needs considerable updating to be of much use to research students.

Regiments and Corps of the British Empire and Commonwealth 1758–1993: A critical bibliography of their published histories
Roger Perkins, 1994
This mammoth work was produced with the aid of a worldwide network. Even the rarest of items are included.

Saunders, A.J.
'Collecting Books on the Battle of the Somme'
Book Collector, March 1989

Saunders, A.J.
'Memoirs of the First World War'
Book Collector, December 1990

Scott, Peter T. (comp.)
The Great War 1914–1918
Bertram Rota, 1988
This is Catalogue No. 245 and lists 1627 items. The introduction is by Keith Simpson, formerly of the Royal Military Academy, Sandhurst. Catalogues 252 (1989) and 260 (1991) were also devoted to the Great War.

Spaight, Robin
British Army Divisions in the Great War 1914–1918
Private publication, 1978

This is an A4 booklet that lists the histories of the divisions that served in the war.

White, Arthur S.
A Bibliography of Regimental Histories of the British Army
The Society for Army Historical Research, in conjunction with the Army Museums Ogilby Trust, 1965
Arthur White was for many years the librarian of the War Office Library and the book has a foreword by FM Sir Gerald W.R. Templer. This is a scholarly work which was never intended for the general reader. It was updated in a rather slipshod way in 1988 and in 1992, and is available from its present publishers, the Naval & Military Press.

PUBLISHED WRITTEN SOURCES:
JOURNAL ARTICLES

Anon
'Rivers of Mud and Craters: An illustrated record of October and early November'
The Sphere, 18 November 1916, pp. 118–19

Anon
'Report on the Defence of Gommecourt on July 1st, 1916'
Royal United Service Institution, Vol. LXII (1917), pp. 536–56
This is the war diary of the 55th Reserve Infantry Regt. (2nd Guard Reserve Div.) for the period 24 June to 1 July 1916.

Anon
'The British Attack on Beaumont-Hamel, July 1st, 1916'
Journal of the RUSI, Vol. 66, No. 211, February 1921, pp. 137–41
Extracted from the 'History of the Württemberg Reserve Infantry Regiment', No. 119.

Anon
'Delville Wood: 14th–19th of July, 1916'
Army Quarterly, October 1925, pp. 58–69
Part V of the series 'The Other Side of the Hill', with map.

Anon
'The German Defence of Bernafay and Trones Woods: 2nd–14th of July, 1916'
Part 1
Army Quarterly, October 1926, pp. 19–32
From 'The Other Side of the Hill' series of articles, with map.

Anon
'The German Defence of Bernafay and Trones Woods: 2nd–14th of July, 1916'
Part 2
Army Quarterly, January 1927, pp. 252–60
From 'The Other Side of the Hill' series of articles, this deals with the German counter-attack on Trones Wood, 11 July 1916. With map.

Anon
'The Somme: 15th of September, 1916'
Army Quarterly, July 1933, pp. 300–8
From the 'The Other Side of the Hill' series of articles, with map.

Anon
'The Capture of Thiepval, 26th of September, 1916'
Army Quarterly, January 1934, pp. 215–24
From 'The Other Side of the Hill' series of articles, Part X. With map.

Anon
'In Front of Beaumont-Hamel: 13th of November, 1916'
Army Quarterly, April 1934, pp. 27–36
From 'The Other Side of the Hill' series of articles, Part XI. With map.

Anon
'The Battle of the Somme' July 1st, is a day
to be remembered by London Territorials
The Territorial, July 1937, pp. 15–16
This article describes in brief the role of
the 56th London Division on the first day
of the Somme battle.

Anon
'Aiguillette First Tank Attack! An eye
witness'
This article, with map, tells the story of the
entry of the tank into warfare in September
1916.
Marine Corps Gazette, 1963, pp. 32–6

Anon
'Over the Top Under Fire – "A Sunlit
picture of Hell" at the Somme'
Life Magazine, 1964, pp. 40–1
In the summer of 1964 *Life Magazine* ran a
series of articles to commemorate the
fiftieth anniversary of the start of the First
World War. The series title was 'The
Struggle that Shaped our Century
Exploded 50 Years Ago – The First World
War'. This article was one of a series on
the land battles and used photographs
reproduced from the famous Battle of the
Somme film.

Anon
'Delville Wood. S.A.'s epic stand.' The first
phase of the slaughterous Battle of the
Somme was over
The Springbok, July 1974, p. 9

Anon
'3153 Went In – And Only 770 Came Out'
The Springbok, Vol. 59, No. 7, July 1976, p. 7
The South African Brigade at Delville
Wood – a short article.

Anon
'Delville Wood.' Imperishable story of
heroism
Canadian Military Journal, Vol. LII, Winter
1985, pp. 17–21
This is a brief and illustrated story of the
battle that took place in July 1916.

Anon
'Mametz Wood and Contalmaison:
9th–10th of July, 1916'
Army Quarterly, n.d., pp. 245–59
With map.

Anon
'The Somme 1916'. A Dragon Battery
Gun Position
Gunner, n.d., pp. 134–6
This illustrated article is a short diary
account of 48th Bty. RFA, situated behind
Montauban at Glatz Redoubt, in the
period July to August 1916.

Anon
'The Somme 17th–22nd September, 1916'
Gunner, n.d., pp. 227–8
This article is taken from the diary of a
member of the RFA, 2/Lt. B.G. Mason,
which was kept at the time.

Allinson, Sidney
'War's Worst Day: on the first day of the
Somme, ordered ranks stepped out into
locking fields of fire . . . and simply kept
on stepping out as those in front went
down'
Military History, Vancouver, June 1989, pp.
27–33
This illustrated article is written in the style
of a popular tabloid by the author of *The
Bantams*, and indulges in denigration of
FM Haig.

Atwater, James D.
'Survivors of the Somme. Newfoundland veterans relive a World War 1 massacre, the hellish morning their regiment was annihilated'
Smithsonian, November 1987, pp. 196–234
This article is illustrated.

Badsey, S.D.
'Battle of the Somme; British war-propaganda'
Historical Journal of Film, Radio and Television, Vol. 3, No. 2, 1983, pp. 99–115
Dr Badsey was on the staff of the Imperial War Museum when he wrote this article, which discusses the background to the making of, and the authenticity of, the famous Battle of the Somme film.

Balck, Gen.
'The German Defence of Combles. September, 1916'
Journal of the RUSI, Vol. 70, February 1925, pp. 137–9
Extracted from an article by General Balck in Vol. 2 of *Im Felde Unbesiegt*. At the time of the Battle of the Somme General Balck commanded the 51st Reserve Division.

Bateman, H.C.
'Wounded on the Somme'
Stand To!, Winter 1986, p. 29
This short article related to a Mr H.P.H. Davies, who was a member of the 6th Bn. Royal West Kent Regt. He tells of his being wounded on 7 October 1916 when he was nineteen years of age.

Baumgartner, Richard
'Survivors. Vignettes on the German experiences on the Somme. Leipzig Salient 1–7 July, Delville Wood–Ginchy 8–13 September, Rancourt 27 September–3 October and Sailly–Saillisel 14–30 October'
Stand To!, No. 18, Winter 1986, pp. 15–20
Baumgartner translated and edited these short accounts of the German experience of the Battle of the Somme.

Baumgartner, R.A. & Sluys, Reid Van & Smith, Paul M. (comps.)
'The Somme 1 July 1916'
Der Angriff, No. 13, July 1981, pp. 4–23
This illustrated article was commissioned to commemorate the 65th anniversary of the first day on the Somme. The tragic story of 1 July 1916 is recalled by 176 British and German participants of the battle. The British accounts and narrative were compiled and written by Paul M. Smith and Reid Van Sluys, and the German accounts were compiled by R.A. Baumgartner.

Becker, A.
'From Sydney to the Somme: Australians remember the Anzacs'
Journal of the Australian War Memorial, No. 21, 1992, pp. 30–4

Belloc, H.
'The Obstacle of the Somme Valley'
Army Quarterly, Vol. 1, 1920
Belloc describes the Somme valley and its military importance as an obstacle.

Below, Gen. von
'Experience of the German 1st Army in the Somme Battle'
This is an English translation of a German document which was originally issued by the German General Staff (Intelligence) General Headquarters on 3 May 1917. Its

24 pages give full coverage to the lessons learnt by the Germans as a result of the battle. A copy of this translation can be consulted at the Imperial War Museum, ref. K.40504.

Bidwell, S.
'The Unique Experience'
Journal of the RUSI for Defence Studies, Vol. 121, No. 4, 1976, pp. 69–70
A review of John Keegan's *The Face of Battle*.

Blunden, E.
'The Somme Still Flows'
The Listener, 18 January 1979, pp. 99–100
Reprinted from a broadcast Blunden made on 10 July 1929.

Carrington, C.E.
'Kitchener's Army: The Somme and after'
Journal of the RUSI for Defence Studies, Vol. 123, No. 1, 1978, pp. 15–20
Charles Carrington, who was a member of the Royal Warwickshire Regt., was not only a survivor of the Somme battle but was one of its most frequent commentators. He was also a biographer of Rudyard Kipling. What is of special interest in this article, which was first given as a talk at the Imperial War Museum on 8 October 1977, is Carrington's view of the first day of the battle of the Somme. Carrington says that in his opinion the BBC programme first presented in 1976 along with the views of Martin Middlebrook is fundamentally flawed. Carrington writes, 'The BBC conception, that is the Middlebrook version of the battle, is that the whole army was so disillusioned and dismayed by their losses on the first day that they were never the

same men again. The heart went out of the "Pals" Battalions. Then why did they go on fighting?' Later, he writes, 'Most recent books on World War I fall into the same abyss of misunderstanding, more or less deeply.'

Cave, Col. Terry, CBE
'The Canadian Corps'
Stand To!, No. 22, Spring 1988, pp. 14–15
This article is the first part of a brief history of the Canadian Corps and concludes with a short piece on the Somme battle which the Canadians were involved in from 3 September 1916.

Cornwall, Richard
'Delville Wood – The South Africans in France (April–July 1916)'
Militaria, Vol. 7, No. 2, 1977, pp. 1–5

Croft, Maj. Revd John, MC (late the Royal Deccan Horse)
'The Somme: 14 July 1916 – A great opportunity missed?'
Army Quarterly, Vol. 116, No. 3, 1986, pp. 312–20
Croft, who was son of Brig.-Gen. W.D. Croft, tells of the chance that was missed of the British capturing High Wood when it was virtually undefended in mid-July 1916.

Dawnay, Maj.-Gen. G.P. & Headlam, Cuthbert
'The German Defence During the Battle of the Somme, July, 1916, derived from German sources of information'
Army Quarterly, January 1924, pp. 245–59
This was the first of a series of articles issued under the title of 'The Other Side of the Hill', published in the 1920s. With map.

Doitsh, Cpl. E., 1st S.A.I.
'Reminiscences of the Delville Wood Armageddon'
The Springbok, July 1938, pp. 9–10
These memoirs were abridged from *The First Springbok Prisoner in Germany*.

D.R.H.
'Diary of Delville Wood.' A South African officer's jottings during the battle
The Springbok, September 1933, pp. 4–5
This article is signed by D.R.H. It is particularly useful because the notes for it were made at the time, and cover the period 1–24 July 1916.

Dunning, Richard
'Lochnagar Crater Pilgrimage 1st July'
Stand To!, No. 5, Summer 1982, p. 4
In this short piece Dunning describes the service at the famous crater on the Somme which he did so much to preserve for posterity by purchasing it from its French owner. In the years since, it has become a significant place of pilgrimage and is especially associated with the sacrifice of the 34th Division.

Edmonds, A.H.
'An Anzac and France Veteran recalls the Somme Bloodbath'
Reveille, Vol. 30, No. 12, 1 July 1957, pp. 9, 38–41
Edmonds was a member of the Australian 2nd Div. Signal Coy. Illustrated.

Eliot, C.R.
'Veterans Go Back to the Somme'
Royal British Legion Journal, Vol. 56, No. 8, August 1976, pp. 2–3
A party of Royal British Legion veterans returned to the battlefield in 1976. Fifteen illustrations are included.

Emmett, R.G.
'The Taking of Thiepval – A personal account'
Stand To!, No. 6, Winter 1982, pp. 12–15
The author was a member of the 11th (Service) Bn., Royal Fusiliers. With illustrations and map.

Fidler, T., MM
'On the Somme September 1916'
Firm and Forester, Vol. 5, No. 3, April 1979, pp. 217–18
This very short article was written by a member of the 2nd Sherwood Foresters.

Fitchett, W.B.
'Muddy Grave of an Army.' A New Zealand platoon commander at the Somme
Reveille, Vol. 30, No. 3, 1 October 1956, pp. 11 & 32

Ford, Lt.-Col. C.W., *p.a.c.* (late R.A.)
'The Bloody Somme'
The Fighting Forces, Vol. X, No. 2, 1933, pp. 143–50
This article was written as a response to the publication of the 'Official History of the War' and concludes that 'in no uncertain manner that the Britisher knows how to die gloriously for his country'.

Forde, Capt. Frank M., MAR
'36th (Ulster) Division at the Somme'
An Cosantoir, Vol. XXX, No. 6, June 1974, pp. 165–9
This article includes an Order of Battle for the division.

Forde, Frank
'Tyneside Irish Brigade'
Irish Sword, Vol. 16, No. 63, 1985, pp. 117–22

This tells the story of this brigade, which was part of the 34th Div. and was decimated in the struggle to capture La Boisselle on 1 July 1916.

French, D.
'"Official But Not History?" Sir James Edmonds and the Official History of the Great War'
Royal United Services Institute Journal, Vol. 131, No. 1, 1986, pp. 58–63

Gaffen, Fred
'Canada on the Somme 70th Anniversary'
Stand To!, No. 18, Winter 1986, p. 32
This one-page article contains one illustration.

Gill, B.J.
'Sapper on the Somme'
Stand To!, No. 2, Autumn 1981, p. 12
This one-page article gives information on how the Royal Engineers coped with the problem of providing water during the Somme battle.

Gompertz, Capt. A.V.
'The Battle of the Somme'
Journal of the United Service Institution of India, Vol. XLVI, No. 209, October 1917, pp. 350–76
This article was first given as a lecture at the Officer Cadet Unit, Lower Topa, and later at Murree. It was published less than a year after the Somme battle was finished, and it is hardly surprising that it takes an optimistic approach to the campaign.

Green, H.
'Kitchener's Army'
Army Quarterly, July 1966, pp. 89–96

Hall, William
'The Lone Terrier (3500 Cpl. 1st/4th Bn. King's Shropshire Light Infantry)'
The Cadre (King's Shropshire & Herefordshire Light Infantry), 1969
Includes an illustration.

H.C.B.C.
'The Battle of the Somme, 1916'
The Stafford Knot, n.d., pp. 20–1
This article is the first of two signed by H.C.B.C. and tells of the involvement of the 1st South Staffs in the capture of Mametz on 1 July 1916. A map is included.

H.C.B.C.
'The Battle of the Somme, Delville Wood 1916'
The Stafford Knot, n.d., pp. 14–16
This article is signed by H.C.B.C.

Hose, Anthony
'Heroes of Delville Wood Return'
The Springbok, Vol. 59, No. 10, October 1976, p. 12
This article deals with the battle briefly and commemorates the return of twelve South African veterans to the wood.

Hudson, R.
'Gommecourt'
Queen's Westminsters and Civil Service Rifles Retired Members Association Newsletter, October 1975, pp. 148–9
This relates the experiences of Rifleman Ron Hudson (13 Platoon) of the 1st Bn. Queen's Westminsters.

Hyde, V.M.C.
'Twenty Years After – The "Blood Bath" ground is still red. We visit "Lousy", Bernafay and "Devil's" Woods, and find skyscraper of Picardy'

Ypres Times, October 1936, pp. 168–72
Illustrated.

Ludlow, Brig.-Gen. W.R.
'A Visit to the Somme Battlefield. Story of the gallantry of the Warwicks. How the officers and men attacked the enemy'
[n.p.], 1 July 1918
This is a short description of the experiences of the 8th Bn. the Royal Warwickshire Regt. at the Battle of Beaumont-Hamel on 1 July 1916. It is compiled from accounts of the survivors and of a visit to the field of battle on 12 March 1918.

May, R.K.
'July 1, 1916'. The First Day of the Somme
The Lion and the Dragon, Vol. 6, No. 9, Spring 1976, pp. 46–7
This is a short article on the role played by the 1st Bn. The King's Own on 1 July 1916.

Methuen, Lt.-Col. J.A.
'The Taking of the Schwaben Redoubt.' Keeping the Germans out of their own trenches
The Springbok, December 1933, pp. 19–22

Mielke, Friederich
'1916. The Crisis of World War 1'
Military Review, Vol. 67, No. 5, 1987, pp. 70–9
This article, written by a German academic, describes the year of the battles of Verdun and the Somme, and 'cautions us against letting them fade from our memories'. Illustrated.

Moreman, T.R.
'The Dawn Assault: Friday 14 July 1916'
Journal of the Society for Army Historical Research, Vol. 71, No. 287, pp. 180–224

Morrell, Col. D.W.
'17th Battalion. The Sherwood Foresters on the Somme'
Firm and Forester, Vol. 4, No. 4, October 1977, pp. 31–6
This article, published when the writer was eighty-five, gives a brief account of the experiences of the battalion on the Somme, with particular reference to the second battle of Beaumont-Hamel which took place on 3 September 1916.

Officer, D.
'Re-presenting War: the Somme Heritage Centre'
History Ireland, Spring 1995, pp. 38–42
Illustrated. This article is a critique of the new Somme Centre north of Belfast.

O'Flaherty, J.F.
'Albert (Beaumont-Hamel) 1916'
The Caribou, Vol. 2, No. 1, September 1978, pp. 55–66
This article discusses the history of the Royal Newfoundland Regt.'s role on 1 July 1916 and includes battle honours. Three photographs taken in 1925 are included and one of them is of the log cabin in Beaumont-Hamel Park, which was taken down many years ago.

O'Flaherty, J.F.
'Guedecourt 1916'
The Caribou, Vol. 3, No. 1, December 1979, pp. 39–47
This covers the role of the Royal Newfoundland Regt., with map and illustration.

Parsons, Dr W.D., MD, FRCP (C)
'The Newfoundland Regiment'
Stand To!, No. 22, Spring 1988, pp. 16–17
Analysis of those wounded on 1 July 1916.

Pigg, Lt.-Col. C.H., OBE, MC
'Mametz, la Boisselle and High Wood, 1916'
Firm, Vol. 16, No. 4, January 1950, pp. 200–4
This deals with the experiences of Capt. Pigg as related in diary extracts while serving with the 2nd Worcesters.

Richards, Maj. P.
Royal Signals. 'The first day on the Somme' – A communications battle?
Journal of the Royal Signals Institute, Vol. 16, No. 6, Winter 1984, pp. 268–76

Roy, R.H.
'The Battle for Courcelette, September 1916: A soldier's view'
Journal of Canadian Studies, Vol. 16, Fall & Winter 1981, pp. 56–67
This article is based on a journal written up from a diary and kept by Pte. Donald Fraser, a Scot who served in the Canadian Infantry. A book of the journal which was published later is one of the most vivid accounts of life in the trenches.

Simkins, P.
'Somme Footnote: the Battle of the Ancre and the struggle for Frankfort Trench, November 1916'
Imperial War Museum Review, No. 9, October 1994, pp. 84–101

Smart, Capt. M.C.K. (British Army of the Rhine)
'Looking Back: Picardie, Hell's Fury on Earth.' A battlefield tour presented to the Western Front Association

The Wire, November 1982, pp. 487–9
This is billed as a tour but the author's emotional involvement rather gets in the way. With one map.

Smither, R.
'A Wonderful Idea of the Fighting: The question of fakes in "The Battle of the Somme"'
Imperial War Museum Review, No. 3, 1988, pp. 4–16
This is an article on the Somme film of August 1916 by a member of the staff of the Imperial War Museum. Illustrated.

Spagnoly, A.
'Delville Wood: Somme South African Brigade 9th Scottish Division 15–20 July 1916'
Stand To!, No. 19, Spring 1987, pp. 25–7
This illustrated article briefly tells the story of the heroic stand of the South Africans at Delville Wood.

Stevenson-Jones, Capt. S.
'Thiepval'
Regimental Chronicle South Lancashire Regiment, Vol. 20, No. 2, pp. 83–7
This article was based on the experiences of the 8th South Lancashire Bn. on an attack against Thiepval on 3 July 1916. Based on notes kept in a field service message book, it was written up long after the events described, at the invitation of an editor named George.

Taylor, M.
'"Two Fusiliers": The First World War friendship of Robert Graves and Siegfried Sassoon'
Imperial War Museum Review, No. 7, 1993, pp. 4–14

Terraine, John
'The Texture of the Somme, 1916'
History To-Day, Vol. 26, 1976, pp. 559–67
In this article Terraine describes how the battle was not so much an Allied failure as the beginning of the end of the German Army, for which it marked the 'ruddy grave'. Illustrated.

Terraine, John
'The Year of the Somme'
Army Quarterly and Defence Journal, Vol. 116, No. 4, 1986, pp. 441–60
Ten years later Terraine published a greatly expanded article with the same title as the earlier one in *The Times*.

Travers, Tim
'Learning and Decision-making on the Western Front, 1915–1916: The British example'
Canadian Journal of History, Vol. 18, No. 1, 1983, pp. 87–97
This article was written by a young Canadian academic who, unlike so many writers who had gone before, produced a fresh angle on the conflict by going back to primary sources. In this article he devotes several pages to the planning for the Somme offensive.

Veitch, Colin
'Play up! Play up! and Win the War! Football, the nation and the First World War 1914–1915'
Journal of Contemporary History, n.d., pp. 363–77
This article examines the role of sport in the war and in the escapades of Capt. Wilfred Nevill in particular.

Weisemann-Remscheid, R.
'Delville Wood, Ginchy (German side)'
Stand To!, No. 18, Winter 1986, pp. 20–1

Williams, M.J.
'The Treatment of German Losses on the Somme in the British Official History: "Military Operations France and Belgium, 1916"'
Vol. 2
Royal United Services Institution Journal, February 1966, pp. 69–74
In this article Williams proves the incorrectness of the casualty figures of both sides during the Battle of the Somme. Sir James Edmonds, the official historian, not only 'cooked the figures', but also made actual mistakes in his figure work.

Youell, Capt. E.W.
'Operations at Longueval and Delville Wood, July 1916'
The Britannia (journal of the Royal Norfolk Regt.), 1937, pp. 80–7
This article gives a brief history of the fighting at Delville Wood with particular emphasis paid to the 1st Norfolks. With map.

PUBLISHED WRITTEN SOURCES: NEWSPAPERS

Many hundreds of newspaper articles and letters to the press have been published about the Battle of the Somme and each main anniversary – namely those of 1966, 1976, 1986 and 1991 – has produced another crop. New memorials have been erected: a memorial to the 38th Welsh Division was unveiled in front of Mametz Wood in July 1987 and attracted a lot of media interest, particularly in Wales.

The correspondence in *The Times* of June/July 1966 is of particular interest as most of the contributors were participants in the battle fifty years before. Contemporary references in *The Times Index* are located under War, European (Operations). The volume for July–September 1916, pp. 490–4, covers the Somme–Ancre region, allied offensive. The volume for October–December 1916, pp. 544–7, covers the Somme–Ancre front.

The following is a very small selection of articles published in the British press on the Battle of the Somme. Unfortunately it has not always been possible to quote complete references. The list is alphabetical by author.

Anon
'Our Losses Light: The offensive cheaply carried out'
Headlines, *Evening Standard*, 3 July 1916, p. 2

Anon
'1914–1918. The Battlefields Revisited. The Somme and the Meuse'
Sunday Times Magazine, 23 February 1964, pp. 22–9
In 1964 the *Sunday Times* in its new *Sunday Times Magazine* published two articles on the 50th anniversary of the outbreak of war. They did not contain much text, but visually showed what remained after the war in the form of landscape and human tragedy. As well as period photographs, the contemporary pictures taken by Robert Freson were quite outstanding.

Anon
'1914–1918. What was it like?'
Sunday Times Magazine, 22 March 1964, pp. 7–29
This is a companion article to the previous entry, with photography by Robert Freson.

Anon
'When the Barrage Lifted'
The Times, 1 July 1966, p. 15
This was a lead article which pointed out the effect that the battle had in shaping the pacifist views of the postwar generation and its effect on the soldiers and politicians who directed the Second World War.

Anon
'Somme Slaughter. Recalled after 70 Years'
East Anglian Daily Times, 2 July 1986

Anon
'The Taking of High Wood'
Weekend Guardian, 1–2 September 1990
An article about Bert Steward of the 6th London Rifles, then aged ninety-three, who 'went over' with the tanks.

Anon
'A Tale of the Tanks: Vision of fleets of mastodons before the war is over. Terrified Germans. Prisoners really angry on the subject'
Headlines, *Evening Standard*, 19 September 1916, p. 12

Arnold-Forster, Mark
'An Arrangement for Killing Soldiers'
The Guardian, 1 July 1966
This article was based on a study of the minutes of the British War Cabinet on 30 June 1916.

Beddington–Behrens, Sir Edward
'Battle of the Somme'
The Times, 1 July 1966
This letter criticized Sir John Elliott's letter of 30 June 1966. It pointed out that the tactics of the British High Command resulted in his division suffering almost 70 per cent casualties in the attack on Beaumont-Hamel.

Boston, R.
'Why Old Soldiers Never Forget'
The Guardian, 18 June 1983, p. 19
This article was written as a result of a visit to the Somme battlefield.

Brown, Claire
'Grim Days Louise Will Never Forget. From soldier to pacifist'
Bury Free Press, 4 July 1986

Browne, Sir Denis
'The Battle of the Somme'
The Times, 4 July 1966
This letter suggested that the only lesson of the battle was that each side should suffer an equal number of casualties.

Buxton, N.
'Quiet Flows the Somme'
Sunday Telegraph, 29 June 1986, p. 12

Crookston, P.
'Death of the Pals'
Sunday Times, 1988, pp. 66–72

Dunlop, Brig. Sir John K.
'The Battle of the Somme'
The Times, 4 July 1966
This letter was written by a former machine-gun officer with the 18th Div. He pointed out that his division made a breach in the enemy line on 1 July, and that their casualties of 916 on that day were not disproportionate to the division's achievements.

Elliott, Sir John
'The Battle of the Somme after 50 years'
The Times, 30 June 1966, p. 13
This letter argued that the battle must be viewed as part of the overall strategy for destroying the German Army.

Elliott, Sir John
'The Battle of the Somme'
The Times, 4 July 1966
In this second letter to the paper the writer replies to Sir Edward Beddington-Behrens' letter of 1 July 1966 and agrees that although the British High Command tactics were wrong, the strategy was right.

Gibbs, Philip
'The Germans on the Somme'
Daily Chronicle, 1917, p. 37

Hamilton, A.
'Quiet Reflections Where Once was a Monstrous Roar'
The Times, 17 June 1983, p. 24

Hamilton, A.
'The Somme Survivors Return. An apocalypse relived'
The Times, 1 July 1986

Hamilton, A.
'Last Farewell to Somme 70 Years On'
The Times, 2 July 1986
This was a report from Thiepval.

Hargrove, C.
'Protecting the Half-million Silent Witnesses to the Horrors of Two World Wars'
The Times, 11 November 1977
This newspaper article was written on the work of the Commonwealth War Graves Commission and refers to those graves in the Somme region.

Haves, Alison
'Three Who Came Back'
Newmarket Journal, 10 July 1986

Lewis, Cecil
'The Battle of the Somme after 50 years'
The Times, 2 July 1966
This letter was written by the author of *Sagittarius Rising*, who took part in air patrol activity before and during the Battle of the Somme. From a Morane Parasol he witnessed the blowing of the mines at La Boisselle, which he argued were wrongly sited.

Mellersh, H.E.L.
'I Was There . . . on the Somme'
Observer Magazine, 27 June 1976, pp. 9–10
An article based on the experiences of a second lieutenant in the East Lancashire Regt., which tells of his experiences on 6 July 1916.

Minogue, J.
'The Somme: Tactics which exhaust the enemy'
The Guardian, 1 July 1966
This was an examination of contemporary accounts of the start of the Battle of the Somme.

Salisbury-Jones, Maj.-Gen. Sir Guy
'The Battle of the Somme'
The Times, 5 July 1966
This letter argued that all front-line troops lacked faith in the general staff.

Terraine, John
'The Year of the Somme'
The Times, 13 November 1976, pp. 6–7
This article was published on the 60th anniversary of the capture of Beaumont-Hamel and in part expresses similar views to those of Charles Carrington in 'Kitchener's Army: The Somme and after'. Terraine describes the first day of the battle as being a 'fearful blow', but 'The Army recovered from it almost immediately; the nation never recovered. It is possible to say with assurance that the Army recovered, because the Army proceeded to continue the battle implacably for 141 more days.'

van der Vat, Dan
'At Last, the Scars of the Somme are Healing'
The Times, 18 October 1980

Watkins, M.
'The Somme's Undying Echoes'
The Times, 27 June 1986, p. 14

Williamson, Henry
'The Return to Hell'
Evening Standard, June–July 1966
Williamson, who served on the Somme, was invited to write a series of articles on the occasion of the fiftieth anniversary of the Battle of the Somme. They also covered other parts of the Western Front. The articles were incorporated in the Gliddon Books edition of Williamson's *The Wet Flanders Plain*, see pp. 139–40.

MEDIA: FILM/TELEVISION AND RADIO

The following is a selection of material on the Battle of the Somme which has been broadcast on radio, television or film. This listing has been made from the author's own records, with the help of the Imperial War Museum's Department of Film, and finally from a listing produced as a result of the Proceedings of the XVth International Conference of the International Association for Media and History in Amsterdam in 1993. The theme at this particular conference was 'Film and the First World War'. The conference listing was produced by Mette Peters and Anouk van der Jagt.

The majority of these films were produced in either Great Britain, Germany or the USA, but some were also produced in France, Belgium, the Netherlands and elsewhere. Most of the films were produced as one-off programmes or were compiled for a series.

One important comment to be made is that many of the television companies are not geared up to historical research and are in the main more interested in selling stock shots relating to the First World War. The example of the faked 'over the top sequence' in the famous 1916 *Battle of the Somme* film is a prime example of the stock shot. One final point to be made is that the author of this book has not viewed every item listed.

Readers who wish to know more about films on the war should consult the *Imperial War Museum Film Catalogue* Vol. 1: The First World War Archive. This is an extremely comprehensive listing of 1,218 items in the museum collection and has been produced by the Imperial War Museum/Flick Books (Trowbridge, 1994).

Film/Television

14–18
Part 60: *Bataille de la Somme I*
Part 66: *Bataille de la Somme II*
Producer: Jacques Cogniaux
Directors: Van Besten, Cogniaux, Deline, Keresztessy, P. Meyer, S. Nay, Podolski, Stamezchkine, D. Vos & Wetelet
First broadcast: Radio-Télévision Belge de la Communauté Française 3, August 1964 – 23 December 1968
Fifty years after the war, Radio-Télévision Belge de la Communauté Française started a week-by-week programme about the First World War, which was broadcast over four years.

The Battle of the Ancre and the Advance of the Tanks
Produced for: The War Office Topical Committee, September 1916
Photographer: Geoffrey Malins
Released: January 1917
Malins was filming on 15 September 1916 when the attack was made on Martinpuich

with the assistance of two tanks. A booklet was produced to accompany this film: further details appear in the next entry.

The Battle of the Somme
Produced for: The War Office Topical Committee, early July 1916
Photographers: Geoffrey Malins & J.B. McDowell
Released: August 1916
This is the most famous of the Somme films and a few years ago was issued on video by the Imperial War Museum. It is undoubtedly fake in places, but nevertheless is a very laudable effort in the circumstances. It has been the subject of several articles. A booklet (*The Battle of the Somme and the Battle of the Ancre and the Advance of the Tanks*, edited by Roger Smither, Film and Video Archive, Imperial War Mueum, 1993) accompanies this and the previous film. It replaces a previous viewing guide first published in 1987. These original films are available on a double video cassette VDO106 under the title of *The Battles of the Somme and Ancre*.

The Battle of the Somme
Producer: Malcolm Brown
Narration: Leo McKern
First broadcast: BBC TV, July 1976, 70 min.
This BBC film on the Battle of the Somme is something of a *tour de force* with the actor Leo McKern simulating the battle by walking the actual front line.

Charlie Brown's Great War
Producer: David Kenten
First broadcast: Anglia TV, 8 November 1976
A First World War veteran is taken back to the Somme to visit the grave of his brother for the first time. At the same time he visits Flanders to recall his own war.

A Day That Shook the World: 1st July 1916
This five-minute film was produced in 1992 by BBC Enterprises Library Sales.

De Eerste Wereldoorlog
Part 2: *Van het front geen nieuws*
Produced for: Nederlandse Omroepprogramma Stichting
Directors: Gerda Jansen Hendriks & Wim van der Spek
First broadcast: Nederlandse Onderwijs Televisie, 18 November 1986
This episode focuses on the events of 1915 and 1916: The Battles of the Somme, Verdun and Gallipoli. The Netherlands keep their neutrality.

An Everyman Special: A game of ghosts
Producer: David Willock
Director: Stephen Walker
First broadcast: BBC TV, 1 July 1991, 50 min.
After 75 years, four men who survived the Battle of the Somme talk about their experiences, feelings and continued anguish, including nightmares and feelings of guilt at surviving when comrades died.

Flashback, at the Front 1914–1916: The story of Kitchener's army, and the men that filmed it
Director: Taylor Downing
First broadcast: Channel 4, 1983

The Great War
Part 13: *The devil is coming*
Producer: Tony Essex
Script: John Terraine *et al.*
Narration: Sir Michael Redgrave
First broadcast: BBC 2, 22 August 1964

The Great War: The Definitive Video Collection
Part 2: *The Technology of War*
This compilation was of six videos first issued for sale in 1995. Part of programme 2 (which runs for 92 minutes) deals with the Battle of the Somme. Ref DD.1032. No further details.

Harvests of Iron/Les moissons de fer
Part 1: *The Watch on the Somme (Experiences of a German Soldier)*
Part 2: *The Theatre of Operations (A French Army Surgeon's Story)*
Producers: Gérard Rougeron & Yves Jeanneau
Directors: Jean-Claude Lubtchansky & Gérard Rougeron
Broadcasts: Antenne 2, BBC, Radio-Télévision Belge de la Communauté Française, RTSR, SVT, Arbeitsgemeinschaft der offentlichrectlichen Rundfunkanstalten der Bundesrepublik Deutschland
Documentary series, being the result of three years research, the discovery of previously unknown library footage and unpublished eyewitness accounts and correspondence. Made in France in 1991, both programmes run for 50 min. They were broadcast in the UK as part of the BBC *Timewatch* series, 1992.

The King Visits his Armies in the Great Advance
Produced for: The War Office Committee
Photographers: Geoffrey Malins & J.B. McDowell
Released: October 1916

Late Night Line-up: Interview with Edmund Blunden
Broadcast: BBC TV, 14 February 1966

Lions Led by Donkeys
Producer: Brian Harding
Director: B.A. Duffy
Script: Peter Crookston
Narration: Robin Bailey
First broadcast: Channel 4, 9 November 1985, 50 min.
The story of the Battle of the Somme told by veterans who were then in their nineties. 'The battleplan was defective and doomed, but the bravery of the British Tommies caused the German General Ludendorff to describe them as "Lions Led by Donkeys".'

Mametz
First broadcast: HTV Wales, 1987, 30 min.

Memorial
Produced for: Mass Media Associates, USA, 1972
Re-enacts the Battle of the Somme with marches over a battleground now covered with grain. It conveys the futility and valour of war.

Newsnight. Haig and the Somme
First broadcast: BBC 1, July 1986
A critical discussion of the issue.

Newsnight. Siegfried Sassoon.
First broadcast: BBC TV, July 1986
A programme about the First World War poet Siegfried Sassoon.

Our Empire's Fight for Freedom
Produced for: The War Office Topical Committee
Released: early 1917

'Pals': The 'Pals' Battalions
Producer: Roger Finnegan
Produced for: Yorkshire TV, 1989, 45 min.

The Ragtime Infantry
Producer: Tony Staveacre
First broadcast: BBC TV, 30 December 1968
A report of the six months of filming, covering the making of the film *Oh! What a Lovely War* from the first day on Brighton pier to the last day in the ruins of Bayham Abbey.

Rails of War
Producer & director: David C. Kenton
Script & narration: John Huntley
First broadcast: Anglia TV, 1986, 25 min.
The story of the narrow gauge railway that ran from the back area to the Somme front lines.

Railways
Producer: David Kenten
First broadcast: Anglia TV, 7 November 1988
A film made on location in the Somme featuring an extant narrow gauge railway dating from the First World War when the whole front was dotted with such railways. Great use is made of library film showing these rails in action bringing up troops and supplies.

Robert Graves
First broadcast: BBC TV, 10 November 1969
An interview in which Graves discusses his First World War experiences.

A Slow Walk Over No Man's Land
Produced by: DBA TV (Belfast), 1986
Director: Michael Beattie
First broadcast: Channel 4, Ulster TV
A docudrama based on reminiscences of the Battle of the Somme. An evocation of the Ulster Division's experience at the Somme.

Soldiers' Tank
Produced for: BBC TV, in association with RKO Pictures & ABC Australia
Producer: Ian Taylor

Script: Richard Holmes
Narration: Frederick Forsyth
First broadcast: BBC 1, 1994
This film showed a short section on the first tank attack against the village of Flers. It was part of a series called *History of Fighting Man*.

The Somme 1916
Part 1: *Here comes Kitchener's army*
Part 2: *Through dark woods of Picardy*
Part 3: *Friends are good on the day of battle*
Produced for: Tyne Tees TV, 1994
Producer: Ed Skelding
Each part ran for 50 min.

The Somme: 70 years on old soldiers remember
Produced for: Central TV, 1986, 55 min.
This is a programme of personal accounts by survivors interspersed with narration of the battle.

The Somme: A hell on earth
This 1994 video has comments and analysis by Dr David Chandler, formerly of the Department of War Studies at the Royal Military Academy at Sandhurst. The film is introduced by the actor Brian Blessed and is a dramatized account. The accompanying booklet consists of an extract from Conan Doyle's *The Campaigns in France and Flanders 1916*.

Somme revisited
First broadcast: BBC TV, 12 July 1989

Tanks: Wonder Weapon of World War I?
Produced for: BBC/A. & E. Network Co-Production
Producer: Helen Bettinson
First broadcast: BBC 2, 12 November 1995, 45 min.
This programme traces the development of

the tank in the war and shows about ten minutes of the Battle of the Somme. It was broadcast as part of the BBC Timewatch series.

Voices of War
Part 1: *Loss of innocence*
Part 2: *Image and reality*
Part 3: *In the line*
Part 4: *Man to man*
Part 5: *Talisman and crucifix*
Part 6: *Legacies*
Producers: Derek Smith & Heather Ging
Director: Barrie Crosier
First broadcasts: ITV & Channel 4, 9 November & 14 December 1988
A drama documentary series, based on Peter Liddle's archives of private letters, diaries and photographs, which reveal the personal experience of men and women during the First World War. This programme shows how the initial waves of enthusiasm and patriotic fervour soon turned to disillusionment.

The World's Greatest Story
Episode 3: *The Battle of the Somme*
A film made after the war by British Famous Films, it includes tank and mining operations.

World War I. Multimedia history CD-ROM (PC only). Flag Tower.
This CD-ROM appears in the 'From Ancient Civilization to The Space Race' series and lasts for two hours. The Somme is mentioned.

Radio

Mametz Wood
Produced for: BBC Wales
Producer: Sukey First
Script: Vincent Kane
First broadcast: BBC Wales, July 1986

Slaughter on the Somme
Producer: David Woodward
Compiler: Robert Pocock
Introduced by: General Sir Brian Horrocks
Details of broadcast not known.

A Summer Day on the Somme
Producer: Alan Haydock
Narration: Paul Rogers
First broadcast: BBC Radio 4, 1976
This programme was based on Martin Middlebrook's *The First Day on the Somme*.

ARCHIVES

Sound Archives

In the past twenty to thirty years there has been a huge interest in research into family history and a great deal of valuable interviewing has taken place and been recorded. The Imperial War Museum has pursued a very active role in this area, and at the time of writing is preparing a new checklist of their oral records. I am therefore relying on a listing which is frankly out of date, but nevertheless gives readers a clear sample of what material can be consulted at the museum.

When dealing with material provided by elderly survivors it is sensible to think of it as only one source of historical material and that it is unlikely to be without the odd inaccuracy or blemish. It is only what men thought took place and can be easily distorted by hindsight or a selective memory. It is important, therefore, to read as widely as possible in both primary and secondary sources. This, combined with the oral interview, will at least give the most rounded version of what happened that it is now possible to achieve.

Much oral work has been conducted throughout the country and it is not catalogued in an orderly way. Local archive departments and family history societies are worth contacting.

IMPERIAL WAR MUSEUM SOUND ARCHIVE

Adlam, Tom Edwin
Oral 1/IWM 35/5
British Officer, served with 7th Bn. Bedfordshire & Hertfordshire Regt. in UK and Western Front, 1916. Awarded VC for actions during attack on Thiepval, Somme, 1916.

Bell, A.A.
Oral 2/IWM 13672/C/A
British Army soldier, served with 17th Bn. Manchester Regt. on Somme, 1916.

Brady, James
Oral 3/IWM 11387/2
British stretcher-bearer, served with 43rd Field Ambulance, Royal Army Medical Corps, and 14th Light Div. at Flers and the Somme, 1916, and at Arras, March 1917.

Cattell, D.E.
Oral 4/IWM 13673/C/B
British Army soldier, served on Somme, 1916.

Dickinson, A.
Oral 5/IWM 13674/C/C
British Army captain, served with 10th Bn. Lincolnshire Regt. on Somme, 1916.

Duffield, John
Oral 6/IWM 4411/4
British civilian chaplain, served with Lancashire Bn. Bantam Bde. on the Western Front, 1916, including Battle of the Somme.

Durrant, A.S.
Oral 7/IWM 13675/C/A
British Army soldier, served with 18th Bn. Durham Light Infantry on Somme, 1916.

Easton, T.
Oral 8/IWM 13676/C/B
British Army private, served with 21st Bn. Northumberland Fusiliers on Somme, 1916.

Evans, Wally
Oral 9/IWM 13677/C/C
British Army lance-corporal, served with 8th Bn. King's Own Yorkshire Light Infantry on Somme, 1916.

Fawkes, Maj.
Oral 10/IWM 13678/D/A
British Army officer, served with 1st Bn. Hampshire Regt. on Somme, 1916.

Goddard, Robert V.
Oral 11/IWM 303/16
British Naval captain, served as cadet at Naval College, Dartmouth, 1914–15; transferred to Royal Naval Air Service and served as airship pilot in UK and over Channel, 1915–16; served as airship pilot during Battle of Somme, 1916.

Hall, John L.
Oral 12/IWM 14599/5
British soldier in 2/11 Bn. London Regt. (Finsbury Rifles) 1915–17 and 47 Machine

Gun Bn. 1917–18. Fought at High Wood, Somme, July 1916.

Ham, Horace
Oral 13/IWM 12323/3
British soldier, served with 16th Bn. Middlesex Regt. in France, wounded 1 July 1916; served with 12th Bn. Middlesex Regt. in France 1916–17, wounded and convalescent in Ireland.

Harrison, Derek A.C.
Oral 14/IWM 11031/B/B
British civilian journalist's thoughts on visiting Somme in 1986.

Howe, Phillip
Oral 15/IWM 13671/nnn
British Army lieutenant, served with 10th Bn. West Yorkshire Regt. on Somme, 1916.

Jarman, Clarence W.H.
Oral 16/IWM 12925/3
British private, served with 7th Bn. Royal West Surrey Regt. in GB and Western Front, 1914–16. Wounded during Battle of Somme, 1 July 1916. Leg amputated.

Kennedy, P.J.
Oral 17/IWM 13679/D/B
British Army soldier, served with 18th Bn. Manchester Regt. on Somme, 1916.

Pearson, Arthur V.
Oral 18/IWM 13680/D/C
British Army soldier, served with 15th Bn. West Yorkshire Regt. on Somme, 1916.

Price, Thomas John
Oral 19/IWM 9350/
British NCO, served with 14th Bn. Welch

Regt. in UK and Western Front, 1915–17 including Somme, 1916.

Senescall, Pte.
Oral 20/IWM 13681/D/D
British Army private, served with 11th Bn. Suffolk Regt. on Somme, 1916.

Tansley, Cpl.
Oral 21/IWM 13682/B/A
British Army corporal, served with 9th Bn. Yorks & Lancs on Somme, 1916.

Wiffen, Arthur Edward
Oral 22/IWM 3959/2
British NCO in Essex Regt. in France and Belgium 1914–16, including Loos and Somme campaign.

Wilson, Charles A.
Oral 23/IWM 32/6
British Army officer, served in the infantry during First World War with the Corps of Army Schoolmasters, the Reserve Gloucester Bn. and the 1st Bn. Gloucesters. Involved in action on the Western Front: at Loos and the Somme in 1916, Festubert in 1918. Conditions of trench warfare.

Wood, A.
Oral 24/IWM 13683/B/B
British Army corporal, served with 16th Bn. West Yorkshire Regt. on Somme, 1916.

Yuille, Archibald B.
Oral 25/IWM 320/4
British captain, transferred from 8th East Lancashire Regt. to Royal Flying Corps in 1917 after being wounded on the Somme, 15 July 1916.

MISCELLANEOUS

The Battle of the Somme
Castle, n.d., ref: 1860740634
This is a double cassette. No further details.

Photographic Archives

The largest collection of photographs concerned with the Battle of the Somme in 1916 is housed in the collection at the Imperial War Museum.

The Battle of the Somme was the first major offensive on the Western Front to be covered by official photographs. Nearly 2,000 photographs were taken during the battle by British, Australian and Canadian photographers. These and other photographs of the First World War are now preserved in the Imperial War Museum, London, and may be viewed by appointment in the visitor's room of the museum's Department of Photographs. To assist those unable to visit the department, lists of selected images are available free of charge. Lists currently available on the Battle of the Somme include:

206. The Battle of the Somme: The First Day, 1 July 1916

207. The Battle of the Somme: 1 July – 18 November 1916

220. Photographers at the Battle of the Somme: 1 July – 18 November 1916

If readers wish to view the collection or to receive copies of the above lists then they should contact:

Department of Photographs
Imperial War Museum
Lambeth Road
London SE1 6HZ
Tel: 0171-416 5000

TANKS

It is generally known that the Battle of the Somme saw the entry of the tank into warfare for the first time in September 1916, and it seems worthwhile to give prominence to this new weapon, as it has been written up in the history books. (Official histories have been excluded.)

Anon
A Short History of The Royal Tank Corps
Aldershot: Gale & Polden, 1938
The Somme, pp. 9–14
The well-illustrated book includes a list of commanders of the battalions and a list of different tank types.

Anon
Historical Record of the 4th Battalion Royal Tank Corps
Aldershot: Gale & Polden, 1925
This small book describes the use of the tank for the first time in battle.

Anon
Narrative History of 'G' and 7th Tank Battalion 1919
Aldershot: Gale & Polden, 1919
The Somme, pp. 16 & 17
This is a small booklet.

Baker-Carr, C.D.
From Chauffeur to Brigadier
Benn, 1930
Service with tanks, pp. 186–99

Baldwin, Hanson
World War 1: An outline history
Hutchinson, 1963
Tanks on the Somme, pp. 79–80

Boyle, Andrew
Trenchard
Collins, 1962
The Somme is mentioned on p. 200 in connection with destruction by 60 Squadron of three enemy observation balloons overlooking British tank parks on 15 September 1916.

Browne, Capt. D.G., MC
The Tank in Action
Edinburgh & London: Blackwood, 1920
The Somme pp. 30–41 & 42. Lessons learnt on the use of the tank in battle, pp. 45–56
This book is illustrated.

Carey, G.V. & Scott, H.S.
An Outline History of the Great War
Cambridge University Press, 1929, 2nd edn
Tanks, pp. 111–12 & 114

Carrington, Charles
Soldier from the Wars Returning
Hutchinson, 1965
First use of the tanks on the Somme, pp. 3–5

Chadwick, K.
The Royal Tank Regiment
Leo Cooper, 1970 (Famous Regiments series)
The Somme, pp. 9–12

Charteris, John
At G.H.Q.
Cassell, 1931
Tanks on the Somme, pp. 164–8

Churchill, W.S.
The World Crisis, 1911–1918
Thornton Butterworth, 1931, abridged and revised edn
Tanks on the Somme, pp. 651–3

Conan Doyle, Sir Arthur
The British Campaign in France and Flanders, 1916
Hodder & Stoughton, 1918
First appearances of tanks on the Somme, pp. 241, 245, 249, 261, 269, 272, 283, 285, 288, 293 & 320

Cooper, Bryan
The Ironclads of Cambrai
Souvenir Press, 1967
The Somme, pp. 35–46
This book is illustrated.

Cooper, Bryan
Tank Battles of World War One
Ian Allan, 1974
The Somme, pp. 22–3 & 25–32
This book is part of a series and is numbered as Armour in Action 3. It includes a Somme map and some illustrations.

Cruttwell, C.R.M.F.
A History of the Great War 1914–1918
Oxford University Press, 1936, 2nd edn
Tanks, pp. 270–3

Dewar, George A.B. & Boraston, J.H.
Sir Douglas Haig's Command: December 19th 1915 to November 11th 1918

Vol. 1
Constable, 1922
Tanks on the Somme, pp. 155–6

Duff Cooper, Alfred
Haig
Vol. 1
Faber, 1935
Tanks, pp. 359–63
This covers the use of tanks at Flers–Courcellette on 15 September 1916. The views of Churchill, Elles, Fuller, Haig, Robertson, Swinton and Williams-Ellis are all quoted.

Duncan, N.W.D.
An Illustrated Record of the Development of the British Armoured Fighting Vehicles, 'Tanks': 1915–1918: The First World War
Bovington Camp, Dorset, RAC Tank Museum, 1967

Ellis, Clough Williams Maj., MC & Ellis, A. Williams
The Tank Corps
Country Life & G. Newnes, 1919
The Somme, pp. 24–38
This book is well illustrated.

Esposito, Vincent J. (ed.)
A Concise History of World War 1
Pall Mall Press, 1964
Tanks on the Somme, p. 90

Falls, Cyril
The First World War
Longmans, 1960
Tanks on the Somme, pp. 174–5

Farrar-Hockley, A.H.
The Somme
Batsford, 1964

Tanks on the Somme, pp. 179–82, 188–9 & 191–202

Fletcher, David
Landships: British tanks in the First World War
HMSO, 1984
The Somme, pp. 15–17
This paperback book includes many good photographs.

Fletcher, David
Tanks and Trenches: First hand accounts of tank warfare in the First World War
Stroud: Alan Sutton Publishing, 1994
The Somme, pp. 1–20
This fully illustrated book is concerned more with the tank in action than with technical details.

Foley, John
The Boilerplate War
Muller, 1963
The use of tanks in the Battle of the Somme is mentioned in Ch. 1, 2 & 3. The postcript offers a personal account of first tank action by Capt. H.W. Mortimore, who commanded tank D1 on 15 September 1916.

Forty, G.
The Royal Tank Regiment: a pictorial history 1916–1987
Guild Publishing/Spellmount, 1988
The Somme, pp. 20–3 & 25–9

Forty, G.
Tank Action – From the Great War to the Gulf
Stroud: Alan Sutton Publishing, 1995
The Somme, pp. 19–27
The book includes a map of Flers.

Fuller, J.F.C.
Tanks in the Great War
John Murray, 1920
The Somme, pp. 16–17, 33–4, 54, 58–9, 61, 98, 134, 166, 169, 172–7, 199–201, 205–6, 212, 223, 225–6, 251–2, 287 & 303–4. (Falls★)

Gardner, Brian
The Big Push: A portrait of the Battle of the Somme
Cassell, 1961
Tanks on the Somme, pp. 123–31

Gibbs, Philip
Now It Can Be Told
Harper & Brothers, 1920
Tanks on the Somme, pp. 384–7

Gough, Sir Hubert
The Fifth Army
Hodder & Stoughton, 1931
Tanks on the Somme, pp. 146–7

Haig, Sir Douglas
Despatches December 1915 – April 1919
Dent, 1920
Tanks on the Somme, pp. 42–3

Haig, Sir Douglas (ed. by Robert Blake)
The Private Papers of Douglas Haig 1914–19
Eyre & Spottiswoode, 1952
Tanks on the Somme, pp. 166–7

Hammerton, Sir John
World War 1914–1918: A pictorial history
Amalgamated Press, n.d.
Tanks on the Somme, pp. 943–4

Hankey, Maurice
The Supreme Command, 1914–1918
Allen & Unwin, 1961
Views on the use of tanks on the Somme, pp. 510–16

Hogg, Ian V.
Armour in Conflict: The design and tactics of Armoured Fighting Vehicles
Jane's, 1980
The Somme, pp. 26–8
This book is illustrated.

Jones, Lt. Paul
War Letters of a Public School Boy
Cassell, 1918
This book contains letters written from the Somme battlefield, pp. 202–12. The author was in the Tank Corps.

Jones, Ralph E., Rarey, George H., & Icks, Robert J.
The Fighting Tanks Since 1916
Washington, USA: National Service Publishing, 1933
The Somme, pp. 5–9
This book includes some superb drawings of tanks and their development by country.

Liddell Hart, Capt. B.H.
The Tanks: The history of the Royal Tank Regiment and its predecessors Heavy Branch Machine Gun Corps, Tank Corps and Royal Tank Corps. 1914–1945
Vol. 1: 1914–39
Cassell, 1959
'The baptism of the Tank Corps', pp. 71–9
The author was well placed to write this history, as he knew many of the personalities involved in promoting or opposing the tank as a war-winning weapon. It has very good illustrations and a foreword by FM Viscount Montgomery.

Lloyd George, David
War Memoirs of David Lloyd George
Vol. 1
Odhams Press, 1938

This book covers the production and development of the tank on pp. 381–8

Low, Prof. A.M.
Tanks
Hutchinson, n.d.
The Somme, pp. 31–4
This small book is illustrated.

Macksey, Kenneth
To the Green Fields Beyond: A short history of the Royal Tank Regiment
Royal Tank Regiment, 1965 (private publication)
The Somme, pp. 2–6
The book includes citations for VCs.

Macksey, Kenneth
Tank Warfare: A history of tanks in battle
Hart-Davis, 1971
The Somme, pp. 34–8

Martel, Lt.-Col. G. Le Q, DSO, MC, REMI, Mech E, PSC
In the Wake of the Tank
Sifton Praed, 1935
The Somme, pp. 6 & 9
This book includes many pictures of armoured vehicle development.

Maurice, Maj. R.F.G. (late 13th Bn. Tank Corps)
Tank Corps Book of Honour
Spottiswoode Ballantyne, 1919
This book is mainly a roll of honour of officers and other ranks, together with honours awarded to the Corps. There is Somme information in the first four pages. In 1982 Midland Medals of Birmingham reissued the book as *The Tank Corps Honour and Awards 1916–1919*. It included additional material, two appendices of medal citations and also a short history of the Tank Corps.

Mitchell, Frank, MC
Tank Warfare: The story of the tanks in the Great War
Nelson, 1933
The Somme, pp. 25–42
The author gained the MC in April 1918 in the first ever tank versus tank battle.

Murland, J.R.W.
The Royal Armoured Corps
Methuen, 1943
The Somme, pp. 21–2
The appendix gives technical details of tank designs.

Norman, T.
The Hell They Called High Wood
William Kimber, 1984
Tanks on the Somme, pp. 32, 184, 185, 198–200, 204, 205, 213, 214, 216–19 (and footnote), 221–3, 228, 229, 236, 237, 238, 242 & 244
This fully illustrated book has one tank photograph and maps.

Palmer, Frederick
With the New Army on the Somme: My second year of the war
Murray, 1917
Tanks on the Somme, pp. 287–310
The author was an American correspondent at the British Front.

Parker, Ernest
Into Battle
Longmans Green, 1964
Tanks on the Somme, pp. 50–61

Pidgeon, Trevor
Tanks at Flers: An account of the first use of tanks in war at the Battle of Flers–Courcelette, the Somme 15 September 1916

Cobham, Surrey: Fairmile Books, 1995
This two-volume book was self-published and was a real labour of love. It is 290 pages long and includes 130 illustrations, 40 of which are in colour. The book also includes 12 coloured maps in folders.

Rogers, Col. H.C.B.
Tanks in Battle
Seeley Service, 1965
The Somme, pp. 36 & 40
The book has illustrations and maps.

Smithers, A.J.
A New Excalibur: The development of the tank 1909–1939
Leo Cooper, 1986
The Somme, pp. 86–108
This book describes the teething troubles and first experiments with the tank in battle in September 1916, and the lessons learnt.

Steele, Harwood
The Canadians in France, 1915–1918
Fisher Unwin, 1920
The use of tanks with two brigades of the 2nd Canadian Div. is mentioned on p. 70.

Stern, Albert G.
Tanks 1914–1918: The log-book of a pioneer
Hodder & Stoughton, 1919
Tanks on the Somme, pp. 93–108

Swinton, Maj.-Gen. D., KBE, CB, DSO, RE (retd.)
Eyewitness: Being personal reminiscences of certain phases of the Great War including the genesis of the tank
Hodder & Stoughton, 1932
The Somme, pp. 282–99

Taylor, A.J.P.
The First World War: An illustrated history
Hamish Hamilton, 1963
Tanks in the Battle of the Somme, p. 105

Terraine, John
Douglas Haig: The educated soldier
Hutchinson, 1963
Tanks on the Somme, pp. 218–28

Thompson, P.A.
Lions Led by Donkeys: Showing how victory in the Great War was achieved by those who made the fewest mistakes
Werner Laurie, 1927
Tanks on the Somme, pp. 229–32

Ward, C.H. Dudley
The 56th Division (1st London Territorial Division)

Murray, 1921
Introduction of tanks to the division, pp. 50–51. Tanks in the battle of Flers–Courcelette, pp. 69–94

Whitehouse, Arch
Tank: The battles they fought and the men who drove them – from Flanders to Korea
Macdonald, 1960
The Somme, pp. 40–54
This book is illustrated.

Wilson, G. Murray
Fighting Tanks: An account of the Royal Tank Corps in action 1916–1919
Seeley Service, 1929
The Somme, pp. 37–41 & 45–52
This book is the work of various contributors and has five good illustrations.

COMMONWEALTH WAR GRAVES REGISTERS

This list includes most of the cemeteries in the care of the Commonwealth War Graves Commission in the Department of the Somme area that contain the remains of men killed during the 1916 Battle of the Somme. The registers for these cemeteries contain brief information about the casualties.

The number represents the cemetery number. Grouped entries indicate cemeteries contained together in one register.

4	Acheux Brit. Cem.	150	Bapaume Post Mil. Cem., Albert
239	Adanac Mil. Cem., Miraumont	386	Bazentin-le-Petit Com. Cem.
		387	Bazentin-le-Petit Com. Cem. Ext.
744	A.I.F. Burial Ground, Grass Lane, Flers	388	Bazentin-le-Petit Mil. Cem.
		837	Beaumetz Com. Cem., Cartigny
430	Albert Com. Cem. Ext.	1892	Beaumetz Com. Cem., Somme
882	Allonville Com. Cem.	221	Beaumont-Hamel Brit. Cem.
339	Ancre Brit. Cem., Beaumont-Hamel	515	Bécourt Mil. Cem.
35	Auchonvillers Mil. Cem.	399	Quarry Cem., Montauban
36	Auchonvillers Com. Cem.	400	Bernafay Wood Brit. Cem., Montauban
702	Authuile Mil. Cem.	5	Bertrancourt Mil. Cem.
251	Aveluy Com. Cem. Ext.	745	Bienvillers Mil. Cem.
252	Aveluy Wood Cem. (Lancashire Dump), Mesnil-Martinsart	246	Blighty Valley Cem., Authuile Wood, Aveluy
748	Bailleulmont Com. Cem.	210	Bonnay Com. Cem. Ext.
306	Bancourt Com. Cem.	295	Bouzincourt Com. Cem.
307	Bancourt Brit. Cem.	296	Bouzincourt Com. Cem. Ext.

516	Bouzincourt Ridge Cem., Albert	203	Couin Brit. Cem.
		204	Couin New Brit. Cem.
394	Citadel New Mil. Cem., Fricourt	205	Couin Com. Cem.
395	Bray Hill Brit. Cem., Bray-sur-Somme		
		280	Courcelette Brit. Cem.
396	Bray Vale Brit. Cem., Bray-sur-Somme		
		133	Courcelles-au-Bois Com. Cem. Ext.
164	Bray Mil. Cem., Bray-sur-Somme		
		397	Dantzig Alley Brit. Cem., Mametz
329	Bronfay Farm Mil. Cem., Bray-sur-Somme		
		118	Daours Com. Cem.
		119	Daours Com. Cem. Ext.
577	Bucquoy Com. Cem.		
		188	Dartmoor Cem., Bécordel-Bécourt
198	Buire-sur-Ancre Com. Cem.		
		402	Delville Wood Cem., Longueval
277	Bull's Road Cem., Flers		
		176	Dernancourt Com. Cem.
7	Bus-les-Artois Com. Cem.	177	Dernancourt Com. Cem. Ext.
1505	Sunken Road Cem., Contalmaison	330	Devonshire Cem., Mametz
1506	2/Canadian Cem., Sunken Rd, Contalmaison	331	Gordon Cem., Mametz
		141	Dive Copse Brit. Cem., Sailly-le-Sec
513	Carnoy Mil. Cem.		
		62	Doullens Com. Cem. Ext. No. 1
432	Caterpillar Valley Cem., Longueval		
		1012	Englebelmer Com. Cem.
639	Chipilly Com. Cem.	1013	Englebelmer Com. Cem. Ext.
640	Chipilly Com. Cem. Ext.		
		156	Euston Road Cem., Colincamps
785	Combles Com. Cem. Ext.		
786	Guards' Cem., Combles	453	Flatiron Copse Cem., Mametz
215	Connaught Cem., Thiepval	281	Foncquevillers Mil. Cem.
703	Contalmaison Château Cem.	2	Forceville Com. Cem.
		2	Forceville Com. Cem. Ext.
59	Contay Brit. Cem.		
		533	Frankfurt Trench Brit. Cem.
22	Corbie Com. Cem.	534	New Munich Trench Brit. Cem., Beaumont-Hamel
23	Corbie Com. Cem. Ext.		

207	Méricourt-l'Abbé Com. Cem. Ext.	1491	Redan Ridge Cem. No. 1, Beaumont-Hamel
1503	Mesnil Ridge Cem., Mesnil-Martinsart	1492	Redan Ridge Cem. No. 2, Beaumont-Hamel
197	Millencourt Com. Cem. Ext.	1493	Redan Ridge Cem. No. 3, Beaumont-Hamel
383	Mill Road Cem., Thiepval	314	Regina Trench Cem., Grandcourt
1504	Miraumont Com. Cem.	1705	Ribemont Com. Cem. Ext.
633	Morlancourt Brit. Cem. No. 1	342	Sailly-au-Bois Mil. Cem.
634	Morlancourt Brit. Cem. No. 2, Ville-sur-Ancre	216	Sailly-Saillisel Brit. Cem.
217	Morval Brit. Cem.	1014	St Amand Brit. Cem.
152	Munich Trench Brit. Cem., Beaumont-Hamel	742	Serre Road Cem. No. 1, Hébuterne
153	Waggon Road Cem., Beaumont-Hamel	743	Serre Road Cem. No. 3, Puisieux
189	Norfolk Cem., Bécordel-Bécourt	1890	Serre Road Cem. No. 2, Beaumont-Hamel
393	Ovillers Mil. Cem., Ovillers-la-Boisselle	535	Stump Road Cem., Grandcourt
580	Owl Trench Cem., Hébuterne	643	Sucrerie Mil. Cem., Colincamps
151	Peake Wood Cem., Fricourt	1891	Thiepval Anglo-French Cem.
630	Péronne Road Cem., Maricourt	41	Varennes Mil. Cem.
637	Point 110 Old Mil. Cem., Fricourt	635	Ville-sur-Ancre Com. Cem.
638	Point 110 New Mil. Cem., Fricourt	385	Warlencourt Brit. Cem.
832	Pozières Brit. Cem., Ovillers-la-Boisselle	120	Warlincourt Halte Brit. Cem., Saulty
74	Puchevillers Brit. Cem.	43	Warloy-Baillon Com. Cem.
		44	Warloy-Baillon Com. Cem. Ext.
514	Queen's Cem., Bucquoy	1490	'Y' Ravine Cem., Beaumont-Hamel

INDEX OF PLACES

Places which appear in book titles are indicated by (T)

INDEX OF AUTHORS AND OTHER PEOPLE

Unless otherwise noted, names refer to authors/editors of the books listed

(A) = author

(C) = mentioned in the commentary (including writers of Introductions)

(O) = contributor to oral records

(P) = poet

(S) = subject of biography

INDEX OF TITLES

'History of/Short History of' and similar phrases are inverted. Where entries begin with numbers of Regiments etc, they are filed at the beginning of the appropriate letter of the alphabet in numerical order.

(J) = journal or newspaper article

(F) = fiction